S0-BQW-717

UTSA BT LIBRARY RE   ALS 452-2410

Common Ground, Common Future

Moral Agency in Public Administration, Professions, and Citizenship

WITHDRAWN
UTSA LIBRARIES

Library
University of Texas
at San Antonio

PUBLIC ADMINISTRATION AND PUBLIC POLICY

A Comprehensive Publication Program

Executive Editor

JACK RABIN
Professor of Public Administration and Public Policy
School of Public Affairs
The Capital College
The Pennsylvania State University—Harrisburg
Middletown, Pennsylvania

Assistant to the Executive Editor
T. Aaron Wachhaus, Jr.

Library
University of Texas
at San Antonio

Available Electronically

Common Ground, Common Future

Moral Agency in Public Administration, Professions, and Citizenship

Charles Garofalo
Texas State University
San Marcos, Texas, U.S.A.

Dean Geuras
Texas State University
San Marcos, Texas, U.S.A.

Taylor & Francis
Taylor & Francis Group

Boca Raton   London   New York   Singapore

A CRC title, part of the Taylor & Francis imprint, a member of the
Taylor & Francis Group, the academic division of T&F Informa plc.

Published in 2006 by
CRC Press
Taylor & Francis Group
6000 Broken Sound Parkway NW, Suite 300
Boca Raton, FL 33487-2742

© 2006 by Taylor & Francis Group, LLC
CRC Press is an imprint of Taylor & Francis Group

No claim to original U.S. Government works
Printed in the United States of America on acid-free paper
10 9 8 7 6 5 4 3 2 1

International Standard Book Number-10: 0-8247-5337-2 (Hardcover)
International Standard Book Number-13: 978-0-8247-5337-5 (Hardcover)
Library of Congress Card Number 2005048402

This book contains information obtained from authentic and highly regarded sources. Reprinted material is quoted with permission, and sources are indicated. A wide variety of references are listed. Reasonable efforts have been made to publish reliable data and information, but the author and the publisher cannot assume responsibility for the validity of all materials or for the consequences of their use.

No part of this book may be reprinted, reproduced, transmitted, or utilized in any form by any electronic, mechanical, or other means, now known or hereafter invented, including photocopying, microfilming, and recording, or in any information storage or retrieval system, without written permission from the publishers.

For permission to photocopy or use material electronically from this work, please access www.copyright.com (http://www.copyright.com/) or contact the Copyright Clearance Center, Inc. (CCC) 222 Rosewood Drive, Danvers, MA 01923, 978-750-8400. CCC is a not-for-profit organization that provides licenses and registration for a variety of users. For organizations that have been granted a photocopy license by the CCC, a separate system of payment has been arranged.

Trademark Notice: Product or corporate names may be trademarks or registered trademarks, and are used only for identification and explanation without intent to infringe.

Library of Congress Cataloging-in-Publication Data

Garofalo, Charles.
    Common ground, common future : moral agency in public administration, professions, and citizenship / Charles Garafalo [sic], Dean Geuras.
        p. cm. -- (Public administration and public policy ; 115)
    Includes bibliographical references and index.
    ISBN 0-8247-5337-2
    1. Public administration--Moral and ethical aspects. 2. Public administration--Moral and ethical aspects--United States. 3. Ethics. I. Geuras, Dean. II. Title. III. Series.

JF1525.E8G369 2005
172'.2--dc22   2005048402

Taylor & Francis Group
is the Academic Division of T&F Informa plc.

Visit the Taylor & Francis Web site at
http://www.taylorandfrancis.com

and the CRC Press Web site at
http://www.crcpress.com

Preface

The aim of this book is to examine the public and private roles of the citizen as a moral agent. We define the moral agent as a person who, rather than merely behaving in a manner consistent with morality, recognizes morality as a motive for action. The moral agent not only follows moral principles but also acknowledges morality as his or her principal.

In developing the notion of the moral agent, we accord a special significance to public administration. We argue that public administration is a fundamentally moral enterprise that exists to serve values that society considers significant enough to support. It is dedicated to the provision of goods and services that society recognizes as important enough to justify the expenditure of our collective resources. It is committed to the creation and cultivation of the admittedly elusive but nonetheless central concept of the public interest. Therefore, public administration is, by definition, inherently moral, and public administrators are, again by definition, moral agents.

We maintain that its inherently moral nature makes public administration a plausible prototype for other professions to emulate as they pursue their own objectives. Thus, as illustrative cases, we explore business, particularly corporate social responsibility; the practice of medicine, especially managed care; higher education; and the legal profession. In our view, all of these professions and others are experiencing moral distress and confusion that can be alleviated by recognizing public administration's moral nature and the compelling need for reciprocity and trust across all sectors of our society. Although moral public administration remains a work in progress, its essential purpose can serve as a gyroscope or centrifuge to stabilize and direct our collective moral development. But we are not utopians, proposing the removal of politics from politics. Instead, we are proposing that individuals and institutions acknowledge the presence and power of universal values embodied in public administration as the central expression of moral agency and citizenship. We are proposing that public administration become the model of moral governance in American society.

In the process, we offer the unified ethic — a combination of the major strands of philosophical ethical theory — that we contend can help elucidate and enhance our individual and institutional moral identities. Just as we call for a shift from business to government as the institutional embodiment of central values, we, once again, call for a shift from a disparate approach to moral thinking and action to an integrated one in which principle, consequences, and character are understood both in their own right and as inseparable from each other. This holistic perspective, we believe, can provide intellectual and moral clarity and the impetus for still another shift, this time in ethics training, away from the legalistic, procedural, and superficial and toward reasoning and judgment, as well as toward morally grounded decision-making skills and the exercise of discretion.

This book is intended to appeal to practitioners in various professions; to academics responsible for research and graduate teaching in administrative, applied, and professional ethics; and to citizens interested in clarifying the inevitable and insistent moral ambiguities and perplexities associated with their personal and professional lives, including their responsibilities as members of the polity. Its title, *Common Ground, Common Future: Moral Agency in Public Administration, Professions, and Citizenship*, signifies our principal purpose and our abiding hope: the development of a broad perspective on our individual and collective roles and responsibilities as citizens, professionals, and moral beings, as well as the recognition of our mutual obligations to the large and small challenges inherent in the processes of governance.

The initial chapter provides a general overview of the book's central themes, including the notion of the moral agent, moral agency in the professions and in citizenship, and the concept of the unified ethic, which is intended to help moral agents in making moral decisions. The second and third chapters discuss the special status of the public administrator as a moral agent. Chapters 4–7 concern moral agency in the important professional fields of business, medicine, law, and higher education. Chapter 8 examines the unified ethic, while Chapter 9 applies the unified ethic to moral agency. Chapter 10 presents a critique, from a conservative and liberal perspective, of our respective positions on the public administrator as a moral exemplar. Chapter 11 concludes with a proposal for meeting the conditions required to establish moral agency in public administration, across professions, and in the citizenry.

Table of Contents

1 The Moral Agent, Moral Organization, and the Public Administrator

This chapter introduces the main issues with which the book is concerned: the notion of the moral agent, the application of that notion to the different sectors of society, and the special roles of the public administrator as moral agent and as moral exemplar for the private citizen. The chapter also discusses the notion of the "unified ethic," which provides the means of clarifying and applying universal values for both the public administrator and the private citizen.

WHAT IS A MORAL AGENT?

In this book, we argue that the public administrator is a moral agent and, therefore, a moral exemplar for the private citizen. The claim that the public administrator functions as a moral agent cannot be fully understood unless the term "agent" is carefully examined. The literatures of moral philosophy, law, management, and public administration use the term differently, so to settle on a single definition, we refer to the term's etymology. "Agent" comes from the Latin term "agere," which simply means "to do." Such a general definition helps us, but only minimally — any activity is a doing of some kind.

The matter is clarified, at least somewhat, when we add the preposition "of," which usually accompanies "agent" in spirit, if not in writing. An agent does something for some person or thing. Although one could speak of being one's own agent, as one could speak of being one's own attorney or doctor, one would naturally speak as though one person, A, is an agent of another, B. In philosophical jargon, "agent" is a two-place (A and B) relation. In more natural language, an agent relates two things: the actor, commonly called the agent, and something or someone in behalf of which the actor performs the action. If Jack is an agent, then there must be a Jill for whom Jack acts. Jack and Jill may be people or impersonal entities, as when we say that soap is a cleaning agent or that necessity is an agent of change. Furthermore, "Jack" and "Jill" may, like "Louis Armstrong" and "Satchmo," refer to the same thing. Thus, we can say that success produces success or that Arthur is his own best friend. But enough of the odd cases. We may begin by thinking of the agent, or actor, as being a person who acts in behalf of another person, whom we will call, according to the current fashion in public administration literature, the principal.

A morally upright agent would therefore serve his or her principal in a moral manner. Such an agent would be morally bound to pursue the aims of the principal but would do so without violating anyone else's rights or otherwise doing anything immoral.

It would seem a rather simple matter in most cases for the agent to identify the principal. The attorney, for example, would identify the client as the principal, as the political campaign manager would identify the candidate, and as the booking agent would identify the celebrity. But in some cases, the identification becomes more complex: An attorney who works for a union in defending one of its members may be unsure of whether the union or the defendant is the "real" principal; the campaign manager may be unsure of whether the principal is the candidate or the political party.

The issue becomes more complicated still when the agent has multiple principals. A member of the U.S. House of Representatives is the agent of the district from which he or she is elected; the group of voters who, in good faith, voted for him or her because of his or her promises; the people who contributed to his or her campaign; the interest groups within his or her district; his or her political party; and the nation as a whole, among other potential principals. The multiplicity of principals invites conflict and requires an ordering of priorities among them. The greater the number of principals and the more diverse their interests, the less the agent can be considered an agent of any specific principal. If the principals become too numerous, the alleged agent may cease to be an agent at all.

A deeper complication arises when something abstract becomes an agent's principal. An agent may be regarded as acting on behalf of a country, a society, or a cause. The addition of such abstractions to an already diverse class of principals would make the task of resolving conflicts of obligation more complex.

Morality itself is among the abstract principals. If someone believes that he or she is under a moral obligation, independent of or in addition to any obligations to individuals or groups, morality becomes his or her principal. But morality, as a principal, has a different status from other principals — both abstract and human — that may form the complex structure of one's obligations. When obligations to multiple conflicting principals need to be balanced, morality is not merely one principal among many, to be balanced against the others. When one evaluates the relative strength of competing obligations, the evaluation itself should be founded on moral considerations. If, for example, a physician recognizes his or her family's material needs, his or her patients' health, his or her profession's prestige, his or her career advancement, and his or her moral obligations all as principals, he or she must decide, in a particular instance, which among them should be best served. But to decide what "should be" is to determine the moral course of action. Thus, morality becomes the supreme principal.

Agents can therefore be subject to morality in two senses. In one sense, everyone is subject to morality in all pursuits because they should be conducted in a moral manner. In the second sense, one may also pursue morality itself as the goal. Any person functioning as an agent should behave morally, in the first sense, while seeking some good that may be morally neutral. An agent is subject to morality in the second sense when he or she acts with the purpose of promoting morality and thus functions as an agent of morality. The morally observant pipe fitter is an agent of the first kind, whereas defenders of civil rights are agents of the second kind. To distinguish between the two kinds of agents, we will refer to the agent who acts morally, though not necessarily with morality as a principal, as an ethical agent. We will use the phrase "moral agent" to designate an agent who recognizes morality as a principal.

The different perspectives of Robert Bork and both Elliott Richardson and William Ruckelshaus during the Watergate investigation exemplify the distinction between the moral agent and the ethical agent (Moore and Sparrow, 1990, pp. 136–150). President Nixon asked Richardson, the attorney general of the United States, to fire Watergate Special Prosecutor Archibald Cox because Cox was a threat to the administration. Richardson refused because he did not wish to interfere with the implementation of justice. After Nixon fired him, Ruckelshaus, who assumed Richardson's duties, also refused Nixon's demands on the same grounds as Richardson. After firing Ruckelshaus, Nixon asked Bork, the solicitor general, to fire Cox. Bork complied with Nixon's request on the grounds that his function within the government was different from those of Richardson and Ruckelshaus. He argued that although Richardson and Ruckelshaus were primarily members of the legal profession and, therefore, owed their primary allegiance to the law and its principles, the solicitor general was an agent of the president and was obligated to execute the president's will. In Bork's reasoning, he was an ethical agent of the president and Richardson and Ruckelshaus were moral agents.

The moral agent acts in a manner that expresses concern for moral values as final ends. Therefore, the moral agent would often act against self-interest to advance something that he or she considers morally worthwhile. Moral agents include Socrates, in taking the hemlock; Mohandas Gandhi, in engaging in passive resistance for the sake of human rights; and Albert Schweitzer, for dedicating his life to service to the poor. Although most people never attain the notoriety of these historically important figures, whoever acts in behalf of a moral value is, at least momentarily, a moral agent.

There is ambiguity in our concept of a moral agent. Let us suppose, first, that a person acts on a genuine moral value, such as the equality of all people or the abolition of all war, though without complete, unquestionable proof for the validity of the value. Such a person would seem clearly to qualify as a moral agent. But let us now suppose that another person questions the validity of the motivating value. Should the second individual still regard the first person as a moral agent because of his or her sincere belief in the validity of the questionable value? Or must one be considered a moral agent only if acting on the basis of a provably genuine value? Is it enough for one to believe in the morality of a cause, or must the cause be objectively moral?

To require proof of the objective validity of a moral value is too demanding. Although most people would agree that equality of human beings is a worthy moral value, few could begin to give a philosophically compelling argument for human equality. Even those who offer such proof will differ among themselves about what is the truly valid proof. Kantians and Utilitarians both, for example, recognize human beings as equal, but for different and disputable reasons. Most of us acknowledge the validity of the notion of equality without a need for proof. Moreover, some would question whether any value is objectively provable. Such people would never recognize anyone as a moral agent if we insist that a moral agent act on an objective moral value.

Other problems arise if one is considered a moral agent merely for having a subjective belief in the moral validity of a value. Stalin, for example, was probably convinced that his eradication of millions of people was moral. Nevertheless, few would consider him a moral agent in any sense.

Difficulties arise whether one defines a moral agent on the basis of an objectively provable value or a subjectively held value. For this consideration, we designate a moral agent as one who, on sincere conscientious grounds, considers morality as his or her principal, even if he or she cannot prove its validity. We will later examine the factors that render grounds sincere and conscientious.

We have seen that it is possible to be an ethical agent without being a moral agent. To be an ethical agent, one need merely pursue any goal in a morally correct manner, such as the ice cream merchant who goes about his or her business without cheating anyone, but a moral agent has a moral goal, such as the promotion of human equality. It is also possible to be a moral agent without being a fully ethical agent. A witness who is certain of the innocence of a defendant but uncertain of the jury's willingness to acquit might take it on himself or herself to lie in support of ultimate justice. The witness would be a moral agent because he or she regards justice as a principal but would not be fully ethical by virtue of his or her dishonest behavior. More extreme examples are easily imagined. Few would doubt the moral validity of the principal that the abolitionist John Brown pursued, but his murderous methods were ethically questionable at best. Even the most just of just wars can be conducted by unethical methods.

If it is possible to be a moral but not ethical agent, and an ethical but not moral agent, one might ask whether it is possible to be an ethical immoral agent. If someone is motivated by an immoral value, can he or she pursue that value in an ethically pure manner? Let us suppose that, in persecuting a political opponent, Cesare Borgia did nothing immoral except intentionally murder him. The very statement of the case has an aura of absurdity: One cannot murder in a moral manner. People who have immoral intentions in their actions can be neither moral nor ethical agents.

The concepts of moral agency and ethical agency, which apply primarily to individuals, can be extended to organizations. Some have a moral mission. They exist not merely to provide a service that people want but also to perform a morally justified task. Other organizations may have morally neutral missions, though their employees may act in a perfectly ethical manner. We designate a profession founded on a moral purpose as inherently moral. The dedicated employee of such an organization, who acknowledges its moral purpose as his or her own in all of his or her professional activities, is a moral agent. If the organization allows only ethical behavior in pursuit of its moral goal, the organization is also ethical. An agency is ethical but not inherently moral if it allows only ethical behavior but exists for a morally neutral purpose. A third possibility, which one would hope does not exist, is the inherently immoral profession, in which one is an agent of immorality.

We examine several professions to distinguish those that are inherently moral from those that, though ethical, are not inherently moral. Inherently moral professions will most likely serve as sources of moral exemplars because in those fields, dedicated, ethical professionals who are motivated by the values that their organizations exist to serve are both moral agents and ethical agents. Our examination of professions is inescapably broad. It is likely that, in the daily work of professionals in all areas, as in life in general, acts of moral agency arise, but some professions have moral agency deeply embedded into their very fabric. Public agencies are among them, though not exclusively. Different professions can promote exemplarship in various ways, but the public agency will be shown to provide the most comprehensive source of moral exemplars.

THE SPECIAL ETHICAL ASPECTS OF PUBLIC ORGANIZATIONS

There are several reasons for the special moral status of public organizations. First, private companies and corporations exist explicitly to make a profit, whereas public organizations exist to serve the public good. Although in a free-market society the profit motive is thought to provide ultimate social benefits, the private organization is created and sustained to provide material advantage for itself and its members. The public organization, in contrast, exists to serve a value that the society deems significant enough to fund. The public organization is not allowed to make a profit but must dedicate itself entirely to the public good. The administrator of a private organization can justify lack of altruism by saying, "We are in business to make money." The public administrator cannot use such a statement as either a justification or an excuse. We may therefore initially suppose that public organizations are inherently moral professions, though that tentative supposition may require reexamination and refinement later.

Second, private organizations are not required to establish that their product has significant social value to justify their existence. Although a society might outlaw the sale of some products, such as narcotics, and limit the sale of others, such as alcoholic beverages, the manufacturers of most products, such as Frisbees, lava lamps, or hip-hop videos, have no need to prove that these products are of significant value to the society. If there is a market for a harmless product, private businesses can provide it. Public organizations, however, are most often dedicated to the provision of goods and services that they recognize as valuable enough to justify their collective efforts and resources. It would be difficult, in most democratic societies, to justify the existence of a public organization with the responsibility of producing Halloween costumes.

We do not suggest that private organizations need not be ethical or moral, but some moral aspects of public organizations are not generally present in private firms. There are exceptions: Some private entities have strong foundations in social values, and some public organizations do not. For example, the medical and legal professions can claim as firm a basis in social values as most public organizations, whereas the state-owned liquor stores may have little moral justification except as sources of state revenue.

The exceptions are noteworthy for two reasons. First, in some societies, both medicine and law are under the public sector. Even where they are largely under private control, they are heavily regulated by government. Second, professions such as medicine and law are, like much of public administration, concerned with matters of vital importance to the society. As a consequence, it is possible that the moral context of public administration is derived at least in part from the generally important missions that public organizations have. One might be tempted to conclude, therefore, that they may be more inherently moral because they are socially significant and not solely because they are public.

Still, the mere public quality of public organizations accounts for some of their especially moral nature. Public organizations must publicly justify their expenditures and activities on the basis of their relation to their missions. Private corporations can be much freer with expenses (e.g., travel funds) than public organizations, which must demonstrate that they are not wasting public funds. Private companies can branch out into entirely new ventures, whereas public agencies are confined to their assigned missions. The owner of a private company may hire his wife as vice president, but in a public organization, such behavior would constitute nepotism. The requirement that a public organization remain responsible to the general public provides an ethical dimension.

Because of the special moral aspects of public administration, public organizations are under more extensive regulations than most private organizations. Those regulations are intended to ensure that the organization is responsible to the public and conducts its activities within the scope of the public charge. In addition to legal regulations, most public organizations have ethics codes with which members of the organization are expected to comply. Relatively few private firms have ethics codes, and many of these private codes are clearly intended to promote good public relations and thus to ensure the popularity of the company (Geuras and Garofalo, 2002, pp. 15–42).

Both ethical and unethical behaviors exist in all organizations. Public organizations are not ideals of moral perfection, and private organizations are not havens for the amoral. Nevertheless, there is ample evidence to indicate that ethics are more central to the organizational culture of the public organization than to that of the private firm.

The centrality of ethics is also a significant factor in private, nonprofit institutions. Such institutions are private, and they thus have a common element with the private corporation, but they serve a moral goal and are therefore morally dedicated organizations. They provide a rich potential source of moral exemplarship but in a subtly yet significantly different manner from that of public administration. This difference will emerge as we consider the relation between the public administrator and the citizen.

CITIZENSHIP AND PUBLIC ADMINISTRATION

We have argued that the public administrator serves as an exemplar for private individuals because public administration is inherently moral. But our argument might be questioned on the grounds that it makes a faulty analogy: Although public administration may be inherently moral and public administrators may be moral agents, private individuals may not regard themselves as necessarily motivated by any moral goal. They may consider themselves perfectly adequate members of society who conduct their affairs in an ethical manner but not as agents of any moral value. They thus would consider themselves ethical agents rather than moral agents. If they are not moral agents, public administration would appear to be no more a source of exemplars for them than any other profession would be.

However, our analogy proves valid because the private individual in a civil society is also a citizen. The status of citizen, in at least the formal sense, is a political office. It is the foundation of political authority in a democracy. The nature of public administration — with its explicit responsibility to the public, formalized ethical rules and codes, and general organizational culture — situates the public administrator as an appropriate moral teacher by example. Public administrators must justify their professional goals and the manner in which they pursue them as advancing the values of the society. The public administrator derives his or her professional existence from those values and is professionally dedicated to them. This professional dedication of the public administrator is identical to the social dedication conferred and demanded by the status of citizen.

As exemplar for the private citizen, the public administrator is also indirectly an exemplar for the private firm and its members. In addition to their corporate responsibilities, members of private firms, and perhaps even the firms themselves (French, 1994), are also citizens. As such, they may find themselves in conflict with their interests as professionals. As citizens, their ethical behavior may be professionally unprofitable, as in the case of managers of a paper plant who sacrifice funds to avoid polluting a river or executives of an automobile company who sacrifice profits for safety and fuel efficiency. Ideally, laws should prevent such conflicts, but in reality, the legal system cannot carry the complete burden of anticipating and sanctioning all potential unethical behavior without the risk of regulating to excess. If the employees in such a conflict act only in the corporate interest, the public good will be sacrificed, but if they act as good citizens, the society will be best served.

Although we maintain that the public administrator is an exemplar for the public citizen, the corporation and its members, nevertheless, can model an aspect of citizenship better than can the public administrator. The very conflict between citizen and member of a private corporation gives the corporate employee the opportunity to choose between corporate and social interest. The public employee's job, at least theoretically, requires that he or she act in the public interest because his or her organization exists to serve the public, whereas the private employee's job exists to serve corporate interests. To oversimplify to the point of crassness, the public employee is paid by the public, but the private employee is paid by the company. The private employee thus has the opportunity to choose against the interests of his or her organization and in the interests of good citizenship.

However, this advantage to the private employee as an exemplar must be tempered. Public employees, despite their organizations' dedication to the public good, can still find themselves in ethical conflicts similar to those of the private employee. Public agencies and divisions within them vie with each other for funding and other benefits. Often, organizations and their members will seek money, that could be better used in another unit for their own advantage. In such cases, the public employee can be in conflict with the public interest. Another common example of the conflict of public interest with public organizational interest is the frantic use of "leftover" funds at the end of a fiscal year. In such cases, the public employees have the opportunity to demonstrate citizenship over personal and organizational self-interest. But how often do they?

Another area in which, at least on the surface, the private corporation may serve better than the public organization as an ethical exemplar is in the area of voluntary contribution. Private firms can, and often do, donate corporate funds to charities, universities, and other nonprofit organizations. Public organizations are barred from using public funds in this manner. Nevertheless, the public organization, as a collection of public citizens, can assume some of the exemplary function of the private organization. Even if public organizations cannot use their publicly allocated funds as contributions, members of the organization can contribute individually. The organizations can encourage and facilitate the process.

Earlier we noted the potential for employees of private nonprofit organizations to function as moral exemplars, though in a manner different from that of the public administrator. A specific nonprofit agency is dedicated to a set of voluntarily assumed moral responsibilities that define its activities. Although the public employee is also a member of an organization with a specific charge, the public administrator is, above all, an agent of the entire society. The public administrator's organization is part of a much larger governmental structure to which the specific organization belongs and to which it is responsible. That governmental structure represents the society as a whole. The nonprofit employee therefore serves his or her own private moral values, but the public administrator serves the values sanctioned by the entire society. The nonprofit employee is an agent of his or her own values, but the public administrator is an agent of public value as well as his or her private values.

The citizen is more like the public administrator acting in his or her professional capacity than like the nonprofit employee acting in his or her professional capacity. Private citizens, similar to both nonprofit employees and public administrators, have their own moral values and are free to pursue them. But *qua* citizen, each person has a responsibility to honor the values of the society as a whole. As a citizen, one is beholden to the entire society. The dual responsibility to both one's own values and those of the society characterizes both the citizen and the public administrator. The employee of the nonprofit organization is beholden to the society because he or she is a citizen rather than because he or she works for a specific type of organization.

The public administrator does not automatically, by virtue of employment, become a good moral exemplar. His or her status as public employee, the social goals of the organization, and the highly developed system of specific ethically based rules governing public organizations give the public administrator an opportunity to serve as an exemplar. Only an ethically concerned, ethically knowledgeable, and ethically practiced public administrator can take best advantage of the opportunity. We must examine the current state of public administration to determine how well the profession is performing in that regard.

THE ETHICAL ENVIRONMENT OF PUBLIC ADMINISTRATION

A municipal department's sick-leave policy is regularly used by employees for a number of reasons other than illness. For example, employees use sick leave to supplement their vacations, whereas others, nearing retirement, use it in their last weeks as vacation and to avoid returning the unused time to the department. However, these uses of sick leave are not seen by employees as improper. Rather, they consider them to be entitlements that help to compensate for relatively low salaries or simply to be their due as public employees. Management, in contrast, may consider these practices as an abuse, but it either is at a loss as to how to prevent or control them or is unwilling to exercise its authority. Proving abuse can be difficult, and in some cases, managers themselves plan to use sick leave in the same way when their own retirement dates approach.

Although the use or misuse of sick-leave policy in a local government department may appear far removed from the important ethical problems in public administration, it is, nonetheless, one type of problem with which many public managers struggle every day, and that raises a number of significant ethical, management, and policy questions for public service as a whole. The other type of problem is that of knowing and doing the right thing under the circumstances surrounding public organizations. As participants in a world of competing values and competing priorities, multiple stakeholders, vague legislative intent, relentless budgetary pressures, and shifting mandates, public managers are jugglers, keeping many balls in the air while striving to make reasonable judgments and decisions. In this world, the ethical dimensions and implications of these judgments and decisions are generally obscured by the familiar and pressing issues of the moment. In this connection, we might recall the aphorism that the immediate drives out the important. In any event, systematic and sophisticated ethical analysis and dialogue are the exception, rather than the rule, in public organizations. Whether it is abuse of authority, avoidance of responsibility, improper use of resources, or ethical ambiguity in policy and management, these concerns tend to receive short shrift in the daily diet of budgets, procedures, and deadlines. The goal is to get the job done, and the legal supersedes the ethical.

As a number of observers have noted, ethics in the public service tends to be compliance oriented, meaning taking the "low road," or "adherence to formal rules," in John Rohr's (1989) terms. It is often interpreted as staying out of trouble and understood as sanctions, scrutiny, and controls rather than independence, judgment, and character. In contrast, as Carol Lewis (1991) has said, "Compliance is fundamental to the way the public business is conducted. As guardians of political relationships and political goals, *controls are accountability implemented (p. 10).*" The problem is that compliance, including a legalistic approach to moral challenges, tends to be the dominant — or even the only — perspective in public service. As Bowman and Williams (1997) argue, the majority of public organizations have no consistent approach to ethics, which in turn means that employees often flounder when confronted with ethical issues.

Administrative ethics are inseparable from organizational structure and culture, which reflect and reinforce the organization's moral choices and commitments. Thus, the creation and cultivation of ethical public organizations are complex undertakings, involving all rungs of the hierarchy, from top management to street-level bureaucrats, as well as initiatives in the legislative and judicial arenas and the larger culture.

The key question is how we conceive of politics. Is it strategic competition for power and advantage? Or is it an ethical enterprise in which interests and strategy are subordinated to the public interest? If politics is fundamentally ethical, it cannot be justified on the basis of strategy and interests alone. As Richard Dagger (1986) maintains, "Political justification is a form of ethical justification," requiring a compelling theory of ethics (p. 271). We also must note, however, that public justification, as Stephen Macedo (1990) says, is not simply a philosophical or intellectual exercise. Rather, its purpose is the establishment of "a transparent, demystified social order" (p. 295).

THE NEED FOR ETHICAL REASONING IN PUBLIC ADMINISTRATION

It is virtually axiomatic that citizens should be ethical, but recent scandals in business and government have highlighted the need for a more ethical populace. If public administrators are to function as exemplars for the private citizen, the need to develop the moral commitment and understanding of public administrators is paramount. The public service has responded at both the national and local levels by establishing ethics training programs. However, although such programs are laudable, they often emphasize adherence to specified rules rather than ethical reasoning and decision making. The participant often completes the program knowing organizational policies but not understanding the ethical underpinnings behind them. The graduate of such a program may be better equipped to act ethically in cases to which the preestablished rules clearly apply but have little understanding of how to address the new and ambiguous cases that inevitably arise. Perhaps more important, the graduate may be unable to explain decisions in such cases, or even in more common ones, with reference to a sound ethical foundation.

More important than ethics codes, training programs, or other methods to ensure compliance to formal rules is an understanding of basic universal values and how to apply them. A better method of imparting ethical awareness is needed, and we here give the broad outlines of a structure that proceeds beyond mere compliance to rules. Our purpose in describing the structure is not to suggest a formal education method but to examine the important elements of any attempt, formal or informal, to develop more effective ethical decision-making skills. We call this structure the "unified ethic," because it combines different philosophical ethical approaches into a single process. That process forms the means of resolving ethical problems both in public service and in the life of the citizen, for whom the public servant serves as an exemplar.

The clarification of universal values is especially important for public administrators because their status as moral agents requires them to justify the policies, programs, and practices of public organizations. Policies, programs, and practices must be examined in terms of the extent to which they further the core values and broad goals embodied in legislation, court decisions, or institutional regulations. For example, public administrators must be prepared to determine whether a policy is inconsistent with the advancement of human rights, environmental protection, or democratic governance. The public administrator, as moral agent, must be able to justify the policy or show why it should not be instituted.

For perspective on justification, we may turn to Douglas Yates (1981), who argues that as the American bureaucrat occupies a significant position in the policy-making process, the bureaucrat's value choices should be justified. Such justification, according to Yates, is especially important, given the lack of bureaucratic legitimacy in policy making compared with the legitimacy enjoyed by elected officials, who are exempt from justification by virtue of being elected. The policies, programs, and practices of public organizations are sufficiently significant to warrant systematic examination and justification from an ethical perspective. Their value premises and their obligations, the implications and effects of their decisions, must be explicit and legitimate if the concept of moral citizenship is to have any meaning and any future.

Yates, however, limits himself to the bureaucrat's choices, whereas our model entails justification of laws, policies, and programs themselves — an admittedly controversial shift that appears to move us away from procedural democracy and toward substantive democracy and what might be called moral due process. When we envision the public administrator *qua* moral exemplar acting as a moral agent whose position potentially may trump that of an elected official or organizational superior, we are reconfiguring the role, responsibility, and boundaries of public administration. We are making explicit and legitimate the moral autonomy of public servants as professional citizens. However, we also recognize the likelihood of disagreement, principled or otherwise; that the public administrator may not prevail; and that moral authority, in our current constitutional system, may sometimes have to yield to political or organizational authority if, as John Burke (1986) says, the public administrator, in the end, is committed to the enterprise as a whole.

The unified ethic is intended to enable the public administrator to justify his or her decisions regarding policy and thus to exemplify moral agency. However, we cannot propose a formula to resolve all ethical problems definitively. Different people using our procedure may come to different ethical conclusions on the same issue. Using the procedure conscientiously does not guarantee the morally perfect conclusion, but it will provide strong ethical justification.

Philosophical ethical theories may be divided into four classes. First is the teleological theory, which determines whether an action is good or bad on the basis of its consequences. According to this theory, which is also called consequentialism, the end justifies the means. The predominant theory of this kind is utilitarianism, which aims at the maximization of universal happiness as its desirable consequence. From this theory, we derive the following questions that should be asked: What are the consequences of my action? What are their long-term effects? Do they promote the greatest happiness? Answers to those questions may be difficult to ascertain with certainty, but the important consideration is that they be answered as fully as possible.

The second theory, deontology, is somewhat more complex. Deontological ethical theories consider actions to be good or bad in themselves, regardless of their consequences. The prevalent deontological theory is that of Immanuel Kant, who argues that actions must conform to rational, consistent principles. He gives three formulations that each attempt to capture the concept of rational consistency, though no single formulation and perhaps not a single set of them, can specify the concept perfectly for all instances. His three formulations, stated summarily, are as follows: Act according to a rule that can be willed to be a logically consistent universal law, treat all rational beings equally as ends in themselves, and act as a legislator in a kingdom of ends (i.e., in a society in which the aims of all members form a consistent, conflict-free whole). From Kantianism, we may derive the following questions: What principle applies in this case? Can this principle be applied consistently in this case and in all similar cases? Can this principle be considered a possible universal principle of behavior? Which course of action best exemplifies the ideal of treating all people as ends in themselves? Which course of action best exemplifies and most fully promotes the ideal of a society of free, responsible people whose ends promote each other rather than conflict with each other?

Deontology and teleology are often considered to be at odds with each other. Take, for example, the case of someone who is faced with lying to save innocent human lives. The teleological utilitarian would seem to favor telling the lie, whereas the rule-based deontologist would seem to favor telling the truth. However, the two theories may not be as distinct as first appearances suggest.

Consider, for example, President Lincoln's decision to sign the emancipation proclamation (Garofalo and Geuras, 1999, p. 96). Suppose, first, that he used only utilitarian considerations, concluding that humanity would be better off if slavery were eliminated. Would a deontologist be justified in dismissing Lincoln's decision as amoral because deontological considerations did not enter into it? However, it would be equally absurd for a teleologist to fault a deontological Lincoln who operated on the inviolability of the principle that human beings are ends in themselves.

Most likely, we would expect a fully moral Lincoln to approach the question from both teleological and deontological perspectives because, in the end, they are not all that different. The utilitarian's belief that people should be happy surely presupposes the inherent value of human beings. The deontologist's treatment of human beings as ends in themselves and consideration of legislation in a kingdom of ends surely must take human happiness into account. Principle and consequence are so interrelated as to be impossible to disentangle. Therefore, the ethical thinker's consideration of both teleological and deontological questions entails no ultimate contradiction.

The third ethical theory is called virtue theory. According to the virtue theorist, an action is considered good or bad on the basis of the character trait evidenced in the action, regardless of the principle or utility that the act serves. According to the virtue theorist, if an act expresses a positive trait such as honesty, generosity, or courage, the act is to be considered good, but actions expressing negative traits such as egocentricity, spitefulness, or rashness are bad. From the virtue theorist, we derive the following questions: What character traits does this action express? What effect will this action have on my character? What effect will this action have on the character of other people?

However, virtue theory can easily be folded into the deontology–teleology unity when one asks why certain traits are considered virtues whereas others are considered vices. Invariably, the virtuous traits are related to either utility or principle, and usually to both. For example, to risk one's life to save strangers from a fire is courageous, and such courage both promotes social utility and expresses the moral principle that human life is inherently valuable. However, risking one's life to prove that one can survive multiple cobra bites is asinine; such an action does no good for anyone and expresses no moral principle. Traits are evaluated as virtues or vices because of teleological and deontological considerations.

The final ethical theory is intuitionism. The intuitionist determines whether an act is good or bad on the basis of a kind of sixth sense or intuition that observes a moral property inherent in the action. Whether such a property exists or not, however, it is evident that some actions just feel good or bad morally. From the intuitionist, we borrow the following questions: Do I feel good about this action? What does my conscience tell me about this?

Like virtue theory, however, intuitionism cannot be separated from the other moral theories. Although feelings are subjective, if one were to examine how one feels about a moral issue, one would probably discover that the feeling is not baseless but is related to the factors included in deontology, teleology, and virtue theory. It is difficult to imagine a moral issue that is not related to them.

The unified theory asks the ethical decision maker to consider all of the questions suggested by the four theories and to attempt to find a consistency among his or her answers. The exercise will not always be easy. On occasion, consideration of one or two of the four aspects will lead toward a different conclusion from the others. In such cases, the decision maker must use judgment in determining the relative weight of the conflicting factors. Regardless of the final conclusion, however, the decision maker will be able to give good, if not unassailable, reasons for the action. One can ask nothing more.

An example is needed to demonstrate the application of the unified ethic. The previously mentioned case of the use of medical leave for vacations will serve this purpose. In that case, management was unwilling or unable to stop the practice among employees but also occasionally engaged in it themselves. The order in which the unified ethic's questions are asked is not significant, but we will begin with those of the intuitionist.

It would appear that initially the nonmanagement employees would have little discomfort in answering the intuitionist's questions. Because those employees are untroubled by the practice, they would likely say that they do feel fine about it and that it does not bother their consciences.

Furthermore, the employees may find even the utilitarian questions unthreatening to, if not supportive of, the practice. The employees may argue that the practice is harmless and improves morale by allowing more vacation time, but the deontologist's and the virtue theorist's questions may prove more troublesome.

One of the more difficult deontological questions for the employees is the one that asks, "Can this principle be considered as a possible universal principle of behavior?" To explain their absences on an official document, the employees must lie. The principle "It is acceptable to lie whenever it is to your advantage" cannot be sustained. Such a principle would make asking and answering questions in such cases an empty enterprise, and the answers themselves would be devoid of credible content. The question concerning treating people as ends in themselves rather than as means would also threaten the practice. It would appear to treat taxpayers and legislators, and policy makers, who devised the restrictions on vacation time, as means rather than as ends in themselves.

The most difficult questions for the employees to answer may be those of the virtue theorist, who asks, "What character traits does this action express?", "What effect will this action have on my character?", and "What effect will this action have on the character of other people?" Lying with impunity for self-interest displays and encourages dishonesty, both in the liar and in those who observe the common and successful use of the practice.

Apparently, then, the answers to the four types of questions are inconsistent with each other. The intuitionist and teleological answers conflict with the deontological and virtue theorist answers. The next step is to attempt to reconcile all into one solution. In this case, the conflicts are easily resolved.

In light of the answers to the virtue theorist questions, the teleological questions deserve reconsideration. One of those questions asked about the long-term consequences of the practice. But a general dishonesty, or at least a lack of respect for honesty, within an organization is certain to cause long-term problems, both within the organization and with the society that the organization serves. Also, it would not be helpful to either the society or the organization itself if it acquired a reputation for lying. And what could happen if the taxpayers, legislators, or framers of the policy discovered what was going on? Even if no obvious on-the-job problems occur, it is difficult to relinquish one's dishonesty as soon as the working day ends. It is very difficult to argue that dishonest people are good for a society.

We may now return to the formerly untroubled intuitions. In light of the deontological, virtue theorist, and reexamined teleological considerations, the employees' intuitions might now be different from what they were originally. Let us at least hope so.

The case that we have just considered is a relatively easy one that is chosen to illustrate the application of our unified ethic. Not all cases will be so simple. We examine some much more complex examples later in this book.

MORAL AGENCY, THE PUBLIC ADMINISTRATOR, AND THE PRIVATE CITIZEN

Although we have concentrated on the significance of the unified ethic for public administrators, this ethic is meant to apply to all moral agents, whether they are public servants, private entrepreneurs, or public/private citizens. In the course of this book, we examine a broad range of issues that the unified ethic can address. The issues include the following: What are the moral limits of governmental authority? What are the moral limits of private corporate activity? What responsibilities do members of the society have to the natural and social environments? Do citizens of local communities have global responsibilities? Does globalism change the nature of the citizen's moral responsibilities? How can the individual moral agent resolve conflicting obligations to different principals? Public administrators, in their professional capacity, grapple with all of these issues and thus can serve as exemplary moral agents.

The early stages of this book develop the notion of moral agency in the public, private, and nonprofit sectors. We proceed to discuss the common moral core that they share both among themselves and with the private citizen, for whom the public administrator serves as the most significant, though not sole, exemplar. We then outline the challenges of moral agency, including its moral conflicts, and provide strategies, based on the unified ethic, to meet those challenges.

In the course of this book, we encounter disturbing issues, including ethical problems in all of the aforementioned sectors. It is not our intention to expose, in an accusatory manner, elements of moral decay. Our purpose is to describe problems as they exist and to suggest how the conscientious citizen, as a moral agent, might respond to them, with the public administrator as the most noteworthy model.

REFERENCES

Bowman, J. S., and R. Williams. 1997. Ethics in Government: From a Winter of Despair to a Spring of Hope. *Public Administration Review*. 57:517–526.

Burke, J. P. 1986. *Bureaucratic Responsibility*. Baltimore, MD: Johns Hopkins University Press.

Dagger, R. 1986. Politics and the Pursuit of Autonomy. In *Justification*, eds. J. R. Pennock and J. W. Chapman, pp. 270–290. New York: New York University Press.

Garofalo, C., and D. Geuras. 1999. *Ethics in the Public Service: The Moral Mind at Work*. Washington, D.C.: Georgetown University Press.

Geuras, D., and C. Garofalo, 2002. *Practical Ethics in Public Administration*: Vienna, VA: Management Concepts.

Lawton, A. 1998. *Ethical Management for the Public Services*. Buckingham: Open University Press.

Lewis, C. W. 1991. *The Ethical Challenge in Public Service*. San Francisco: Jossey-Bass.

Macedo, S. 1990. The Politics of Justification. *Political Theory*. 18:280–304.

Moore, M. H., and G. Sparrow, 1990. *Ethics in Government, The Moral Challenge of Public Leadership*. Englewood Cliffs, NJ: Prentice Hall.

Rohr, J. A. 1989. *Ethics for Bureaucrats*, 2nd ed. New York: Marcel Dekker.

Yates, D., Jr. 1981. Hard Choices: Justifying Bureaucratic Decisions. In *Public Duties: The Moral Obligations of Government Officials*, eds. J. L. Fleishman et al., pp. 32–51. Cambridge, MA: Harvard University Press.

2 Moral Agency in the Public Sector

In this chapter, we examine moral agency in the public sector by considering public servants in their ideal forms. We discuss the ideal public administrator, elected official, political appointee, and member of the judiciary. We argue that although each of these trustees of the public differs in the details of his or her professional activity, they all function as moral agents. The public administrator is the most suitable as a moral exemplar because the professional activities of the public administrator most resemble those of the public at large. The public administrator's moral agency, and thus his or her moral exemplarship, is most demanded in cases of evaluation, conflicts of obligations, unclear obligations, bending and breaking of the rules, and moral whistle blowing. In such cases, especially those in which the public administrator's moral judgment conflicts with standard procedures, a sophisticated level of moral analysis is required.

One should not be fixated with the ideal. It may be so unattainable as to intimidate us and discourage us from even attempting to instantiate it in the imperfect world and in our imperfect selves. Also, as the history of utopian schemes indicates, an ideal is not a roadmap to perfection. Ideals, at best, tell us where we would like to go, but they seldom provide directions concerning how to get there.

Nevertheless, ideals can be useful in their proper context, as scholars since at least the time of Plato have recognized. Ideals tell us what things should be, even if in reality they fall short of perfection. As a consequence, the ideal provides us with something for which to strive. By examining things in their perfect state, one recognizes the respects in which things as they exist could be improved. Second, the ideal provides a criterion by which existing, imperfect instances can be evaluated. Even if none approximates the ideal, some are closer to it than others and can therefore be deemed better. Third, studying things in their ideal form helps us to understand them better, even if at the cost of simplification. One could, for example, imagine how difficult it would be to understand geometry or physics if not isolated from the hidden variables of the "real" world. Finally, we should not discount Nathaniel Hawthorne's observation in *The Great Stone Face* (1985) that one's admiration for ideals may, in some unconscious, indescribable way, cause one to approximate them. If Hawthorne were right, he alone would provide sufficient reason for our examination.

THE IDEAL PUBLIC ADMINISTRATOR

In the earlier days of public administration theory, under the influence of Woodrow Wilson, the public administrator was regarded as a tool of the public will, avoiding exercising evaluative judgments by only executing those of the public as represented through their elected officials. Wilson (1887) argued that public administrators should merely execute the policies that the political process dictates. The ideal public administrator, in the Wilsonian sense, would therefore be a public "servant," in at once both the fullest and the emptiest senses of the word: fullest in its sense of absolute commitment to its designated task, but emptiest in its absence of personal autonomy. The Wilsonian model entails the public administrator's acting as an agent of a single principal: the legislator.

George Frederickson (1980, p. 17) includes Wilson's concept of public administration, together with those of Max Weber and Frederick Winslow Taylor, under the "Classic Bureaucratic Model." According to this model, the public administrator functions as an element in a bureaucratic structure that demands obedience within a hierarchical system governed by a legislative body. This model dictates the values of efficiency, economy, and effectiveness in carrying out legislative aims.

Other models that, according to Frederickson, subsequently developed provided a more complex environment for the public administrator but still provided little, if any, room for administrative moral judgment. These models include the "Nonbureaucratic Model," (p. 22) which included greater emphasis on impartial rationality and productivity than the Classic Bureaucratic Model, and the "Institutional Model," (p. 22) which was most concerned with merely describing the behavioral patterns within organizations without prescribing moral values.

Although the Institutional Model attempted to maintain a scientific objectivity, it may have, perhaps unintentionally, encouraged a less value-free examination of public administration. The Institutional Model revealed the resistance of bureaucracies to change, with the exception of incremental change, as well as their tendency to become inefficient. Thus, the Institutional Model, although purporting to make no evaluative judgments, presented a reality about which observers would make judgments.

Frederickson's "Human Relations Model," (p. 25) eschewed the perhaps untenable value-free concept of public administration. This model, similar to the Institutional Model, examined the internal functioning of the organization, but with an emphasis on the interests and working conditions of the members of the organization. According to Frederickson, the values embedded in this model included worker and client participation in decision making; reduction in status differentiation; reduction in internal competition; and emphasis on openness, honesty, self-actualization, and general worker satisfaction. Although the Human Relations Model may have been largely motivated by the attempt to make organizations more efficient and effective by improving the working conditions of members of the organization, the interest of those members became, at least in part, ends in themselves.

The fifth of Frederickson's models, the "Public Choice Model," permits a variety of diverse organizations, structured in different ways, to provide services in the ways that they find best. The Public Choice Model allows for different organizational cultures and accommodates different ways of accomplishing organizational goals, including outsourcing and privatization. This model encourages experimentation and originality. It also permits citizens, albeit to a limited extent, to choose among different organizations: If someone does not like the manner in which services are delivered in his or her own location, one can move to another place, where a different set of organizations offer the services.

The Human Relations Model is the only one of the five models that explicitly espouses values other than mere efficiency and effectiveness. The other four interpret the public organization as answering only to the values imposed on it by a hierarchical structure, with the electorate acting as the ultimate source of authority. Those models, in their efforts to avoid moral decision making within the organization, would not likely favor the notion of the public administrator as moral agent. The Human Relations Model values the employee of the organization and thus expresses a value, but it would still not encourage moral agency. The concerns of the Human Relations model include the welfare and self-actualization of the employee but would not, at least explicitly, suggest that the employee should be making moral decisions in carrying out professional duties.

Although all five models might presuppose the employee to be an ethical agent, and the Human Relations Model may be seen to be encouraging ethical agency by promoting self-actualization, no model evidently supports the notion of moral agency. All five would conform to Robert Bork's notion of the public employee, as demonstrated in his decision to support President Nixon's removal of the Watergate Special Prosecutor. Bork understood his position as that of an agent of his superior in the structural chain of command and not as that of a moral agent.

In contrast to those five models, The New Public Administration, which, according to Frederickson, developed in the late 1960s and early 1970s, encourages moral agency. The "new" aspect of the New Public Administration was its addition of the pursuit of social equity to the already recognized expectations of efficiency and economy in Public Administration. The New Public Administration encouraged changes in static bureaucracy by means of such devices as decentralization, evaluation, and termination while promoting organizational tools such as zero-based budgeting and productivity measurement. The aim of such changes and innovations was not only to increase efficiency and "bang for the buck" but also to restructure public organizations so that they could better meet public needs. Advocates of the New Public Administration also favored a more activist stance among public administrators in forming, rather than merely executing, more equitable public policy.

If public administrators have a responsibility to advance social equity, they are, *ipso facto*, moral agents. Although their moral agency may be restricted to the seemingly single value of equity, they would have at least begun to recognize a moral value, rather than an authority in the bureaucracy, as a principal.

Furthermore, the value of social equity is not really a single value, because innumerable values are interwoven into the fabric of an equitable society. Those values include equality, respect, dignity, security, opportunity, and the meeting of at least basic material needs. Equity includes the entire range of morally significant social values.

John Rawls (1971) provides philosophical support for the New Public Administration. According to Rawls, government must adhere to two basic principles of justice. The first requires that each person have an equal right to the most extensive possible system of basic liberties that are compatible with liberty for all, and the second allows a society to tolerate inequalities if necessary to provide the greatest possible benefits to the least advantaged in the society (p. 135). Rawls therefore believes that all people have a right to equal liberty as long as no group, including the whole, would suffer to preserve the equality. For example, few would demand total equality if the only way in which it could be attained would be to require that everyone be equally destitute. If equality were the only value to be considered, killing everyone and committing suicide would attain it. Rawls would therefore favor a productive but heavily regulated capitalism over an unproductive but total egalitarianism. But he would favor such a capitalism, or any system that permits inequality, only if it benefited the least advantaged members of the society better than any other system. The concern for those least advantaged and the emphasis on equality both contribute to the notion of equity that is central to the New Public Administration.

The normative nature of public administration, evident in the New Public Administration, finds a culmination in the second Minnowbrook conference. In the essay that has come to be known as the Blacksburg Manifesto (Wamsley et al., 1990), the authors argue that the facile dichotomy of fact and value leads to an overly simplified dichotomy of the political from the administrative functions of a governmental system. They maintain that "we need to recognize that at the highest level, speaking descriptively and conceptually, there is no dichotomy. Public administration at this level of abstraction is an integral part of the governance and political process" (p. 43).

The code of ethics of the American Society for Public Administration includes normative considerations, especially the concern for equity, as evidenced in the following entries:

- Exercise discretionary authority to promote the public interest;
- Exercise compassion, benevolence, fairness, and optimism;
- Promote constitutional principles of equality, fairness, representativeness, responsiveness, and due process in protecting citizens' rights; and
- Subordinate institutional loyalties to the public good (Geuras and Garofalo, 2002, pp. 34–35)

If the code is to guide the professional behavior of public administrators, they must act as moral agents, as evidenced in the admonition to use discretionary authority and the emphasis on concepts such as equality, fairness, and the public good.

There are several aspects of the public administrator's professional activities that admit of moral agency, but the most debated and perhaps most significant is that of the exercise of discretion. Discretion is one of the thorniest issues in public administration theory and practice. Many scholars have addressed discretion with various aims, approaches, and assumptions. Some have argued for expanding the scope of administrative discretion, and others have argued for limiting it. Some have discussed discretion from a normative perspective, others from an empirical perspective. Some scholars approve of administrative discretion, at least as a practical matter, whereas others find it problematic on the basis of democratic theory. Thus, discretion has proved to be a fertile source of discourse and debate.

The belief that bureaucracy is instrumental and that bureaucrats are agents, not principals, is an important element in much of the thinking about political–administrative relations across ideologies, cultures, and countries. As Aberbach, Putnam, and Rockman (1981) suggest, "The official norm in every state is that civil servants obediently serve their political 'masters'" (p. 5). However, at the same time, we encounter routine dismissal of the politics–administration dichotomy. Robert Behn (2001), for example, argues not only that discretion is necessary but also that "without discretion, there can be no accountability" (p. 82), which, in turn, "requires both discretion and trust" (p. 83). Thus, we confront a conundrum: On the one hand, administrative discretion is feared across the globe (Behn, 2001, p. 93), and, on the other hand, it is exercised in every administrative setting across the globe. Therefore, an important challenge facing administrative scholars is to understand and, perhaps, resolve this conundrum so that responsible discretion can be incorporated as an organizational reality into public service ethics education and training programs and, ultimately, into administrative practice.

A major aspect of this conundrum is the question of what alternative to administrative discretion is either available or possible. For example, Aberbach, Putnam, and Rockman (1981) examine the roles and relationships of bureaucrats and politicians in Western democracies (specifically, Great Britain, France, Germany, Italy, the Netherlands, and the United States) and conclude that "the distinction between discretionary (political) and nondiscretionary (administrative) decisions is ultimately untenable" (p. 5). The authors argue that "even if civil servants wanted merely to follow orders — and there is some evidence that many honestly do — that is a practical impossibility" (p. 5) because politicians lack the expertise, information, and time to decide the thousands of policy questions in modern government. In their view, "discretion, not merely for deciding individual cases, but for crafting the content of most legislation, has passed from the legislature to the executive, . . . and within the executive branch elected politicians are everywhere outnumbered and outlasted by career civil servants" (p. 6). Thus, to these three scholars, as a practical matter, no alternative to administrative discretion appears to be possible or even desirable under the circumstances of modern governance.

Clearly, however, given the constitutional, cultural, and ethical features of the debate, justification of administrative discretion on practical grounds alone is insufficient. Therefore, to broaden our understanding, we consider the work of Donald Warwick (1981), John Burke (1986), Gary Bryner (1987), James Wilson (1989), Arthur Applbaum (1999), Christian Hunold and B. Guy Peters (2001), and Richard Lehne (2001). Warwick (1981) probes the ethics of administrative discretion because the gap between the image of the civil servant as executor and the reality of the civil servant as initiator underscores the need for such ethics. According to Warwick, the most significant ways that public officials exercise discretion are policy formulation, implementation, and evaluation. They seize the initiative in a policy domain, draft legislation, and negotiate broad interpretations of policy, thus raising ethical questions about the limits of administrative entre- preneurship. As Warwick puts it: "Should administrative responsibilities regularly be 'up for grabs' by skilled operators, or do assigned responsibilities have some moral claim?" (p. 97).

Warwick also offers what he calls "An Ethics of Discretion" and suggests five questions that he believes are real for many administrators but that "have rarely been discussed in essays on ethics and the public service" (p. 111). First, should bureaucratic entrepreneurs seize the initiative in a policy domain when they see a compelling need, or should they follow established procedures? Second, should public officials mobilize outside constituency support to strengthen their bargaining position, or should they act only within their agency's hierarchy? Third, how far should a program manager press for results when some individuals may be harmed as a consequence of strong pressures? Fourth, is it morally justifiable for officials to do nothing when they oppose a program, to obstruct or subvert it, or to carry out only those parts they approve of? Fifth, are officials obligated to design a completely fair evaluation of their programs and to present the findings in an accurate and evenhanded manner, or should they have some latitude for slanting the design and results? According to Warwick, these are ethical dilemmas that "arise from the pulls on the administrator created by different conceptions of the good to be promoted through public service" (p. 111). Although posed two decades ago, these questions seem quite germane to contemporary governmental reforms, especially New Public Management (NPM). In any event, to Warwick, the key issue for administrative discretion is responsibility in the generation and use of power, for "it is not whether officials should have discretion but when, how, and for what purposes it should be used" (p. 125).

In *Bureaucratic Responsibility* (1986), John Burke traces the development of the major positions on discretion, pointing out, for example, that proponents of formal legalism argue that bureaucrats should have no discretion in either making or implementing policy. "For advocates of this approach, the political and moral considerations that might inform an official of his obligations and duties are already expressed in existing laws, rules, administrative regulations or other dictates of higher authorities" (p. 11). Action beyond these dictates violates the public trust, usurps authority, and interjects individual, group, or institutional bias into the policy process.

Burke, however, suggests that "there are situations . . . where discretion can serve as a means to legitimate policy ends" (p. 12). It may be granted to officials to use their own expertise and skill, which have become more and more necessary given the growing intricacy and interrelatedness of governmental programs. "[T]he increasing technical complexity of public policy and the concomitant need for professional autonomy, hence discretion," Burke observes, "probably account for much of the expansion of the discretionary power of the bureaucracy" (p. 13). However, he argues that it is not only the complexity of government that requires administrative discretion: "The exercise of discretion may also serve the spirit and purposes of public policy, while strict adherence to rules and regulations, paradoxically, may not" (p. 13). Discretion, for example, may be necessary to secure the intent of legislation when strict adherence to formal dictates would result in undesired consequences or unanticipated outcomes.

Gary Bryner (1987) notes that the scope of agency responsibility and authority almost always exceeds the resources provided. Agencies are given little guidance in their enabling statutes concerning how they should shape their regulatory agenda, set priorities, allocate scarce resources, and distribute costs and benefits in the rules and regulations that they issue. Therefore, Bryner believes that bureaucratic discretion is appropriate, even essential, in ensuring that policies are developed by experts and that scientific expertise and technical calculations determine environmental, health, and safety regulations — the focus of his book.

Arthur Applbaum (1999) poses the following question: "May government officials create and exercise discretion to pursue their dissenting views of good policy (constrained only by political prudence and a reasonable interpretation of the law), or should officials faithfully serve the will or the interests of those who have formal authority over their actions or over the disputed policies?" (p. 207). His answer: "It depends" (p. 207). Applbaum argues that an account of when a public official may legitimately act on his or her judgment of good policy is similar to an account of when legislators may act on their judgments in the face of disagreements with their constituents or when presidents can act on their judgments in the face of congressional disagreement. The common consideration in all of these cases is this question: If substantive judgments conflict, when should an actor subordinate his or her conduct to the authority of others?

Applbaum suggests that on the obedient-servant view, one's own beliefs about the good are never good reasons for action. Public roles are to be impersonal, and public figures are to be interchangeable. Discretion, though often necessary, is regrettable. Applbaum, however, describes this view as an "accountant's version of public control and accountability" and argues that it "is grossly inadequate as a description of political life" (p. 214). A public administrator who wants to do nothing but obey his or her superiors or a governor who wants only to respond to the will of the people faces a serious problem: Mandates of public officials to act are ambiguous, conflict-ridden, forever changing, and shaped in part by the very actions of these intendedly obedient public officials. In this regard,

Applbaum's position is analogous to the view articulated by Aberbach, Putnam, and Rockman (1981).

We may group the arguments that establish that the complete, ideal public administrator must be a moral agent into two categories. The first, which includes the positions of Frederickson, Wamsley, Burke, and, in general, those of both the advocates of New Public Administration and of the participants in Minnowbrook II, recognizes the moral responsibility of the public administrator individually and public administration as an entity to promote social equity and related values. We may therefore refer to the first category as the argument from the viewpoint of social justice. The second category, which includes the positions of Bryner and Applbaum, acknowledges the reality that value-free public administration is a practical impossibility. We may refer to the second category as the argument from the viewpoint of practical experience. The two categories, both individually and in combination, as they appear in Warwick's writings, provide strong support for the role of the public administrator as a moral agent.

THE LEGISLATOR'S MORAL AGENCY

The legislator is a moral agent in the fulfillment of his or her duties, but the legislator's moral agency differs from that of the public administrator in several respects. First, the legislator makes the laws and supplies the funding for the public service. However, this difference may not be as great as it appears on the surface. In formulating laws, at least in a democracy, the legislator is ultimately responsible to the citizenry, as is the public administrator. Though the public administrator is further removed from the public in the structural "chain of command" than the legislator, both the public administrator and the legislator answer to the same ultimate authority. Still, one might argue that because of the legislator's more proximate responsibility to the public, the legislator expresses the public will more directly.

A second difference lies in the nature of the public administrator's discretion, as we discussed earlier. There is no question of whether the legislator should exercise discretion in formulating legislation. The exercise of the legislator's judgment is so essential that it could hardly be called discretion. The public administrator exercises judgment when formulations do not apply clearly, but legislators are relatively unfettered in their exercise of moral judgment because they create the formulations.

A third difference suggests a reason for which the public administrator may serve as a better model of moral agency than the legislator. Whereas legislators enact measures for the benefit of the entire society, they also represent smaller constituencies, such as their states or districts. Legislators are expected to assist specific constituents in seeking governmental benefits, but public administrators are generally barred by ethical rules from "going outside of the system" to benefit an individual. Furthermore, legislators are expected to compete or bargain for favors for their districts, but public administrators do not have legislative districts to serve. As a consequence, the public administrator is an agent of the entire unit, be it a country, state, county, or community, but representative legislators serve both the whole unit and, often, smaller geographic units.

However, even in this third respect, the difference between the public administrator and the legislator may be smaller than it appears. Although the public administrator does not have a geographic constituency that is distinct from the entire political unit, or a constituency that elects public administrators, public organizations are beholden to groups that could be called constituencies. They include the groups, such as indigent people, people with disabilities, and public school students, whose interests the public administrator is intended to serve. Those constituencies, if we may use that term, deserve the public administrator's special concern but may conflict with the interests of the general public. A second set of constituencies are the organizations, which are themselves public, that are created to serve those agencies. For example, a consolidated school district is itself a public agency, but it is also the constituency of the state educational administration. In addition, unions and other employee organizations may exert pressures on public administrators and thus be considered another constituency. Although the constituencies of public administrators may be distinctly different from the electorate of a legislature, they may not be so distinct as to obviate any analogy with legislators.

However, there remains one important respect in which the moral agency of legislators is different from that of public administrators. The professional life of the public administrator resembles that of the public citizen much more than does that of the legislator. In comparing public administrators with legislators, the average citizen would say that public administrators, bureaucrats as they may be, are more "like us." Few citizens can look to the legislator as a model for their professional behavior: Citizens do not spend most of their time debating laws, engaging in political strategy, soliciting contributions, and campaigning for office. Public administration is so vast and multifaceted that it includes activities comparable to those of nearly any form of gainful employment.

It may be argued that although the activities of the public administrator are similar to those of many employees in the general populace, the public administrator often functions under different structural rules than would his or her counterpart in the private sector. Many of the structural rules of the public sector are intended to ensure that the general public is properly served, but most private concerns function to benefit themselves. When the public organization favors itself over the people that it serves, it betrays its mission. When a private organization favors its interests over those of its customers — or even the people collectively — it engages in business as usual. For example, public organizations, to protect the public from the private interests of employees, have nepotism and consanguinity rules that are not always imposed within private organizations. Budgets of public organizations are matters of public record, but private organizations are generally not required to reveal all of their internal fiscal allocations. One might therefore argue that public employees labor under a layer of rules and regulations with which private organizations need not concern themselves.

The absence of that layer of rules and regulations does not mean that they should be of no concern to the private organization, however. Although they may not have the force of law in private organizations, these rules and regulations may yet have the force of morality. Even if, for example, a private organization has no rules regarding nepotism, the practice should still be discouraged. Similarly, although good arguments may be advanced against requiring organizations to reveal all of their financial details to the public, morally concerned decision makers would do well to ask themselves whether they would take pride in their organizations if their books were made public. Although many of the rules and regulations of public organizations generally are not, and perhaps should not be, imposed by law on private organizations, the explicit moral formulations of the public sector in many cases can serve as moral recommendations in the public sector.

Both the function of the public administrator as a moral agent and the similarity of the public agent's work to that of the general populace are related to the inclusion of most public organizations in the executive branch. Legislators devise laws and policies, and judges interpret and apply law, but public agencies perform the services that government provides to the populace. Public agencies are the doers of public good, and therefore to them the term "agent" best applies. Their services are so varied and numerous that, among their broad array, nearly every profession can find affinity.

THE JUDICIARY AND MORAL AGENCY

The question of whether judges can act as moral agents is a matter of significant debate. Some theorists, such as Alan Goldman (1980), argue that the role of the judge is only that of interpreting and applying the law while withholding any moral values that he or she might privately hold. But even Goldman allows that there may be cases in which the law, because of its inevitable flaws and inabilities to anticipate all possible circumstances, is clearly at odds with morality. In such cases, though they may be rare, Goldman suggests that a judge may have the authority to impose a moral judgment.

Those who would dispute Goldman and argue that judges can impose their own moral judgments — as perhaps Judge Taney should have in the Dred Scott case — suggest that a judge could still be a moral agent. However, even if Goldman is correct, the moral agency of the judge would still not be removed entirely. In making a moral judgment to suspend his or her other moral beliefs to uphold the law as it is written, the judge would function as a moral agent.

Aside from the issues of whether a judge is ever a moral agent, or under what conditions the judge may function as a moral agent, it is evident that the judge is not the best model of moral agency for the common citizen. The work of a judge resembles that of most citizens only to a slight degree. In any organization, rules must be interpreted and applied, but such activities constitute the entire professional function of very few employees.

CLASSIFICATION OF MORAL DECISIONS IN PUBLIC ADMINISTRATION

The general charge to act in the public interest is the unifying factor in the public sector, interpreted broadly to include public servants, legislators, and judges. That charge distinguishes the public sector from much, if not all, of the private sector. Within the public sector, the public service most resembles the general public. The public administrator, who oversees and implements the function of the public service, is therefore the best candidate to model moral agency for the public as a whole.

We cannot describe all possible situations in which the public administrator displays moral agency. We can, however, enumerate different classes of cases that public administrators commonly face.

EVALUATION

Public agents are constantly in the process of evaluating programs, projects, and individuals, including themselves. Responsible evaluation requires ethical agency, as do all other functions of one's professional life. But evaluation involves moral agency when questions arise concerning whether the public is best served by an agency, its divisions, its projects, or its personnel.

Evaluations often arise in cases of funding reduction, where if "across the board cuts" are not instituted, assessment of the relative importance of divisions and sometimes entire agencies becomes necessary. Even under normal fiscal conditions, however, agencies do not have the resources to do all of the things under their charge with equal commitment. Carol Lewis (1991, p. 72) mentions an unfortunate case in which a police department failed to enforce a building violation on a structure that eventually burned and cost the lives of 87 people. In explaining the failure, a police lieutenant implied that violent crime such as murder was a higher priority than building infractions, which are extremely common. One can sympathize with the police in such a situation, though in this case, the consequences of a seemingly reasonable priority were tragic. Most agencies, like the police department, have to make choices concerning the relative importance of different concerns. Even when resources are sufficient to encompass all of the potential tasks that an agency must perform, they cannot likely be attended at the same time. One must decide what to do first.

Evaluation of a division is also morally necessary to protect the public's right to responsible oversight of its investment. A division may be acting in a perfectly moral manner, and its employees may perform their duties in an exemplary manner, but the division may not produce sufficiently significant benefit to the public to justify its existence. In such a case, the moral public administrator may find it necessary to recommend termination of the agency, even under no financial exigency.

Let us take, as an example, a division that once served a good purpose but is no longer needed. We may imagine a public institution of higher learning, which, in a period of expansion, needed an office to oversee construction. The office may function well for many years, but when the campus has grown to its limits, and funding for new buildings is drastically reduced, the office may no longer be needed as an independent entity. It would be difficult to terminate such a division, but the moral agent must decide on moral grounds.

CONFLICTS OF OBLIGATIONS

Conflicts of obligations, which also may involve evaluation of priorities, form another category of decisions that moral agents must make in public administration. In such cases, there are moral claims on the agent that, by themselves, would demand satisfaction but that conflict with other worthy demands. In a classic case (Leazes and Campanelli, 1996), two moral or legal principles conflict, as when a right to privacy of an AIDS patient conflicted with the rights of others who cleaned her blood from her body and from the immediate surroundings to be informed of a potential health risk. Cases of conflict between written rules, although difficult for those caught between them and interesting to contemplate, are not as troublesome as cases of conflict between less specific principles and obligations. Because the person caught in the conflict can demonstrate the flaw in the rule structure, he or she cannot be blamed. After becoming evident, a conflict of written rules can be resolved, at least for future cases, with a new formulation.

Some conflicts of obligation, however, cannot be so easily resolved by reformulation of written laws or regulations. In determining the sites of highways, drug rehabilitation centers, homes for the elderly, and other needed structures, administrators must balance their obligations to different affected groups. Often economic benefits of projects such as power plants must be balanced against environmental concerns. No reasonable written rule would likely replace human discretion in resolving such issues.

When conflicts exist between the public interest and the private interests of the administrator and his or her organization, the moral agent would, as is virtually self-evident, favor the public interest. Such is not a true conflict of obligations but conflict between a moral obligation and a private benefit. Conflicts of obligation pit the legitimate interests of one portion of the public against another. Here, the moral agent must discern the overall public interest, as opposed to that of specific factions. As difficult as such discernment may be, another class of conflicts of obligation is even thornier. Sometimes the public interest conflicts with another legitimate moral goal, which may, in some cases, even outweigh the public interest. In such cases, the public administrator is called on to become either a public agent or a moral agent.

Rawls's second principle of fairness is meant to address such conflicts. Some governmental policies may favor the interests of the overall populace while being unfair to a deserving minority. Reductions in programs for the disabled, for example, may reduce taxes and, let us say for the sake of argument, benefit the overall economic condition of the society. Although it may be argued that such programs should eventually benefit everyone, let us suppose that they, in a specific instance, do not. Rawls would argue that even at the expense of the society's best interest, fairness, as expressed in his second principle, would require that those disadvantaged members of society be served. According to Rawls, decisions made under the veil of ignorance would require that the least advantaged be at least as well off as they otherwise would be. The disabled would, in the example as constructed, be worse off. The conflict in such cases is that between the public interest, understood as the overall interest of the society, and fairness.

The public interest can also be at odds with fairness in the case of public employees. Regulations requiring the payment of the "prevailing wage" to municipal workers, if not unionization itself, may put strains on government budgets and those of taxpayers. Other measures that may be harmful to the most efficient possible functioning of government include preference to seniority in personnel reduction, affirmative action programs, and strong retiree pension programs. Unless one defines "public interest" as identical to the ultimate moral right on any public issue, there may be conflict between the public interest and fairness, which, in Rawls's theory, constitutes justice. The agent of the public would, in such conflicts, favor the public interest, whereas the moral agent would favor the just.

UNCLEAR OBLIGATIONS

Rules are written and principles are formulated for cases that can be anticipated. Sometimes odd cases arise to which the rules and principles do not apply in any easily discernible way. In public administration, with its rich experience and well-codified policies, such cases may be uncommon, but they can arise. Let us consider, for example, the bizarre. Suppose that an intelligent extraterrestrial survived a crash landing in Ohio. If he could not return to his home planet, would he be required to file for a Green Card? Would he be eligible for welfare payments? If his species has an average life span of 900 years, would he still be eligible for Social Security at age 65 years?

Such cases seem remote, but peculiar events occur even to lifelong earthlings. For example,* a man eligible for Social Security benefits was recoded as deceased by the Social Security Administration. Although he tried several times to prove that he was alive, he did not receive his Social Security checks. He requested and received the assistance of a neighbor who, by the elderly man's good fortune, worked for the Social Security Administration. Is the effort to help the elderly neighbor a case of influence peddling? Would it become a case of influence peddling if the two neighbors had, independent of the incident, financial dealings with each other?

Although the cases of the extraterrestrial and the undead elderly man may seem so rare as to be negligible, new situations that do not fit the established

---

* We are indebted to Stuart Gilman for this example, which he presented at a lecture on ethics in the public service.

rules inevitably arise in a dynamic world. When VCRs first became popular, they temporarily caused confusion concerning copyrights, and the development of the personal computer has introduced a range of issues concerning intellectual property and privacy. In time, rules will be developed to accommodate such novelties, but in the meantime, discretion and judgment are necessary.

BENDING AND BREAKING THE RULES

As Carol Lewis notes, bending the rules can be appropriate or not, depending on the circumstances (1991, p. 129). We have included breaking the rules, along with bending them, as a single category because their intent is the same: choosing to honor a value higher than that of following either the letter or the intent of specified rules. Furthermore, it is difficult to distinguish bending from breaking in many instances, as rules are not physical objects such as pencils or panes of glass.

The moral agent may have occasion to disobey rules, as evidenced by the experience of Nazi Germany. More recent and proximate cases arose out of the Watergate scandal, in which a moral agent arguably may have, unlike Solicitor Robert Bork, chosen to disobey a presidential directive. More commonly, state rules against strikes by public employees have been essentially disregarded to ensure that governmental services to the public would be provided. Moreover, some rules are broken merely because so little is at stake in violating them. An administrator who, like a modern-day Captain Queeg, strictly enforces rules such as those concerning replacement of office pencils, use of telephones for toll-free calls to doctor's offices, and use of computers for personal e-mails risks creating problems larger than the supposed abuses.

Sometimes rules must be broken because they are poorly conceived. A rule requiring that all Federal Bureau of Investigation agents report any bribes that they are offered seems, on its face, to be reasonable. However, the rule has its problems. Occasionally there are good reasons not to report a bribe. After the bribe offer is extended to the agent, he or she can then threaten to report it to the authorities. He or she then may promise not to report it if the person who offered it will reveal something vitally important. If the rule requiring the revelation of all bribes were universally applied, a valuable tool would be taken away from the legal authorities.

In a well-known case of rule breaking (Moore and Sparrow, 1990) — or bending, if one prefers — Gordon Chase, the head of Health Services in the City of New York, knowingly overestimated the success of a methadone treatment program to increase its chances of being funded. Although the optimistic projections were never met, the project resulted in the successful treatment of many addicts, thus benefiting them and the community. Still, whether Chase deserves the designation of moral agent is a matter of opinion.

MORAL WHISTLE-BLOWING

The issue of whistle-blowing to expose illegal or otherwise nefarious activity has been thoroughly examined in the literature of public administration. Our concern is with another form of whistle-blowing arising from our current discussion. There may be cases in which an individual or an organization has broken no rules but has shown consistently poor moral judgment in cases such as the ones that we have discussed (i.e., evaluation, conflicts of obligation, etc.). In such cases, it becomes incumbent on the moral agent to apprise the organization of its failings, in as tactful and productive a manner as possible. However, if attempts to reform from within the organization fail, the moral agent may find it necessary to appeal to a higher authority. Such appeals would require the same courage as that needed in "garden-variety" whistle-blowing, in which illegality is reported, but would also require another measure of courage because no specific violation has been committed. In the absence of a clear-cut offense, the whistle-blower would have to appeal to the moral judgment of the person to whom the moral deficiency is reported. One would hope that person to be a moral agent.

THE IDEAL AND THE REAL

Ideally, all elements of the public sector are populated with moral agents. Legislators perform as moral agents in formulating laws, judges act as moral agents in applying and interpreting laws, and public administrators act as moral agents in performing public services. Public administration serves best as a model of moral agency because the professional activities of the public agent most resemble those of the general population.

We have seen that the public administrator functions as a moral agent under conditions that we have described as evaluation, conflicts of obligations, unclear obligations, bending and breaking the rules, and moral whistle-blowing. The ideal public administrator, as a moral agent, would make the best moral choices in each of these conditions and, because he or she is ideal, would have complete and justifiable confidence in those choices. Axiomatically, however, no one is ideal. There are occasions in which the flesh-and-blood public administrator, as opposed to the mythical ideal public administrator, would have to decide between a course of action that he or she considers best but is not absolutely certain is best. Such occasions are most troublesome when the option that the public administrator favors is not the "by-the-book" option.

Gordon Chase's misrepresentation of the methadone program is an example of such an occasion. It may be argued that Chase overstepped his moral bounds, even though his actions ultimately benefited the public (Moore and Sparrow, 1990). If Chase could claim inclusion among the morally infallible, everyone, including Chase himself, could rest assured that he did the right thing. But no one can justifiably assume moral perfection. In this and other cases of bending and breaking the rules, the decision maker is faced with the question of whether to replace standard procedure with his or her own judgment.

Before condemning Chase as arrogant, however, we must consider the moral implications of his alternative. If he had "gone by the book," he would have cost the city the opportunity to develop a valuable program and possibly cost some heroin addicts their lives. We then might have condemned him as cowardly.

There is no formula for determining when to bend or break a rule. The public administrator must use his or her judgment in many cases in which the general rules may not prove as useful or as morally proper as they are intended to be. Such judgment is also needed in, among other cases, deciding when to discontinue a program or blow a whistle. The public administrator must be prepared to make such judgments. In many such cases, the public administrator must first make a moral judgment concerning what he or she considers the best course of action. But the moral task may not yet be complete. If the public administrator determines it best to break a rule, blow a whistle, or discontinue a program, he or she must also decide whether he or she is certain enough that he or she is right to override standard procedures.

The legislator and the judge often find themselves in analogous situations. The legislator must decide whether he or she is confident enough in his or her own moral judgment to determine whether to act against the opinions of those whom he or she is elected to represent; the Supreme Court Justice must decide when a statement in the Constitution must be understood differently from its traditional interpretation.

It is not enough, however, simply to apply one's best judgment. One must also be sure that he or she has prepared herself for difficult cases by educating and refining his or her moral discernment. Performing to the best of his or her ability is not praiseworthy when he or she has not properly developed his or her ability. It is therefore incumbent on people in public life, especially public administrators, to learn how to make good moral decisions.

REFERENCES

Aberbach, J. D., R. D. Putnam, and B. A. Rockman. 1981. *Bureaucrats and Politicians in Western Democracies*. Cambridge, MA: Harvard University Press.

Applbaum, A. I. 1999. *Ethics for Adversaries: The Morality of Roles in Public and Professional Life*. Princeton, NJ: Princeton University Press.

Behn, R. D. 2001. *Rethinking Democratic Accountability*. Washington, D.C.: Brookings Institution Press.

Bryner, G. C. 1987. *Bureaucratic Discretion*. New York: Pergamon Press.

Burke, J. P. 1986. *Bureaucratic Responsibility*. Baltimore, MD: The Johns Hopkins University Press.

Frederickson, H. G. 1980. *The New Public Administration*. Tuscaloosa, AL: University of Alabama Press.

Geuras, D., and C. Garofalo. 2002. *Practical Ethics in Public Administration*. Vienna, VA: Management Concepts.

Goldman, A. H. 1980. *The Moral Foundations of Professional Ethics*. Totowa, NJ: Rowman and Littlefield.

Hawthorne, N. 1985. *The Great Stone Face and Other Tales of the White Mountains.* Boston: Houghton Mifflin.

Hunold, C., and B. G. Peters. 2001. *Bureaucratic Discretion and Deliberative Democracy.* Available at: http://www.essex.ac.uk/ecpr/events/jointsessions/paperarchive/ Copenhagen/ws1/hunold_p.pdf

Leazes, F., and S. Campanelli. 1996. My Sister's Keeper. In *Ethical Dilemmas in Public Administration*, eds. L. Pasquarella, A. G. Killilea, and M. Vocino, London: Praeger Publishing.

Lehne, R. 2001. *Government and Business: American Political Economy in Comparative Perspective.* New York: Seven Bridges Press.

Lewis, C. W. 1991. *The Ethics Challenge in Public Service.* San Francisco: Jossey Bass.

Moore, M. H., and G. Sparrow. 1990. *Ethics in Government: The Moral Challenge of Public Leadership.* Englewood Cliffs, NJ: Prentice Hall.

Rawls, J. A. 1971. *A Theory of Justice.* Cambridge, MA: Harvard University Press.

Warwick, D. P. 1981. The Ethics of Administrative Discretion. In *Public Duties: The Moral Obligations of Government Officials*, eds. J. L. Fleishman, L. Liebman, and M. H. Moore, pp. 93–127. Cambridge, MA: Harvard University Press.

Wamsley, G. L. et al. 1990. Public Administration and the Governing Process: Shifting the Political Dialogue. In *Refounding Public Administration.* Newbury Park, CA: Sage.

Wilson, J. Q. 1989. *Bureaucracy.* New York: Basic Books.

Wilson, W. 1887. The Study of Administration. *Political Science Quarterly.* 2(1):197–220.

3 Ethical Breakdowns in Public Administration

We have argued that the public administrator is well suited to function as an exemplar or model of the moral agent. Nevertheless, although the ideal public administrator may fulfill this function perfectly, the actual, flesh-and-blood public administrator may not be taking full advantage of this opportunity to display moral agency in its highest form. If the public service bestows positions of moral leadership on public administrators, they should live up to the task. They cannot ignore morality under the excuse that they are merely doing "as anyone else would have done." No one should use such an excuse, especially not public administrators, because they wear a mantle of moral leadership. Unfortunately, some do not bear the mantle in its full splendor.

The term "breakdowns" is used in this chapter in a manner similar to its use when one speaks of an automobile having a breakdown. Sometimes human beings are responsible for that automotive breakdown, but sometimes no one is to blame; some misfortunes befall even the most careful and fastidious drivers. But even when the breakdown is not a driver's fault, he or she must confront the problem. Thus it is with public administrators: They should do whatever they can to avoid moral problems, but when they occur by the fault of others or, as in the case of many moral issues, by the fault of no one, the public administrator, as moral agent, must be equipped to respond.

In this chapter we examine common flaws in the public administrator's exemplarship. We classify these flaws into several groups according to their salient features. Aristotle (1934) argued that virtue is a mean between two extremes, one of defect and one of excess. Following him, we divide the ethical shortcomings among public administrators into cases of insufficient zeal to fulfill assigned duties and cases of overly fervent pursuit of professional aims.

INSUFFICIENT COMMITMENT

SELF OVER SOCIAL GOOD

We need not linger on this nearly universal failing because it is so common and so familiar. It comprises a range of offenses including sloth, use of public property for personal gain, and use of one's position as a professional stepping stone. This general type of unethical behavior exists in all human endeavors.

The model of public administration that Frederickson (1980, p.25) names "The Human Relations Model" may, if misapplied, foster the elevation of the self-interest of the public agent over the public interest. The model is not intended to have this effect, but its emphasis on worker satisfaction may, in practice, become an end in itself rather than a means to a more effective organization. The model may be based on an overly optimistic assumption about the inherent goodness of human nature (p. 27).

Anthony Downs (1967) presents a classification of five types of decision makers on the basis of their commitments to different goals: climbers, for whom power, income, and prestige are dominant motivating factors; conservers, who consider convenience and security to be most important; zealots, who are loyal to narrow policies; advocates, who are loyal to a broad set of social functions rather than to a narrow set, such as the zealots; and statesmen, who are loyal to the general welfare. The classification may not be complete, but it is valuable for the purposes of reference. To demonstrate Downs's classifications, Timothy Hennessey and Joanne Lehrer (1996) show how members of each classification would behave when faced with budget cuts requested by a politically powerful officer but harmful to the legitimate aims of an organization.

The first two of Downs's groups are among those who would sacrifice the social good for selfish reasons. Under the hypothetical budgetary threat of Hennessey and Lehrer, both the climber and the conserver would carry out the cuts, but not out of concern for fiscal responsibility. Hennessey and Lehrer suggest that, although the climber is solely egocentric, the conserver might, if he or she extends his or her concern for convenience and security to the entire organization, show at least some concern for something other than himself or herself. To the extent that he or she shows such a concern, he or she would be guilty of a different, though perhaps just as damaging, flaw: favoring the organization over the social good.

The Organization over Social Good

This failing, because it is not so obviously selfish, seems less immoral than putting one's own interests over the public good. It is natural and in many cases laudable to take as much pride in one's organization. Furthermore, dedication to an organization usually furthers its goals, which, in the case of a properly functioning public agency, benefit the society.

Sometimes, however, the organization becomes an end in itself and thus betrays its public charge. Evidence of an organization given to this failing includes rigidity, unresponsiveness to the public, undue emphasis on hierarchical structures, and turf battles among different organizations. Frederickson's Classic Bureaucratic (1980, p. 17) and Institutional (p. 23) models may be subject to such problems.

Carol Lewis (1991, p. 78) cites the case of the Washington, D.C., school system, which withheld information concerning enrollment from the general public. The unreported enrollment drop would have cost the system funds, which were allocated on the basis of the number of students that the district served. It is difficult, and often impossible, to infer one's motives. If the system's administrators withheld the information because they feared that disclosure would harm the system, they would not be guilty of favoring the organization over the social good; on the contrary, they would then have supported the public interest, albeit in a paternalistic manner. Such behavior may constitute another offense, which we discuss later as an example of overcommitment to organizational goals. However, if the D.C. administrators were merely protecting their organization from having to endure painful cuts in the budget, theirs would be the offense of elevating their organization over the social interest.

The problem of discerning the true motive is common in cases of favoring the organization over the social good, because the interests of the organization can often be confused with the values that the organization exists to serve. For example, law enforcers may nearly always justify their claims for increased funding on the basis of the insatiable need to defend the citizenry. In many cases the justification is valid, but in others, it might be mere rationalization for increased salaries. But in this case, and in many similar cases, another factor confuses the question of motivation even more. The motive may be to increase salaries for equity; the organization's members may deserve more than they are currently receiving. If so, this would not be a case of elevating organizational interest over public value but of a legitimate moral claim.

Most cases of favoring organizational interest over public value are difficult to prove because of the different possible motives that may be at work, sometimes singly and sometimes in combination. There are therefore common epistemic difficulties in establishing motives. Nevertheless, it is evident that the sacrifice of public interests for those of public organizations is inappropriate, though it may be nearly impossible to tell when it is being done.

ORGANIZATIONAL GOAL DISPLACEMENT

Sometimes the process becomes more important than the product. Bureaucracies can become so conservative that they value the following of customary procedures to the detriment of the public. Mindless rule following, which constitutes organizational goal displacement, can result from numerous organizational weaknesses such as lack of innovation, institutional inertia, and fear of change. This conservatism is most frequently a symptom of insufficient commitment to legitimate institutional goals.

By "organizational goal displacement," we mean the replacement of the legitimate goals of the organization by obedience to the organization's rules and habitual procedures or organizational self-interest. Organizational goal displacement may be confused with elevation of the organization over the social good, but although they overlap, they are not identical. Organizational goal displacement is the betrayal of the socially valuable aims of an organization in favor of adherence to bureaucratic rules. In the case of the elevation of the organization over the social good, the organization as a whole was the aim of its own existence.

In organizational goal displacement, adherence to rules and practices within the organization governs the behavior of members, to the detriment of legitimate goals.

The difference may be put into a crude analogy. High officials in some authoritarian states elevate the political party above all other considerations, but lower-ranking members "just follow orders." Those who elevate the organization over the public interest are similar to the high officials, whereas goal displacers are similar to the lower-ranking members. Frederickson's Classic Bureaucratic Model (1980), with its emphasis on hierarchical structures, and Institutional Model, with its attempt to avoid the normative, may often degenerate into organizational goal displacement.

James Q. Wilson (2000) describes how organizational goal displacement can result from external pressures on organizations and individual bureaucrats. He notes that in three major areas of public concern — armies, prisons, and schools — administrators impose policies on others who actually perform the productive work with which the agency is charged. Those who put the policies into effect are often more concerned with meeting the formal requirements of the policies than with accomplishing the goals that the policies — and the entire agencies — are intended to attain. Wilson summarizes the process as it commonly occurs in schools:

> Especially in big cities, many administrators keep principals weak and teachers busy filling out reports, all with an eye toward minimizing complaints from parents, auditors, interest groups, and the press. Teachers individually grumble that they are treated as robots instead of professionals, but collectively they usually oppose any steps — vouchers, merit pay, open enrollment, strengthened principals — that in fact have given teachers a larger role in designing curricula and managing their classrooms. (p. 476)

Wilson explains this phenomenon as often being the result of a mishmash of regulations, restrictions, and requirements imposed by diverse interest groups, watchdog agencies, and concerned citizens with their own separate agendas for the agency. Often the agenda comes from an executive office that fears an agency's independence and therefore stifles it by redirecting its attention from its natural aims to the mass of imposed constraints. As a result, the sense of the agency's mission loses definition. One can easily expect that, once the members of an agency become accustomed to its procedures, inertia sets in, and the agency floats along with no clear sense of purpose.

Sometimes, the members of the agency can hardly be blamed for the exigencies that lead them to value process over product. In 1970, the United States Congress passed the Migrant Health Act (Aron, 2000), which granted funds to local groups for the purpose of creating programs to assist migrant workers. To ensure that the local groups were representative of those whom the act was intended to aid, it contained an amendment strongly suggesting that the local groups consist of persons "broadly representative of all of the elements of the population to be served." But the act was passed late in the fiscal year, so the funds had to be dispersed quickly. In the case of the city of Bakersfield, California, there were plenty of migrant workers to be assisted, but there were no well-established groups to manage the funds. Officials had the choice of either returning the funds or finding a group with insufficient experience and competence. They chose the latter alternative, with predictable results. The officials were more concerned with meeting procedural requirements than with their stewardship of public funds.

But before we blame the officials too severely, we must recognize the pressures under which they functioned. By returning the funds, they would have given the impression of incompetence; they would have been subjected to the charge that any good administrator should be able to find a way to spend the funds at his or her disposal. The charge would be unfair but might nevertheless have a negative effect on their careers.

There is also the possibility that we have misjudged the motives of the officials. One can never be sure of another's motivation. Perhaps, rather than giving the money to the unqualified group merely to answer to the written regulations, the officials were so intent on helping the migrants that they ignored the problems with the means by which the money was dispersed. Perhaps they figured that it was at least possible that some of the money would end up helping migrants, whereas if it were returned, the migrants would be totally cut off from any assistance. If the officials were thus motivated, they could not be accused of organizational goal displacement, but another complaint might be brought against them. That complaint will be discussed later under the categories of "Organizational Goals versus Public Values" and "Organizational Goals versus Moral Principles."

Personal Loyalties

Loyalty, though often a virtue, can become a vice if it interferes with the proper functioning of an organization, especially a public organization. Managers may, because of personal ties, hire or promote the wrong people and put them in positions in which they will not function optimally. Worse yet, one's loyalty may induce one to overlook inappropriate behavior on the part of the favored colleague. One wonders how different the world would be if President Nixon, John Mitchell, and G. Gordon Liddy had not been so loyal to each other.

The personal loyalties that can weaken commitment to organizational goals take many forms. Among the most sensitive is the loyalty of an appointee to the person who appointed him or her. Aside from any concern that one's job may be jeopardized, people usually feel an understandable and perhaps laudable debt of obligation to those who appointed them. A similar sense of debt may be directed toward superiors who provided professional benefits other than appointment. An especially delicate aspect of such cases is the sense of moral obligation that one feels to those who have helped him or her. The debt may exist, but it should not be repaid, if it is to be repaid at all, by unethical means.

Personal loyalty is by no means exclusively directed to superiors, nor is it always the result of past favors. One can be inappropriately loyal to peers and subordinates who have, often with the best of intentions, bestowed favors. Even apart from any sense of gratitude or identity with one's unit, loyalty based on friendship alone may obscure one's judgment. In all such cases, the public administrator must recognize that, though there may be a moral basis for personal loyalty, it does not outweigh the moral obligation of a public servant to the society.

Sometimes personal loyalty to subordinates attains the level of a professional expectation. Terry Cooper mentions, for example, the common case of the members of a unit who expect their supervisor to stand up for their interests (1990, p. 102).

INSUFFICIENT COMMITMENT AND MORAL AGENCY

The moral flaws resulting from insufficient commitment to the valid goals of an organization reflect a failure in moral agency. The strong moral agent would recognize sufficient moral commitment to those goals to prevent other values from superseding them. Still, we must not too hastily suppose that an organizational failure of moral agency necessarily entails that specific members of the agency are weak moral agents. Often, the sheer weight of an organization's size, complexity, and inertia overwhelms even the best-motivated members, including managers. One can imagine the frustration that the most conscientious public administrators experience in an organization that does not maximize its effort on behalf of the society that it serves. Such a lamentable condition needs strong moral agency throughout the organization, especially at the top.

EXCESSIVE COMMITMENT TO GOALS

People are most often criticized for not taking their jobs seriously enough. However, as Aristotle has noted, one can often overdo a good thing. People can pursue their professionally designated goals to the point of vice: Doctors can prescribe overly costly remedies, attorneys can defend their clients to the point of abusing the legal system, and manufacturers can pursue profits at the expense of environmental concerns. Public agencies are often designated as social watchdogs against such abuses, but they also exist in the public sector.

INTERORGANIZATIONAL CONFLICTS

One form of excessive commitment occurs when the pursuit of one organization's legitimate goals interferes with the work of another organization. The goals of the U.S. Department of Defense may conflict with the goals of the State Department; one must balance the need for military action with the requirements of international diplomacy. An overly aggressive head of either agency could upset the appropriate balance. Conflicts can occur between a department of health and an educational institution as, for example, in the case of an epidemic of measles, when the health department might pressure schools to close. In addition to conflicts between specific agencies, virtually all are in conflict with each other for funding.

Some conflicts may be cases of the aforementioned elevation of the organization over the social good and thus might merely manifest as self-interest. In other cases, however, such conflicts may arise or be exacerbated by administrators whose strong belief in the goals of their own organizations conflicts with the important goals of other organizations.

Such a case arose in the 1990s within the U.S. National School Lunch Program, which was intended to combine the interests represented by the U.S. Department of Agriculture (USDA) with those of public schools (Sims, 2000). Under the program, the USDA would donate food, for which producers had been compensated, to school districts to feed needy children. Depending on their level of need, students would pay either nothing for their meals or a portion of the cost, whereas more affluent students would pay the full amount. Students would be adequately fed, schools would have better-nourished students, and food producers would be paid for surplus food. Theoretically, everyone should have been relatively happy with the arrangement, and they were until the nation became more knowledgeable and more concerned about nutrition.

Unfortunately, much of the food donated to the schools was high in fat, and the nation had protected students from being underfed by promoting obesity and bad eating habits. The school districts would appear to have an easy remedy to the problem: Refuse to accept food that is not nutritious. However, the remedy was not painless. If they rejected the food, the school districts would have to make up for the loss by purchasing food themselves, thus incurring a financial burden that would be difficult for some districts to manage.

There would appear to be another simple remedy for the problem: The USDA should supply only nutritious food for the schools to distribute. But this remedy was not so easily instituted, either. One of the original goals of the program was to provide a market for food producers, many of which supplied the offending products. The goals of the USDA, together with its constituents, were thus in conflict with the school district and its students. A responsible school administrator would therefore be forced to choose between the dietary needs of the students and the financial needs of the school as result of the conflict between the interests, legitimate as they were, of two organizations.

Although the problem still exists, efforts have been made, with significant success, to resolve it. The USDA has cooperated significantly in improving the nutritional value of the donated food, despite pressure from agricultural interests and a reluctance of students to eat the foods that are good for them. The occurrence of the problem, however, indicates how legitimate aims of different organizations can clash, leaving the responsible administrator in the middle.

ORGANIZATIONAL GOALS VERSUS PUBLIC VALUES

A second form of conflict arises when the interests of an organization conflict with those of the public, though not with another public agency. One of the most common of such conflicts occurs in the process of budgeting. An organizational head who believes strongly in the importance of his or her agency's work may, quite naturally, expect more public monetary support than, all things considered, the agency deserves; a characteristic of the zealot, as described by Downs, is that he seldom considers all things (1967). The public pocketbook is not the only potential victim of the zealot. Even the best agencies, such as those concerned with the environment, can endanger other legitimate interests. For example, an excess of concern for a species that is not endangered may unfairly limit some-one's use of his or her own property; an overly aggressive concern for universal higher education may encourage unqualified students to attend a college or university.

We noted that public administrators with insufficient commitment to their organizational goals fall short as moral agents. In contrast, those who are overly zealous are strong moral agents in that they are committed to moral values. The zealot cannot be accused of sacrificing those values out of self-interest or indo-lence. Instead, his or her offense is in pursuing those values in an unduly vigorous manner. Those who display insufficient commitment to organizational goals need a greater sense of moral commitment to the importance of their own organiza-tional values. Those who display excessive zeal for organizational goals need a greater moral regard for other values. The first need greater respect for moral values, and the second need greater moral understanding.

ORGANIZATIONAL GOALS VERSUS MORAL PRINCIPLES

Public administrators have an evident moral commitment to the goals of their agencies. All employees have at least a *prima facie* responsibility to serve those who employ them but, in addition, public administrators should have a moral commitment to the public responsibility that their agencies fulfill. That respon-sibility to a goal — however noble, however, does not justify the violation of moral principles. For example, the manager of an agency responsible for public forests may have a legitimate concern about the ability of his or her agency to conserve and develop the woodlands under his or her charge. He or she may be unable, because of insufficient concern among politicians and the public at large, to convey the urgency of the problems that he or she must face. The situation is frustrating. However, it would not justify the exaggeration of the likelihood or threat of forest fires as a scare tactic to secure the necessary funding.

Conflicts between organizational goals and moral principles are different from conflicts between organizational goals and public values, as the forestry case illustrates. In that case, the administrator was fully concerned about the public interest; he or she was aware that the public did not understand that its interests could be best served by increased funding for his or her agency. The tendency of an administrator in his or her position to exaggerate a threat to secure the public good is an indication of paternalism rather than a slighting of public value. One can be true to one's professional charge and true to the public interest but still be unethical in pursuing that interest.

OVERCOMMITMENT AND MORAL AGENCY

We have seen that public administrators can have both too weak and too fervent a commitment to the goals of their agencies. Those with too little commitment fail as moral agents and perhaps as ethical agents as well. Their failure to strive sufficiently for their agency's important public values constitutes their failure of moral agency. But even moral agents can fail with respect to ethical agency when they use ethically questionable procedures in support of valid goals. The ideal moral agent must have the moral and ethical commitment to avoid both forms of misadventure.

MORAL DILEMMAS

Moral dilemmas are moral conflicts, but not all moral conflicts are moral dilemmas (see Kidder, 2003). A moral dilemma occurs when two legitimate moral claims of roughly equivalent value conflict. Someone in a moral dilemma is forced to choose among morally worthy options and therefore to favor one at the expense of the other or others. Moral dilemmas are distinct from another form of moral conflict, which we call the moral temptation. A moral temptation occurs when one's moral obligations conflict with another, nonmoral concern. The moral breakdowns that we have already considered in this chapter have generally been cases of moral temptation, such as the conflict between moral values and self-interest, personal loyalties, or organizational goals. But someone in a moral dilemma has no clear-cut choice between morality and other values. A moral dilemma pits moral values against each other.

No public administrator can expect a career free of moral dilemmas. Many of them occur as a result of funding limitations. As Carol Lewis observes, most organizations have several stakeholders whose valid interests can conflict when funds are scarce (1991, pp. 120–135). When budgets must be cut, the administrator may be forced to choose between forgoing socially valuable new initiatives and cutting existing programs that also serve the public well. Another difficult budget-cutting dilemma involves choosing between firing older, higher-paid, honorable employees who have lost some of their effectiveness and firing younger, less-expensive employees with bright futures.

An emerging set of moral dilemmas occurs in the area of publicly funded medicine. Some nations with highly developed public health agencies already are faced with such choices as those between providing service or either ensuring fiscal restraint and providing equal access or allowing free access that advantages the more affluent. A fuller account of the dilemmas inherent in health care will be given in Chapter 5.

Although many moral dilemmas involve conflicts within public policy, we must not overlook conflicts between public policy and the private morality of groups or individuals. For example, the publicly funded Brackenridge Hospital of Austin, Texas, is administered by a Catholic health organization. The city would like the hospital to recognize a moral obligation to offer abortions to the indigent, but the morality of the Catholic Church forbids abortion. A case mentioned by Douglas F. Morgan (2000) indicates a possible interesting moral dilemma involving the private morality of individuals. A public library chooses to include among its holdings a book that many members of the community consider to be indecent. The library officials who decide to retain the book may privately agree with the negative assessment of the book but include it nevertheless because they honor the library's commitment to freedom of expression.

Public administrators are subject to the moral dilemma because they are subject to numerous potentially competing moral obligations. Dwight Waldo (2000) presents a "map" of such competing obligations, which is daunting enough even though he suggests that it is incomplete. Moral dilemmas represent inevitable conflicts that administrators did not create and that therefore evidence no personal moral flaw. The dilemmas represent systemic moral breakdowns rather than individual human moral breakdowns, but the public administrator, as moral agent, must be prepared to address them when they occur.

THE PUBLIC ADMINISTRATOR AS STRONG EVALUATOR

The ideal public administrator must be an ethical agent, a moral agent, and a moral exemplar. The failures of excess, defect, and confusion that we have examined in this chapter indicate the need for a more comprehensive ethical perspective that public administrators, as a whole, do not possess. The public administrator, as an important decision maker in the overall functioning of a society, must be committed to the goals of his or her organization but also must recognize the proper context of those goals.

The philosopher Charles Taylor (1982) distinguishes among three types of decision makers, though the first may best be described as a mere decider rather than a maker of decisions. His or her decisions are based on impulse, desire, pressure, or, in general, inclinations. The proverbial donkey between two haystacks would exemplify such a state of decision by inclination. People occasionally decide in such ways as, for example, when they choose between a dinner meal of stuffed fillet of sole or Châteaubriand entirely on the basis of which flavor they prefer at the moment of decision. No decision maker who behaves consistently in such a manner would serve as a model for anyone to emulate. Favoring policies or promoting people merely because of how one feels is not a formula for success.

We may include in Taylor's first group those who make choices without thinking seriously about their evaluative aspects. We may hope or at least wish that no such people exist in public administration, but they might be found among Downs's groups of climbers and conservers.

Taylor's second class of decision makers includes the simple weighers of alternatives. These people do not question or contemplate the worthiness of the goals that they promote but merely choose the options that further the goals. The corporate seeker of the "bottom line" exemplifies the simple weigher. A public administrator who behaves as a simple weigher might fall into Downs's class of zealots, whose devotion to one goal or value determines all of their administrative decisions. Downs's advocate may also fit into the class of simple weighers because, although that advocate's goals may be broader than the zealot's, the advocate still adopts policies that favor his or her complex of goals without placing them in the broader context of a public good.

Taylor's third class of decision makers is the strong evaluator, who does not merely choose among alternative means to an end that is presupposed but assesses the value of the goal:

> The strong evaluator envisages his alternatives through a richer language. The desirable is not only defined for him by what he desires, or what he desires plus a calculation of consequences; i.e. is also defined by a qualitative characterization of desires as higher and lower, noble and base, and so on. Where it is not a calculation of consequences, reflection is not just a matter or registering the conclusion that alternative A is more attractive to me, or draws me more than B. Rather the higher desirability of A over B is something I can articulate if I am reflecting a strong evaluator. I have a vocabulary of worth (1982, p. 116).

The public administrator, as moral agent and moral exemplar, must be a strong evaluator and therefore must rise above considerations of self-interest, personal loyalty, and organizational empowerment to discern the overall moral import of his or her decisions. Moreover, the public administrator, as a strong evaluator, must be neither a zealot nor an advocate for a limited class of social goods but must see the entire array of moral values as a coherent whole.

The general moral perspective into which to fit one's specific activities is a common missing element in the moral breakdowns in public organizations. Breakdowns resulting from insufficient commitment to organizational goals are indicative of a lack of concern for the significance of the public agent's activities in the grand moral scheme. Overcommitment to organizational goals also indicates a myopic moral perspective that does not allow the agent to fully recognize how his or her own values are integrated with other legitimate values.

The absence of a general moral perspective is also a reason for the limited value of institutional moral codes. The rote learning of such codes may help to avoid gross ethical mistakes and illegal activity but does little to broaden one's moral viewpoint. On the contrary, such codes specify what one should do under designated circumstances and thus emphasize the particular rather than the general, though both should be recognized. Formulaic application of codes reduces one below Taylor's simple weigher to his even lower level of someone who responds to a stimulus rather than makes choices. Moreover, ethics training programs that emphasize rule following are of little benefit in developing the skills and perspectives of the strong evaluator, whose moral choices and actions display a coherent moral integrity.

But, as Plato recognized in suggesting in *The Republic* that his Good is ineffable, the full articulation of an ultimate coherent moral whole is virtually impossible (1991, p. 186). The problem is that of explaining the ultimate foundations on which explanation itself is based. Because all ethical understanding rests on that coherent ethical whole, any attempt to explain it by means of other or more specific ethical concepts would be circular, as would any attempt to explain the axioms of geometry by means of the theorems. Understanding all of those moral concepts that purport to explain the whole would logically depend on a prior understanding of the very moral whole that is to be explained. For example, any attempt to use a concept such as equality to explain the ultimate source of value would depend on a prior recognition that equality is morally worthy. The question "What makes equality good?" would then naturally arise.

Taylor recognizes the depth of the problem of evaluating the very ethical structure by means of which people generally evaluate ethical practices:

> Now this engages me at a depth that using a fixed yardstick does not. I am in a sense questioning the inchoate sense that led me to use the yardstick. And at the same time it engages my whole self in a way that judging by a yardstick does not. This is what makes it uncommonly difficult to reflect on our fundamental evaluations (1982, p. 126).

To explain his fundamental moral decisions, the moral agent must articulate that which cannot be fully articulated. However, although a full articulation is not possible, explanations of relative clarity can be given. The moral agent must be able to provide them.

We offer, in our unified ethic, a procedure for the public administrator who seeks to be a strong evaluator and, as such, a model of moral agency. As Taylor suggests, our unified ethic seeks to articulate ultimate moral values as much as possible, without claiming to specify them explicitly, in a manner that is applicable to ethical decision making.

REFERENCES

Aristotle. 1934. *The Nicomachean Ethics*, trans. H. Rackham. Cambridge, MA: Harvard University Press.

Aron, M. 2000. Dumping $2.6 Million on Bakersfield (or How Not to Build a Migratory Farm Worker's Clinic). In *Public Administration: Concepts and Cases*, ed. R. J. Stillman, pp. 88–96. Boston: Houghton Mifflin.

Cooper, T. L. 1990. *The Responsible Administrator* 3rd ed. San Francisco: Jossey-Bass.

Downs, A. 1967. *Inside Bureaucracy.* New York: Harper Collins.

Frederickson, H. G. 1980. *The New Public Administration*. Tuscaloosa, AL: University of Alabama Press.

Hennessey, T., and J. Lehrer. 1996. Ethics Values and "Muddling Through": Strategic Behavior of Agency Leaders. In *Ethical Dilemmas in Public Administration*, ed. L. Pasquarella and A. G. Killilea, pp. 149–160. London: Prager.

Kidder, R. M. (2003.) How Good People Make Tough Choices: Resolving the Dilemmas of Ethical Living: New York: Harper Collins.

Lewis, C. W. 1991. *The Ethics Challenge in Public Service*. San Francisco: Jossey-Bass.

Morgan, D. F. 2000. Madonna's Sex. In *Public Administration: Concepts and Cases*, ed. R. J. Stillman, pp. 513-526. Boston: Houghton Mifflin.

Plato. 1991. *Republic*. Trans. A. Bloom. New York: Basic Books.

Sims, L. S. 2000. Reinventing School Lunch: Transforming a Food Policy into a Nutrition Policy. In *Public Administration: Concepts and Cases*, ed. R. J. Stillman, pp. 457–472. Boston: Houghton Mifflin.

Taylor, C. 1982. Responsibility for Self. In *Free Will,* ed. G. Watson, pp. 111–126. Oxford: Oxford University Press.

Waldo, D. 2000. Public Administration and Ethics: A Prolog to a Preface. *Public Administration: Concepts and Cases*, ed. R. J. Stillman, pp. 501–512. Boston: Houghton Mifflin.

Wilson, J. Q. 2000. Bureaucracy and the Public Interest. In *Public Administration: Concepts and Cases*, ed. R. J. Stillman, pp. 476–485. Boston: Houghton Mifflin.

4 Ethics in Business

Discussion of business ethics has been dominated by the debate over corporate social responsibility, or CSR. One side claims that the sole obligation of corporate managers is to increase profit and shareholder value, and another side argues that corporate managers have multiple obligations to a variety of stakeholders. A third side says that many corporations have adopted CSR as a marketing device, with their real intent being to serve shareholder interests and improve sales. A fourth side, finally, contends that the purpose of CSR is to increase the political legitimacy of corporate power. Thus, CSR is conflicted both in its aims and in its interpretations.

Our goal in this chapter is to suggest a reversal of the cliché that government should be run like a business and to argue that, in a moral sense, business should be run like government. Although we grant that sometimes CSR has been adopted for instrumental purposes, such as profit, political power, or public relations, our focus is on the moral obligations of corporations as a set of major institutions, among others, in civil society. Our position, therefore, is consistent with the stakeholder view of CSR, but our approach is different from those proposed by others. Our thesis is threefold: first, government, particularly public administration, by its very nature is a model of moral agency and citizenship and, thus, a significant societal asset in the discernment and enactment of the public interest; second, CSR is fundamental to moral agency, citizenship, and the identity and purpose of the corporation; and third, public administration, as an exemplar in principle of moral agency and citizenship, can help reconcile the contending positions in the CSR debate by reconceptualizing the main features of the controversy and moving them to a different level at which corporations and corporate managers would be seen as moral agents and citizens in a web of interdependence and cooperation.

We begin by reviewing the contours of the CSR debate. Then, for perspective on the nature and magnitude of the challenge, we examine American perspectives on government, including public administration, and we also explore contemporary business–government relations. Again, our ultimate goal is the moral reconfiguration of those perspectives and relations to resolve the CSR controversy in the context of a redefined business–government partnership.

CSR

The signal oppositional piece in the CSR debate is Milton Friedman's 1970 article, "The Social Responsibility of Business Is to Increase Its Profits." In Friedman's view, the corporate manager is an employee of the shareholders, who are the owners of the business, and in that position, the manager's responsibility is to fulfill the shareholders' desires, which generally are to make as much money as possible while abiding by conventional ethical customs. To do otherwise, Friedman argues would constitute a breach of contract. At the same time, if the shareholders wish to seek goals other than profit, then the manager should comply as well. The essential point is that the manager is the agent of the owners and is, therefore, obligated to meet their requirements. If, on their own, managers divert corporate resources to socially responsible activities, they are engaging in theft and taxation without representation. Friedman concludes that social responsibility is harmful and that, taken seriously, is a fundamentally subversive doctrine in a free society.

Since the publication of Friedman's essay, many critics of CSR have made their voices heard. Three of those critics are John Danley, Michael Novak, and Norman Barry. Here, we first summarize their major arguments and then turn to the other side of the debate by presenting the ideas of three proponents of CSR — Robert Solomon, Alan Reder, and Norman Bowie — before finally considering the respective positions of each side. This sketch then leads to our discussion of perspectives on government, business–government relations, and the establishment of public administration as a model of moral agency and citizenship.

OPPONENTS OF CSR

Danley (1994) maintains, correctly in our view, that the debate over the corporation is fundamentally normative, as the persistent question concerns what role the corporation *should* play. But it is also part of a theory of political economy that addresses the larger question of the legitimate relationship between business and government. According to Danley, the major contending positions consist of the Classical Liberals, who advocate minimal or limited government, free market capitalism, and a laissez-faire governmental stance toward the economy, and the Managerialists, who believe that the corporation, both in itself and via its management, has a responsibility to be a "good citizen." To Classical Liberals, government's sole function is to prevent harm, whereas to Managerialists, acquisitive materialism, individualism, property rights, a limited state, and competition are being replaced by other values such as communitarianism, an active state, interdependence, participatory decision making, and servant leadership. Danley argues, however, that Managerialists are not clear about why these values should be accepted or why they are morally legitimate. We would point out that, interestingly enough, Danley raises no such concerns about the Classical Liberal view. In any event, Danley claims that corporate responsibilities in the stakeholder model are vaguely grounded and, therefore, not entirely convincing, as nothing substantial is offered as a substitute for profit maximization, nor are there criteria for decision making or even a definition of what social responsibility means.

One of Danley's most trenchant arguments against the stakeholder model concerns managerial discretion, a topic of parallel concern in public administration, as we saw in the last chapter. If managerial discretion is assumed, then the corporation may not claim that it has no alternative but to maximize profit. Danley maintains, however, that managerial discretion does not establish a corporation's moral obligations. The real issue hinges on the assumption of a wide range of discretionary abilities that, if true, is inconsistent with our convictions about a liberal democratic society and is, therefore, illegitimate. However, if this assumption is false, then management cannot be said to have any corporate responsibilities other than profit maximization. Given the presence of group decision making, bureaucratization, and the division of labor in corporations, Danley states that the claim of meaningful managerial discretion is false and concludes both that "there is very little room for social responsibility, given the constraints of the market" (1994, p. 222) and that the case of corporations to do anything but maximize profit has not been made.

Michael Novak (1997) suggests that business enterprise is an important social good for four reasons: first, it creates jobs; second, it provides desirable goods and services; third, through its profits, it creates wealth that did not exist before; and fourth, it is a private social instrument, independent of the state, for the moral and material support of other activities of civil society (p. 37). Although the last item seems to imply some type of CSR, Novak believes that in recent decades, this point has been increasingly compromised by command and control regulations and heavy-handed guidance from ambitious politicians. As a result, economic growth has been grinding to slow, fitful levels. We return to Novak later in this chapter in our discussion of the moral nexus between business and government. For now, it is important to note the two meanings that he ascribes to the concept of stakeholder. First, he defines a stakeholder as an owner and private risk taker whose goal is to secure the general welfare and the larger public interest, although these terms are not specified. Second, the social democratic sense of stakeholder refers to those who see themselves as entitled to make demands on the system and to receive benefits from it. It is, of course, the second category of stakeholder with which the critics of CSR find themselves at odds.

The third critic of CSR to be considered here is Norman Barry (2000), whose position is consistent in one respect with ours, that is, in the distinction between ethical and moral agency. Barry rejects the attempt to "moralize corporations," that is, to impose positive moral duties on commercial enterprises, to require them to perform duties not expected of private persons that go beyond observance of basic and conventional rules, such as respect for property, contract, and established rights. In a way, then, we might say that he accepts our concept of ethical agency but denies our concept of moral agency, although the specific language is ours. Furthermore, he argues that the rationale for the imposition of such supererogatory duties on corporations derives largely from the claim that their existence depends solely on a grant of privileges from the state. In this view, corporations must act not only morally but also socially; for example, they must pursue social justice even if it means the sacrifice of profits. In Barry's opinion, the agenda of business ethics, therefore, is inconsistent with the aims of business that, he maintains, are reducible to the major goal of enhancing owners' profits.

The proper venue for advancing desirable social goals is the political sphere, and "the imposition of social responsibilities on business is a substitute for that political action which has failed to attract electoral support" (2000, p. 69).

Like other analysts of CSR, Barry considers the issue of managerial discretion and the separation of ownership from control in large-scale modern corporate enterprises. Unlike Danley, who repudiates the claim of meaningful managerial discretion, Barry appears to accept the reality of managerial discretion and contends that managers, with their discretion, rather than owners, are seen as the prime instruments of social responsibility. Like Danley, however, Barry considers managerial discretion as contradictory and immoral, a breach of fiduciary duties, as CSR attenuates owners' property rights and is nothing more than an example of managerial opportunism. In his view, promoting social agendas is probably easier than maximizing shareholder value.

In his analysis of stakeholder theory, Barry expresses his concern about shareholders. On the one hand, he suggests, stakeholder theory is Kantian in that fulfillment of duties takes precedence over maximization of want-satisfaction. On the other hand, the use of shareholders is un-Kantian, as they are used merely as means to the ends of other stakeholders. Moreover, Barry believes that stakeholder theory represents a futile effort to establish some sort of equality between the groups that constitute an enterprise. It is futile, unless we move toward socialism, inasmuch as commercial arrangements generate inequality according to the value added by various participants.

Finally, the most serious problem with stakeholder theory is the potentially conflicting nature of the demands made by various groups on the organization. In Barry's estimation, adoption of stakeholder theory would paralyze corporate strategy, with the incessant bargaining that reflects the self-destructive activities of pressure groups in parliamentary politics. Barry's objection to stakeholder theory is moral as well as economic, because it would undermine property rights and convert the free-enterprise individualist order to a collectivist system. Because we have no common scale of social values to authoritatively order competing claims, he concludes, with Danley, that there are no alternatives to using profitability as the criterion of value.

PROPONENTS OF CSR

Robert Solomon, Alan Reder, and Norman Bowie support CSR. Solomon (1992) argues, for example, that "corporate responsibilities and obligations involve not only stockholders but embrace a wide variety of affected (and effective) groups" (p. 180). The virtue of the notion of stakeholder, in his view, is its sense of holism or concern for the whole rather than some of its parts. The social responsibility of corporations is not an odd number of extraneous obligations but, instead, the very point of their existence. "Social responsibility does not mean sacrificing profits to 'do-gooding' or fleecing the stockholders. Social responsibility only means that the purpose of business is to do what business has always been meant to do, enrich society as well as the pockets of those who are responsible for the enriching" (pp. 180–181).

Solomon is emphatic in his belief that the corporation is a citizen. Indeed, he argues that corporate citizenship is the first principle of business ethics. The corporation is a citizen, a member of the larger community, and is inconceivable without it (1992, p. 148). However, he recognizes that his position runs counter to the classic arguments for the social responsibilities of business that begin with the assumption that the corporation is an autonomous, independent entity, which then needs to consider its obligations to the surrounding community. According to Solomon, corporations are part of the communities that created them, and their responsibilities do not derive from argument or implicit contracts but are intrinsic to their very existence as social entities (1992, p. 149). For Solomon, corporate citizenship entails a relationship of shared identity and mutual concern. It represents an insistence on the larger moral framework within which all business must be viewed and evaluated.

Clearly, Solomon disagrees with the image of the corporation "merely as a legal fiction created exclusively for the protection of its owners and the pursuit of profits" (1992, p. 133). As long as it is seen in this way, he asserts:

> The notion of 'responsibility' will be limited to certain legal and contractual, merely fiduciary, obligations. But once we appreciate the importance of viewing the corporation as first of all a community (within larger communities) and as a culture with shared values and larger social concerns, then the odd questions Where do corporate values come from? And How can corporations be socially responsible? simply disappear from view (p. 133).

Finally, Solomon suggests that people in business should think of themselves as professionals and that "professionalism means service in return for compensation but not just because of compensation" (1992, p. 144). Making money is not the primary purpose of business. It is necessary, but not primary, for making money, and the need to make money is as common to the practices of medicine and law as it is to business. The emphasis in business, therefore, should be on service and the public good. Trust is essential to professional practice, and business should be as protective of its reputation as are the established professions.

Alan Reder (1994) maintains that social responsibility helps ensure that virtually every quality of a successful company will emerge over time and also that it increases a company's chances of long-term success. In his view, social responsibility refers to both the way a company conducts its internal operations, including the way it treats its work force, and its effect on the world around it. More specifically, the agenda of socially responsible business leaders includes such policies and practices as environmental protection; not doing business with repressive regimes; hiring and promoting women and minorities to upper management and boards of directors; providing healthy and safe work environments; providing dependent care assistance and flexible time; protecting employees against sexual harassment; providing permanent, domestic jobs to the greatest degree possible; not lobbying for narrow corporate ends; treating animals humanely; providing stock ownership, profit-sharing, and incentive pay for employees; and encouraging participatory decision making and community involvement of employees. Reder argues that many corporations that have implemented socially responsible policies and practices as a matter of principle have reaped rewards in improved employee allegiance, productivity, quality, management creativity, and customer loyalty. Finally, Reder posits that unprincipled business behavior is running out of time because of the pace of social change and environmental decay.

The third and last proponent of CSR to be cited is Norman Bowie (1999), who argues that the market must consist of more than purely competitive behavior that does not forbid the use of force or fraud. The world of business, Bowie suggests, is not simply a matter of competition, even regulated competition. Instead, successful business activity depends as much on cooperative behavior as it does on competitive behavior, and the key ingredient for success is trust.

Bowie argues that one principle of a moral firm is that every profit-making firm has an imperfect duty of beneficence. This is based on an extension of the individual's imperfect obligation of beneficence. As Bowie explains, "Perfect duties are duties we are always bound to fulfill, whereas imperfect duties are duties that we need to fulfill on some occasions but not all occasions. Thus, we must never lie, but we need not always act with beneficence to others" (1999, p. 26). More specifically, with respect to Friedman's (1970) argument that no firm has an obligation of beneficence because such beneficence would amount to stealing or spending other people's money, Bowie counters with two common arguments that could be made for a corporate obligation of beneficence: citizenship and gratitude.

The citizenship argument extends the notion that individuals have obligations to support the state. If individuals have an obligation to improve society, corporations, as institutional members of society, have an even stronger obligation because they, unlike individuals, were created by society through charters of incorporation and are totally dependent on society for their existence. "Society," Bowie contends, "would not have created them unless they believed that corporations were in the public interest" (1999, p. 94). Furthermore, in the context of increased demands on corporations, Bowie asks: "If the justification of corporations in the first place is that they contribute to the public good, why shouldn't corporations adapt to changing public perceptions of the public good?" (p. 94).

The gratitude argument has much in common with the citizenship argument, but it focuses on the benefits that society bestows on corporations in addition to their existence. Society protects corporations by providing the means for enforcing business contracts; it provides an infrastructure that allows the corporation to function; it provides an educated workforce, as well as roads, police and fire protection, sanitation, and other services; and, via the political process, it subsidizes corporations in various ways. Although it is true that corporations pay taxes for these services, so do citizens, and paying taxes does not exempt citizens from the obligations of citizenship and gratitude. In this connection, Bowie suggests that corporations also take advantage of state competition to win tax breaks and other benefits. Thus, an argument can be made that many corporations have not paid their fair share of taxes. Finally, Bowie claims that these arguments from citizenship and gratitude are consistent with Kant's argument for an obligation of beneficence.

DISCUSSION

In our view, the positions of both the opponents and proponents of CSR are underdetermined, although as indicated, we find the concepts and values of the proponents' position more compelling. The opponents of CSR appear to see the corporation through an atomistic lens, with the emphasis on profit maximization as the only justifiable corporate goal, reflecting a truncated view of shareholders and managers. For example, despite frequent references to managers as agents of owners, there is no reference to owners as agents of the organization or society. Fiduciary obligations apparently travel in only one direction. Shareholders as owners are presented as a caricature of the robber barons of the past, mindlessly and relentlessly pursuing profits above all else, with no genuine fealty to anything or anyone except their own self-interest and self-enrichment. Given the large and growing number of corporations committed to CSR, it is difficult to believe that their shareholders have all been duped by opportunistic managers or that their commitment is nothing more than a public relations ploy. However, as Dennis Quinn and Thomas Jones (1995) suggest, "The supporters of the wealth maximization view now usually amend their advice to take overtly into account legal, ethical, and social concerns" (p. 22).

We believe, however, that Danley is correct when he argues that CSR needs clarification and that managerial discretion does not establish a corporation's moral obligations. Considering the lengthy list of responsibilities offered by Reder, it is easy to see how choosing from among them can present many decisional difficulties to shareholders and managers. Concerning the charge that managerial discretion does not establish moral obligations, this seems to us to be simply stating the obvious. As far as we can tell, no one has suggested that CSR originates in managerial discretion. What has been suggested, however, is that managerial discretion is significant in reifying a corporation's moral obligations. As noted, though, Danley believes that managerial discretion is a fiction in light of group decision making, bureaucratization, and division of labor.

Turning to Barry's concerns about stakeholder theory and what he calls its major drawback, namely, the conflicting nature of stakeholder demands on a corporation and the consequences of those demands, we disagree with his characterization of stakeholder theory as un-Kantian because it uses shareholders as means to the ends of other stakeholders. Again, Barry, without explanation or justification, privileges shareholders to the exclusion of other groups with, we believe, equally legitimate claims on the corporation. For example, it apparently does not occur to him to ask about the use of managers and communities as means to the ends of shareholders. In any event, the central point in this regard is, once again, the treatment of corporations as special institutions whose sole connection to the outside world is profit maximization. Finally, it is either disingenuous or illogical to base one's opposition to CSR on the practical problem of reconciling stakeholder claims and to maintain that, as we have no common scale of social values to order competing claims, the only criterion of value is profitability. In our judgment, this line of reasoning enjoys apparent validity only if one accepts Barry's basic argument; that is, that the aims of business are reducible to enhancing profits and are, therefore, fundamentally incompatible with CSR. It also ignores centuries of philosophical ethics in which having a common scale of values to order competing claims has been high on the list of priorities.

Last, what distinguishes our model of moral agency is its emphasis on individual, in addition to institutional, citizenship. In the case of CSR, for example, our model aims not only at the corporation as a whole but also at individual employees who are also citizens. Thus, in our view, Friedman's distinction between the responsibilities of an individual as a corporate manager and his or her responsibilities as a citizen is unfortunate. It fractures the manager's individual identity and licenses unethical behavior in the guise of the putatively superior moral claims of the shareholders. We believe that it is artificial, arbitrary, and illogical, as well as unethical. As human beings, we are concerned about the link between our moral identity and the rest of our lives, and as Tom Morris (1997) says, although we may wear different hats at work and at home, we still wear them on the same head.

Quinn and Jones (1995) argue, moreover, that the instrumental and fragmented perspective on ethics is fraught with moral and logical difficulties. For example, instrumental ethics may not be possible to carry out because it negates reciprocity and part of its advantage to the firm. "If the senior managers of a firm employ ethics 'instrumentally' or with 'enlightened self-interest' or any other restrictive caveat, why will not employees at lower levels of the firm (or suppliers or customers) also employ ethics instrumentally?" (1995, p. 28). Shareholders, in other words, cannot expect ethical restraint from managers if they themselves support ethics only as it might contribute to increased profits. Once again, our moral identity is inseparable from the rest of our lives, including the panoply of our civic and organizational relationships and obligations.

PERSPECTIVES ON GOVERNMENT

The acceptance of government, particularly public administration, as a model of moral agency and citizenship clearly represents a major cultural challenge. Shifting from a generally jaded view of government, replete with all of the stereotypes associated with bureaucracy, to a more positive perspective that embraces government's responsibility as the promoter and protector of the public interest will require personal, professional, and institutional approaches coupled with equally complex strategies. But before such approaches and strategies can be developed, it is essential that we are clear about the nature and magnitude of the challenge. The issues of CSR and government as a moral model, together, are formidable indeed. In this section, we discuss perspectives on government and business–government relations. In a later chapter, we offer approaches and strategies designed to reconcile the divisions within CSR and to present public administration as a positive model of moral agency and citizenship.

Garry Wills (1999) writes that in the United States, government is accepted at best as a necessary evil. The state is seen as a threat to our liberty, it is the enemy of the free market, and its power is to be limited and diffuse. Distrust of government is embedded in American culture, and the power–liberty zero-sum game is reflected in numerous policy realms. Health care provided by government reduces our freedom. If government can take away our guns, our liberty is gone. The power to regulate business is the power to crush it. These perspectives are part of a cluster of opposition-to-government values: Government should be minimal, and legitimate social activity should be provincial, amateur, authentic, traditional, voluntary, and rotational.

However, there is also a set of contrasting values that has become an integral part of contemporary business–government relations: Government should be expert, cosmopolitan, elite, secular, regulatory, and progressive. Often, the first cluster of values is treated as endangered by the second. But despite the historical and symbolic significance of this value clash, Wills argues that, in practice, "America's business culture . . . lives by the values of the governmental attitude — efficiency, division of labor, impersonal expertise, the mechanics of the market, secular progress" (1999, p. 20). That is, business should, in principle, resist government regulation and portray itself as a defender of spontaneity and freedom. Thus, traditionalists promote capitalism, that engine of ceaseless change; big business and big government are allies more than adversaries; and ordinary citizens find themselves confused.

Wills maintains that the state can be seen as a positive good, not an invasion of the individual's domain but a broadening of his or her horizons. Taxes, regulations, and restrictions all produce complaints, and bureaucrats, like all of us, sometimes commit arbitrary and petty acts. But taxes, regulations, and bureaucracies are not necessary evils. Instead, they are necessary goods that do not uniformly please everyone. Citizens are selective in their grievances about government behavior. Some complain about seat belts or motorcycle helmets, but they do not complain about being required to drive on the right side of the road, to stop at a red light or stop sign, to have a driver's license, or to drive at mandated speeds.

Still, according to Wills, there is ample reason to fear and distrust government, to probe it, to demand access, and to make it come clean. This is as true of the little lies of the bureaucracy, campaign managers, and crooked legislators as the big lies of high politics and international relations. But the essential point here is that it is entirely possible to defend rights, authenticity, and tradition, for example, "without assailing the other values that government can legitimately embody (expertise, division of labor, authority)" (Wills, 1999, p. 316). Finally, Wills turns to what he believes is the astounding assumption of our political life, namely, that governments should be inefficient and that our representatives should be no more professional than ordinary citizens in political matters. We choose our physicians with the expectation that they are unlike us in their training and skills. No one wants an inefficient physician, attorney, teacher, or pilot. Why, then, do we want inefficient or unprofessional politicians? In passing, we would add public administrators to Wills's discussion.

Wills's answer to the question concerning inefficient politicians is that inefficiency is perceived as a safeguard against oppression. If Wills is correct, then politicians as well as public administrators are trapped in a double bind. As citizens, we want them to be both efficient and not so efficient — and this is without raising the question of being efficient for what? We must remember, in any case, that inefficiency may not protect us from the arbitrary employer, the vindictive teacher, or the arrogant physician, and we must remember, too, that although amateurism may have virtues in some areas of life, expertise is desirable in government. In addition to inefficient or incompetent physicians, attorneys, teachers, and pilots, we do not want inefficient or incompetent soldiers, police officers, firefighters, or other public servants.

Wills's perspective is an appropriate point of departure for a more nuanced understanding of American government, including public administration, particularly with regard to its utility as a model of moral governance. We argued in an earlier work (Garofalo and Geuras, 1999) that central to the resolution of the bureaucratic paradox in the United States is the legitimacy of the administrative state in a democracy. We argued, as well, that this issue must be addressed, fundamentally, on moral grounds rather than merely on the basis of expertise or hierarchical position or status. Thus, we again emphasize the critical elements in this regard, namely, the unified ethic as the foundation for the public servant *qua* moral agent's decisions and actions, the reconceptualization of principal–agent relations (Quinn and Jones, 1995), and the development of a normative framework for a bureaucratic role in governance. In short, public administration is an asset, not a liability; it concerns managing and mediating competing demands and priorities; and it functions in the midst of a number of contradictory commitments.

As Gary Wamsley and his colleagues (1990) have argued, for example, the national commitment to freedom and justice creates pressures for equity, but the national commitment to state capitalism also creates a counterpressure for economic and social differentiation. The requirements of the global economy create pressures for a rational, comprehensive planning and policy process, but our historical and constitutional tradition is based on fractionated power, overlapping jurisdictions, and disjointed incrementalism. Public administration is not the cause of governance problems in this complex system. Rather, the problems of public administration result from the difficulty of governing such a system. In this system, as we suggested earlier (Garofalo and Geuras, 1999), public administration is unlikely to achieve legitimacy in governance without achieving the moral legitimacy originating in the unified ethic and acknowledged by citizens, elected officials, judges — indeed, by the polity as a whole. Finally, however, we must distinguish between public administration's moral legitimacy and its moral nature. Although its moral legitimacy is a kind of work in progress, its moral nature is innate and permanent. By definition, public administration embodies, expresses, and enforces our collective values and collective will. It is concerned with conscience, consensus, and consequences — each undergirded by law and morality, all intertwined and implicated in the process of discerning and enacting the public interest.

In *The Spirit of Democratic Capitalism* (1982, 1991), Michael Novak offers a lively, comprehensive, and occasionally controversial defense of capitalism as an economic system as well as part of a democratic policy and moral community. Political democracy, he argues, is compatible, in practice, only with a market economy, and both are nourished and nourish a pluralistic liberal culture. Modern democracy and modern capitalism spring from identical historical impulses — limiting the power of the state and liberating the energies of individuals and independently organized communities. However, democratic capitalism cannot thrive apart from the moral culture or from a democratic polity. The political system has many legitimate claims on the economic system and many roles to play in democratic capitalism. The moral–cultural system, too, has many legitimate and indispensable roles to play in our economic life, such as encouraging self-restraint, hard work, discipline, sacrifice for the future, compassion, integrity, and concern for the common good. Thus, Novak sees economics, politics, and morality as interdependent and significant features of our lives.

Regarding self-interest, Novak's line of reasoning is similar to that of other writers such as Amartya Sen (1987), who offers a systematic critique of the narrowly conceived utility-maximizing model of human behavior embedded in economic theory. Novak contends that democratic capitalism restrains greed and narrow self-interest while encouraging fiduciary responsibility, reliability, integrity, and fairness. Self-intent encompasses families, communities, benevolence, sympathy, and cooperation. A narrow view of self-interest can destroy companies as well as personal lives. A broad view of self-interest can provide realistic limits. As Milton and Rose Friedman (1980) suggest, self-interest is neither myopic selfishness nor exclusive concern with immediate material rewards, but whatever interests individuals. According to Novak, under self-interest, there are moral, religious, artistic, and scientific interests as well as interests in peace and justice.

Although the United States is a commercial republic, commerce has a moral structure, and moral qualities are required for successful commerce at the center of its social life. Commerce is not the whole of life, but it is given greater freedom than elsewhere, and its prosperity is more central to the purposes of the state than in any previous form of civic order. It enhances the cooperative spirit, increases attention to law, identifies individual self-determination as the main source of social energy, and places limits on the state and other authorities. However, commercial virtues in a market system may degenerate into avarice, meanness, cowardice, and hedonism, meaning that commercial virtues are not sufficient in and of themselves. "A commercial system," Novak (1991) suggests, "needs taming and correction by a moral–cultural system independent of commerce. At critical points, it also requires taming and correction by the political system and the state" (p. 121).

Novak sees, therefore, a consonance between the virtues required for commercial success and natural moral virtues. Economic rationality lacks a basis in character without temperance, fortitude, prudence, and justice. The training of managers is moral training, including self-discipline, attentiveness, regularity, and consistency, reflected, for example, in showing up for work on time every day. The virtues required by economic rationality are indispensable to a self-governing polity and a sound morality. Economic benefits need not be attained at the cost of adherence to spiritual values. Thus, democratic capitalism is a web of equal and interdependent systems — political, economic, and moral–cultural — that guides and inspires citizens to exercise their individual initiative and strive toward the achievement of a free society.

Thus far, Novak's assessment appears rather reasonable, measured, and difficult to contest. We believe that he is clearly correct in his contention that the economic, moral–cultural, and political systems in the United States are intertwined. Our concern, however, is his characterization of government or the so-called administrative state as a threat, an alien power inimical to individual freedom — a necessary evil, to use Wills's words. In our view, the direct and indirect ascription of dark purposes to government, often without attribution, perpetuates the Manichean and, in our judgment, misguided antigovernment hostility that debases our civil culture and obstructs good-faith efforts to serve the commonweal.

Novak's analysis of government or the administrative state is remarkably lacking in texture or subtlety. For example, he writes of an ambitious, adversarial class that revels in the prospect of expanded government empires to conquer, personal security, wealth to accumulate, and power to acquire. Although this class remains unidentified, he argues that it finds allies in those who depend on government payments such as universities, hospitals, and teachers. He also claims, moreover, that this class is led by an elite strong enough to rival the business elite in brains, purpose, and power. Presumably, the presence of the business elite is acceptable, and the presence of a countervailing elite is not. In any event, this rival elite is motivated by *superbia*, or lust for power, which is deeper and more pervasive than *cupiditas*, or lust for wealth. It is not entirely clear, however, whether Novak prefers the latter to the former.

Novak (1991) is especially troubled by what he perceives as increasing bureaucratic power over the economy, the power of coercion that can destroy entire industries as well as confiscate profits, tax, and "harass executives through wiretaps, FBI visits in the night, investigations, and subpoenas" (p. 173). One can only wonder what his reaction might be to the U.S. Patriot Act of 2001. He is concerned that "governmental agencies have further acquired powers over hiring and personnel practices," that a "vast apparatus of mandatory information and secret investigation has been erected," and that "this apparatus extends beyond the economic system into the institutions of the moral–cultural system" (p. 173). Whether it is the role of women, abortion, homosexuality, housing, or education, the so-called new politics, according to Novak, has expanded the reach of the political system.

Novak has legitimate cause for concern. A myriad of controversial issues that he cites as well as others confront American society. Privacy is at risk from both public and private sources, raising significant constitutional questions. Globalization presents new challenges on both the domestic and international fronts. Institutional trust, stability, and legitimacy continue to demand leadership from all sectors of society. All of this is indisputable. What is disputable is whether the villain in the piece is government or the administrative state. Is it helpful or accurate to ascribe sinister motives to a population of citizens who labor under demanding and difficult political and economic circumstances in service of the public good? We believe that it is not. Indeed, our claim is the opposite of Novak's and more in keeping with the position of Wills, who argues, "Our popular mythology makes the state the enemy of the free market. But without the state the free market could not exist. Market exchange is a form of contract, and the contracts would not be binding without some authority to enforce them. . . . The state, far from being an enemy of the market system, is both the market's product and its perpetuator" (1999, p. 303).

This line of argument leads us to consider business–government relations in the United States. For example, according to Richard Lehne (2001), most decisions about employment and production are made by private organizations, markets play a key role in the allocation of resources, and government defines the framework for corporate action. More specifically, government plays four distinct roles in a nation's economy. It serves as the framework state, embodying society's values and, in turn, constructing the legal framework in which the country's economy operates. It serves as the promotional state, using its authority to enhance the nation's economy. It serves as the regulatory state "to ameliorate the unacceptable consequences of market activity without losing the benefits of a competitive economy" (p. 26). Finally, it serves as the social service state by focusing especially on the allocation of material benefits and the effect of private economic activity and public policy on the distribution of wealth and income.

Furthermore, just as government plays multiple roles vis-à-vis the nation's economy, scholars vary in their understanding of what the relationship between business and government is or should be. One model, the business dominance model, sees political authority as an extension of economic power. For example, Charles Lindblom (1993) and E. J. Woodhouse (1993), Thomas Ferguson (1995), and Thomas Dye (2001) argue that business enjoys a privileged position in American politics and policy. According to the pluralist model, the one favored by Novak, American society consists of numerous power centers that compete with one another to shape public policy. David Vogel (1989, 1996), for example, insists that many groups other than business have substantial advantages in the policy process. The market capitalism model embraces the assumptions of market-oriented economists and assumes that corporations operate for the benefit of their shareholders and strive to increase shareholder value. Obviously, this is the model that animates one side of the debate over CSR: "The principal task of government under the market capitalism model is to guarantee that markets function properly" (p. 31). Finally, the stakeholder model, which drives another side in the CSR debate, holds that everyone affected by corporate actions should be considered by managers. It "rejects both the market capitalism assumption that the interests of stockholders alone should guide corporate decisions and the pluralist view that a comprehensive array of societal groups has a say in the public policies that govern firms" (pp. 31–32).

Thus, given the complexity involved in designing and managing a country's political and economic systems, there is no simple dichotomy between governments and markets. Instead, we have a broad array of options that combine governmental and market arrangements in a wide variety of ways. Whether we tend to emphasize market capitalism, pluralism, business dominance, or the stakeholder perspective, the debate over CSR takes place in a multifaceted, multilayered system, and simplistic solutions to complicated problems clearly do not suffice. For example, an intriguing contradiction embedded, at least implicitly, in the CSR debate concerns privatization. Specifically, it is illogical for corporations to claim that they lack competence in public policy to avoid social responsibility and then to accept contracts with government to provide social services or manage criminal justice programs and prisons. This lack of logic, however, is not compelling given the confusion or lack of serious consideration of what is inherently public and what is inherently private — a problem that we address later.

CONCLUSION

We would like to make two concluding observations about our claim that government or public administration, in particular, is an appropriate model of moral agency and citizenship that other professions, including business, may consult for guidance. First, as we noted earlier, the shift in perspective from business as the prototype for government to the reverse, at least in the moral sense, is likely to be a monumental cultural challenge on both the individual and institutional levels. At this juncture, however, we are making the claim for an ideal, a different relationship between business and government, that may appeal to citizens, corporate executives, and public officials for different reasons. For citizens, who are accustomed to considering the public interest, the advantages attached to this new moral partnership between business and government should be patently preferable, for example, to the cannibalized commonweal characteristic of pluralism. For corporate executives, both as employees and as citizens, enhanced clarity and coherence surrounding their professional and personal roles and responsibilities should be much more fulfilling than a parochial focus on profit or self-serving justifications of CSR as an asset to the bottom line. In this vein, with regard to those corporations that already participate more broadly in CSR, we believe that the model we offer speaks very clearly to an aspect of CSR that is generally ignored, namely, the clarification of citizenship. Finally, for public officials, our model should be of interest for essentially the same reasons we think it would be for citizens and corporate executives, as public administration, in practice, tends to be as morally anemic as other sectors of American society — a point that takes us to our second observation.

In our view, government or public administration has by no means reached the level of moral agency and citizenship embodied by our claim. Therefore, the shift we recommend must occur simultaneously in different venues. Educational and training initiatives need to be designed, developed, and implemented in both the private and public sectors if the innate moral nature of public administration is to be reified and extended across organizations and professions. Many issues remain on the ethics agenda in both sectors. In a later chapter, we propose an education and training model that we believe has the potential for success in this effort.

REFERENCES

Barry, N. 2000. *Business Ethics*. West Lafayette, IN: Purdue University Press.

Bowie, N. E. 1999. *Business Ethics: A Kantian Perspective*. Malden, MA: Blackwell Publishers.

Danley, J. R. 1994. *The Role of the Modern Corporation in a Free Society*. Notre Dame, IN: University of Notre Dame Press.

Dye, T. R. 2001. *Top Down Policy Making*. New York: Chatham House Publishers of Seven Bridges.

Ferguson, T. 1995. *Golden Rule: The Investment Theory of Party Competition and the Logic of Money-Driven Political Systems*. Chicago: University of Chicago Press.

Friedman, M. 1970. The Social Responsibility of Business Is to Increase Its Profits. *New York Times Sunday Magazine*. Reprinted in *Business Ethics*, 1996, ed. T. L. Roleff, pp. 11–17. San Diego, CA: Greenhaven Press.

Friedman, M., and R. Friedman. 1980. *Free to Choose*. New York: Harcourt Brace Jovanovich.

Garofalo, C., and D. Geuras. 1999. *Ethics in the Public Service: The Moral Mind at Work*. Washington, D.C.: Georgetown University Press.

Lehne, R. 2001. *Government and Business*. New York: Chatham House Publishers of Seven Bridges.

Lindblom, C. E. 1977. *Politics and Markets: The World's Political-Economic Systems*. New York: Basic Books.

Lindblom, C. E., and E. J. Woodhouse. 1993. *The Policy–Making Process*, 3rd ed. Englewood Cliffs, NJ: Prentice Hall.

Morris, T. 1997. *If Aristotle Ran General Motors*. New York: Henry Holt.

Novak, M. 1982, 1991. *The Spirit of Democratic Capitalism*. Lanham, MD: Madison Books.

———. 1997. *The Fire of Invention*. Lanham, MD: Rowman & Littlefield.

Quinn, D. P., and T. M. Jones. 1995. An Agent Morality View of Business Policy. *Academy of Management Review*. 20:22–42.

Reder, A. 1994. Corporate Social Responsibility Benefits Business. In *In Pursuit of Principles and Profit*. New York: G.P. Putnam's Sons. Reprinted in *Business Ethics*, 1996, ed. T. L. Roleff, pp. 18–29. San Diego, CA.: Greenhaven Press.

Sen, A. 1987. *On Ethics and Economics*. Malden, MA: Blackwell Publishers.

Solomon, R. C. 1992. *Ethics and Excellence: Cooperation and Integrity in Business.* New York: Oxford University Press.

Vogel, D. 1989. *Fluctuating Fortunes: Political Power of Business in America.* New York: Basic Books.

————. 1996. *Kindred Strangers: The Uneasy Relationship between Politics and Business in America.* Princeton, N.J.: Princeton University Press.

Wamsley, G. et al. 1990. *Refounding Public Administration.* Newbury Park, CA: Sage.

Wills, G. 1999. *A Necessary Evil: A History of American Distrust of Government.* New York: Simon & Schuster.

5 Managed Care

Different countries finance and deliver health care in different ways. According to Adolino and Blake (2001), for example, at least in industrialized countries, national policy models range from direct governmental provision of health care to minimal governmental activity in providing either care or access to care. The United Kingdom uses a national health service model in which citizens are guaranteed access to most services through a system financed and administered directly by the government. The single-payer model found in Canada guarantees citizens access to privately provided health care via a program funded by the government. A third model, found in Germany, is mandatory health insurance, in which the government guarantees access but with multiple payers and multiple providers. Government in Germany also provides health insurance to the unemployed, the self-employed, and the retired. Finally, there is the market-maximized model found in the United States. Here, except for the elderly and the poor, the government provides no guarantee of either health care or access. Most Americans are covered by private, employment-based insurance, and there are approximately 45 million Americans without health insurance.

Although no system of health care finance and delivery is perfect, the United States is unique in the twin problems of cost and access. In this chapter, we focus on the American response to the cost problem; namely, managed care. Our chief concern, however, is not the strengths and weaknesses of managed care per se but, rather, a moral framework in which managed care can be understood. Like Mary Anderlik (2001), we aim to go beyond the polemic between business and medicine ideologies and offer a framework for inquiry, debate, and decision. Unlike Anderlik's pragmatism, however, which we address later, our framework, we believe, provides more clarity, depth, and moral substance that can inform the policy and professional discourse on possible new directions in health care for all Americans.

Although a moral framework alone is not sufficient to resolve the myriad complexities of health care, it is crucial, nonetheless, to identify the locus of moral agency in the health care system, given the fluidity and uncertainty in American health care today. Managed care, the dominant form of health care financing and delivery, is changing. Some health policy analysts, in fact, believe that managed care is actually either dead or dying; however, a feasible replacement is yet to be identified (P. Cruise, personal correspondence, 2003). Fee-for-service appears to be returning, with managed care organizations temporarily paying what providers demand and then eventually withdrawing from a geographic area, leaving no health care system in their wake. Providers are dropping Medicare HMO (health maintenance organization) patients, regular Medicare patients, and Medicaid patients because of the low fee schedules. This means, among other things, that no one, including the government, guarantees access to health care for any constituents, even the elderly and the poor. At the same time, so-called boutique medicine such as Botox injections and liposuction is increasingly popular among the affluent and semiaffluent. Finally, some argue for the elimination of employment-based health insurance, which was introduced in lieu of salary increases during World War II wage controls. At that time, the government approved of this approach and eventually provided tax incentives to employers who furnished health insurance. Today, health insurance is complicated and problematic for all but the largest employers, with employees having no idea of the true costs of health care, providers taking advantage of asymmetric information, and third-party payers less concerned with individual transaction costs, as they price for groups. Under these circumstances, we believe that a moral framework is fundamental to helping all of us understand and begin to deal substantively with the health care puzzle.

ORIGINS AND STRUCTURE OF MANAGED CARE

Managed care has been the subject of extensive economic and ethical analysis and assessment during the last few years (Morreim, 1995; Anders, 1996; Makover, 1998; Wong, 1998; Gervais et al., 1999; Spencer et al., 2000; Anderlik, 2001). Therefore, a body of literature is available to help us understand the genesis, evolution, operations, and moral dimensions of managed care today. First, however, we must understand what Morreim (1995) calls the most salient feature of health care economics: the exponential rise in the cost of health care since the mid-1960s and concomitant efforts at cost containment.

Four factors — economic, political, social, and normative — have contributed to health care cost escalation. On the economic front, Morreim (1995) argues that extensive government and private investment in medical research, medical education, and hospital construction since the end of World War II has led to a proliferation of high-tech and advanced health care facilities, as well as a shift from a labor-intensive to a capital-intensive enterprise. Furthermore, this investment was accompanied by a significant increase in third-party funding to pay for its use. Fee-for-service insurance coverage meant not only compensation of physicians and hospitals for services rendered but also incentives to provide as many promising interventions as possible. The result, Morreim (1995) maintains, was massive price inflation.

With respect to political factors, Morreim (1995) notes public faith in science and technology, a relentless demand for more and better health services, and the power of the medical profession. In combination, these factors ensured government involvement in health financing, the expansion of government and private insurance, and the dominant role of physicians in controlling both their professional services and overall health resources. Moreover, in the developed nations, including the United States, there was the belief that the cost of health care should not have to be considered at the time of illness. The net effect of this belief, as well as the growth in insurance, was insulation from the economic consequences of health care spending decisions that, in turn, led to larger and larger escalations in premium costs and the overall costs of care.

Among the social factors contributing to the rise in health care costs are the aging of the population, the growing number of uninsured Americans, HIV-AIDS, and litigiousness. Today, the so-called "graying of America" and its policy implications have become a popular topic. The strains that this demographic change places on Social Security, for example, are well known, and in health care, equally well known is that advanced age often brings more illness, including chronic diseases and disability. In the United States, health care for the elderly already consumes far more dollars than for the rest of the population, with no end in sight. In addition, the growing number of uninsured Americans and the growing number of HIV-AIDS patients present formidable economic challenges to our health care system. Last, American litigiousness means that physicians fear malpractice suits, which in turn leads to the practice of defensive medicine or the performance of the maximum number of procedures to minimize the chance of being sued.

Finally, the normative factors underlying cost escalation in health care include values that Morreim (1995) contends are in tension with each other. For example, we believe, on the one hand, that individuals should be able to spend their money as they please, including the purchase of health care. But we also believe that no one should be denied health care because of an inability to pay. Morreim (1995) suggests that within this tension, "we find ourselves supposing that the poor are morally entitled to almost any health care that the wealthy can afford" (p. 13), with the result being an explosion of expenditures. This, coupled with our faith in science and technology, as well as with physicians' insistence that their first loyalty is to their patients, has meant that both providers and patients "have pursued health care largely without regard to its price tag" (p. 13).

To summarize, Morreim (1995) argues that despite the variety of governmental and corporate strategies put in place over the last 30 years to control, let alone reduce, health care costs, economic pressures promise further escalation. In addition to aging, AIDS, and indigency, we face continuing technological growth and our belief in entitlement to limitless care. Ironically, competition in health care may raise, rather than reduce, overall expenditures. Morreim (1995) maintains that, although "competition can . . . reduce the prices of individual products and services, its overall goal and probable effect will be to produce new types of services, greater numbers of services per patient, more (even if briefer) hospitalizations, more ancillary care, and a wider domain of services ranging from sports medicine to wellness to health education" (p. 16). The goal, in her view, is expansion, not contraction, of market share. Finally, Morreim (1995) asserts that "cost containment is not succeeding" and that economic constraints are bound to become even more stringent in the future (p. 17).

Legally, managed care organizations, as insurance companies, are exempt from federal antitrust law, whereas health care organizations enjoy no such exemption (Spencer et al., 2000). Thus, competition or cost containment has been promoted by the federal government through various challenges to health care providers based on antitrust concepts. A second significant legal factor in explaining the strength of managed care organizations concerns the 1974 Employee Retirement Income Security Act. This statute exempts employers who self-insure their health benefit plans from state regulation, taxation, and control. "Under these self-insured plans, the employer pays the healthcare claims directly, rather than purchasing an insurance policy to pay claims, thus escaping dependence on state-regulated insurance companies, which are often more expensive. These companies either formed or turned to MCOs [managed care organizations] to manage their plans" (Spencer et al., 2000).

Managed care integrates the financing and delivery of health care in three ways (Wong, 1998). First, managed care organizations contract with physicians and hospitals to provide health services to enrolled members, either for a fixed monthly premium or for reduced rates on a fee-for-service basis. Second, these providers, called the network, accept utilization and quality controls as part of their contract. Third, patients are given financial incentives to use the designated providers and facilities. For example, out-of-network services either are not covered or require a higher out-of-pocket expense to the patient. Managed care, therefore, represents a direct assault on traditional fee-for-service medicine, raising many issues, including the relationship between medicine and the marketplace as well as the moral implications and consequences of rationing, access, and quality.

Yet, as Peter Cruise (personal correspondence, 2003) observes, after a few years of scandals and unhappy public reaction, state and federal laws began to erode managed care via any-willing-provider laws, patient self-referral laws, and guaranteed hospital stays for certain medical conditions, as well as other measures. Indeed, even the U.S. Supreme Court ruled in April 2003 that states may require HMOs to open themselves to all doctors, hospitals, and other providers who agree to abide by their terms. This decision followed a June 2002 ruling by the high court that upheld state laws requiring HMOs to accept second opinions from medical review boards concerning the necessity of medical procedures. Thus, the system of managed care faces myriad challenges in the years ahead as the United States tries to come to grips with the financing and delivery of health care to all Americans.

MORAL CHALLENGES OF MANAGED CARE

Managed care is rife with moral challenges. In this section, we describe those challenges to set the stage for consideration of alternatives to managed care and, in a later chapter, of our model of moral agency and citizenship in today's managed care environment. We must note, too, that several authors have maintained that managed care organizations are aware that they lack a moral framework to guide their decision making and actions. If this is true, our articulation and application of a model of moral agency and citizenship should not be seen as the imposition of some utopian or alien construct on a resistant or retrograde system. Indeed, our intent here is not to depict contemporary American health care as a contest between good and evil. Rather, it is to sketch the moral dimensions, subtleties, and nuances of an enormously complex assemblage of individuals, institutions, and interests engaged in the financing and delivery of either a critical commodity or a fundamental right, depending on one's point of view.

The moral challenges of managed care can be captured by such terms and oppositions as medical necessity, rationing, financial versus fiduciary, contract versus covenant, gatekeeper, capitation, utilization review, and third-party payer. These terms and others illustrate the seismic shifts that have occurred in American health care in the last few years. Patients, physicians, employers, hospitals, insurance companies, and HMOs are among the key players in the new health care arena, with its changing assumptions, expectations, and processes, and in the midst of all of this churning and shifting are threats to established professional norms, autonomy, and integrity. Conflicts of interest, conflicts of responsibility, and conflicts of commitment are the order of the day.

According to Karen G. Gervais et al. (1999), managed care has focused primarily on cost containment and secondarily on quality improvement and has essentially avoided the issue of access for the uninsured and underinsured. The market-driven managed care system offers no incentives to support research and education or to expand access to the health care system. Moreover, embedded in this system are many ethical challenges, which lie in rationing methods used to achieve cost containment, including definitions of medical necessity, coverage policies, practice guidelines, and risk-sharing arrangements such as capitation. In a general sense, Gervais (1999) argues, health care in the United States is guided by a social ethic that legitimizes the claim that the ethical obligations of managed care organizations extend only to those with whom they have contracted. However, if health care is a fundamental right or a basic good, then a managed care organization is obligated to act as both a fiscal steward and a steward of individual and population health.

This line of reasoning is reminiscent of the debate over corporate social responsibility. Managed care organizations, at least those that are for-profit, are confronted with the same pressures as other for-profit organizations — obligations to the community versus obligations to shareholders — and even some supporters of managed care contend that managed care organizations must be bound by significant ethical responsibilities that transcend the mandate to maximize profit (Wong, 1998). According to Kenman Wong (1998), many physicians adhere to this view as well.

Wong (1998) offers a typology of ethical perspectives on health care that can help order the contending viewpoints in this debate and provide some clarification of the values, assumptions, and objectives at stake. Six types or positions are delineated, along with their respective views toward managed care and profit. We touch on the six types and then describe their perspectives and Wong's in more detail. First, there are patient-centered purists who reject managed care and reject profit. Second, there are market reform purists who reject managed care but support profit. Third, there are explicit rationers who, like the patient-centered purists, reject both managed care and profit, but for different reasons. Fourth, there are cautious supporters of managed care whose support of both managed care and profit is tenuous. Fifth, there are for-profit managed care champions who support both managed care and profit. Finally, there are nonprofit organization supporters who support managed care but reject profit.

Patient-centered purists advocate a return to the older model of medicine under which the influence of third-party payers on care decisions would be minimized and accountability would be ensured by professional norms rather than market forces. This position recognizes the conflicts of interest in fee-for-service but argues that in this model, the interests of physicians and patients are most closely aligned, whereas in managed care, the cost of favoring the patient's interests is much greater to the physician. Patient-centered purists argue that managed care is a rationing scheme, as it limits patient care to preserve resources for others. Rationing drives cost-cutting, and capitation produces rationing, as patients are competing for care provided with limited dollars. Finally, patient-centered purists believe that the patient–physician relationship is abridged in several ways, including the lack of continuity of care that erodes trust, which in itself has therapeutic value; the dilution of informed patient consent; and the fundamental clash between a business ethic and the traditional medical ethic. The purists charge that insurance company executives take no oath and that their morality is profit driven.

Market-reform purists express similar moral concerns, but unlike patient-centered purists, market-reform purists believe that financial considerations should be a primary consideration in the practice of medicine and that the market is the best vehicle to ensure cost-consciousness and monitoring of quality. In the view of market-reform purists, trust in the exclusive use of professional norms to ensure fiscal accountability is misguided. They argue that patients can exercise market discipline and should be given incentives to reduce the use of wasteful procedures and find lower-cost providers. Market-reform purists advocate Medical Savings Accounts in which consumers negotiate prices directly with their choice of provider plans, physicians, and hospitals.

The third category — explicit rationers — holds that fee-for-service is morally suspect because of its exclusive concern with the well-being of individual patients in an age of fiscal scarcity. This results in an unjust distribution of health care because some people use up as much as possible without considering others. Thus, explicit rationers suggest that specific priorities for allocating health care should be established. For example, rationing could be accomplished by age, the idea being that the old should simply die gracefully and that medicine should not be used to extend life beyond a particular chronological point. Rationing could also be accomplished in part by sin exclusions that would limit care based on lifestyle choices that place health at risk. If one willingly engages in behaviors that jeopardize one's health, that person would have no right to receive priority for scarce resources. Such behaviors include smoking, overeating, and alcohol and drug abuse. Last, priorities could be established via community discussion in which categories of injury and disease are ranked with funding for treatment allocated accordingly. The Oregon Medicaid plan exemplifies this approach, in which triage is applied according to quality of life as well as the cost-effectiveness of treatments.

Explicit rationers also believe that explicit rationing with established priorities would protect physicians from ethical dilemmas created by current managed care arrangements that force them to make implicit, *ad hoc* rationing decisions at the bedside. There is no doubt that rationing must occur, given limited resources, but physicians should not be expected to make those decisions, for they are then put into the ethically untenable position of serving as a patient advocate while simultaneously holding the line on costs. Finally, rationing has always been part of health care, but it is hidden in the present system and favors those with means. Indeed, managed care is an implicit rationing scheme with global budgets set by third-party payers and therefore is essentially undemocratic.

On the other side of the debate are managed care supporters of various stripes. In general, supporters of managed care agree with explicit rationers that rising costs must be curbed, but they think explicit rationing is politically and practically infeasible because it negates the freedom required in the practice of medicine. Some managed care advocates embrace market-oriented reforms and incentives for cost consciousness, but in their estimation, physicians, not patients, should be the targets of incentives, as physicians' decisions account for the vast majority of total expenditures. They also maintain that for-profit medicine is ethical because it results from the free choice of consenting adults, that cost-containment measures and denial of expensive benefits do not present ethical conflicts because the consumer has willingly chosen to participate in a particular health plan, and that treating medicine as a business contributes to patient autonomy because it allows freedom of choice in how much of one's resources to devote to health insurance.

Cautious supporters of managed care believe in market-based reforms as well, but they also believe in regulation of managed care organizations. The problem with managed care, in their opinion, is not the concept but the execution. Therefore, managed care organizations must be bound by significant ethical responsibilities that go beyond the maximization of profit. Again, we see at least an implicit reference to corporate social responsibility. Finally, the nonprofit organization supporters advocate some degree of competition in health care but reject pure market discipline in which shareholder profits are at stake. This group of supporters suggests that the profit motive places additional pressure on physicians and further divides physician loyalties. Moreover, they maintain that cost savings should be used for patients or for research, rather than given to shareholders. Some nonprofit supporters believe that medicine is a public good and that to allow corporations and their shareholders to profit from a fundamental human need is immoral and reduces medicine to just another commodity.

Wong's (1998) typology demonstrates the ideological diversity and ethical complexity associated with contemporary American health care finance and delivery. In the United States, health care is embedded in a multifaceted, multilayered public–private system in which individual and institutional interests are conjoined in a multitude of ways. Only now is society beginning to address the ethical issues in managed care through legislation, regulation, and oversight. However, the ethical climate of health care continues to be characterized by uncertainty, confusion, and even fear (Spencer et al., 2000). Many relationships, expectations, and issues remain on our national agenda.

Consider, for example, the various perspectives represented in Wong's (1998) typology. In addition to describing the positions found across the health care debate, Wong (1998) offers a critique of each, beginning with the patient-centered purists who dichotomize the moral objectives of business and medicine. In Wong's (1998) view, the dichotomy of physicians and corporations fails to stand up to scrutiny, as the realms of medicine and business are closer together than a cursory look indicates. Wong (1998) argues that patient-centered purists overestimate the sanctity of the traditional fee-for-service arrangement and the medical ethic under which it has operated and suggests that professional medical norms deserve some degree of skepticism. Physicians, he holds, should not be completely trusted as the exclusive guardians of their patients' health, because medicine, as a profession, has shown itself to be as self-serving as any other. For instance, the medical profession, according to Wong (1998), resists or accepts government and corporate involvement in health care depending on whether it perceives such involvement as enhancing or diminishing its own autonomy. With respect to government and corporate involvement, respectively, the medical establishment has decried socialized medicine but not socialized research or socialized hospital construction, and physicians did not oppose legislation allowing them to form professional corporations to capitalize on favorable corporate tax rates. They have, however, resisted oversight of their billings by third-party payer organizations because this constitutes the corporate practice of medicine. Wong (1998) concludes this discussion with the argument that a return to fee-for-service is implausible, as it was this arrangement that drove up costs in the first place and failed to meet the norms of distributive justice by not addressing the problem of access.

With respect to explicit rationers, Wong (1998) believes that they contribute to the debate by emphasizing fiscal limits and the need for greater societal involvement in acknowledging those limits. But he also believes that their criteria for the allocation of health care resources and services are morally unacceptable and practically infeasible. Whether it is age, lifestyle, or community decision making, serious moral questions concerning the healthy elderly, the slippery slope in applying behavioral factors to health care, and the moral judgment and technical expertise of citizens remain unanswered.

In the end, Wong (1998) sides with the cautious supporters of managed care, arguing, in the spirit of corporate social responsibility, that the stakeholder approach be extended to the managed care system. In his view, the solution to the ethical problems in medicine does not mean the elimination of business values, but it does mean greater transparency; an ethical, not only economic, basis for denial of treatment; and the development of quality and performance measurement tools. Medicine, he maintains, is a public good such as food, safety, and education, and the responsibility for providing it extends to employers, government, and communities, as well as patients themselves.

Other analysts, however, do not share Wong's even cautious support of managed care. Consider, for example, the views of Linda Peeno (1996, 1997), Michael Makover (1998), and Raymond Scalettar (1999) — all of whom are physicians. To these three practitioners, managed care fails in a number of key respects. For example, Peeno, a former medical director and medical reviewer for three health care organizations, testified in 1996 and 1997 before the Subcommittee on Health and Environment, U.S. House of Representatives, Committee on Commerce, that among the moral landmines in managed care are many techniques intended to restrict and obstruct the provision of health care. Benefits restrictions; exclusions; evasions; selection of groups based on economic liability to the plan; mazes of rules for authorizations, referrals, and network availability; harassment of physicians; and denials for "medical necessity" are regularly applied by managed care administrators in the interests of the plan.

According to Peeno, "the core premise underlying any consideration of ethical concerns in managed care is this: every significant medical and health care decision has an ethical component." In this regard, she briefly discusses four categories of ethical concerns in health care — professional ethics, medical ethics, business ethics, and social ethics — and then six claims by managed care — rationing is necessary because of scarce resources, savings occur from cost reduction, cost containment is for the larger societal good, managed care's ethical responsibility is limited to rationing decisions, medical decisions in managed care are made by physicians of good character and competence, and spiraling health care costs justify whatever is necessary to control the decision making of physicians. Peeno concludes her testimony with a number of ethical corrections for managed care.

In regard to professional, medical, business, and social ethics, Peeno raises questions concerning such matters as the meaning of a physician executive and a utilization nurse, what codes of ethics they adhere to, what governing body of peers they submit to, and how the inherent conflict between allegiance to a corporate mission and the commitment to patient advocacy is resolved. She suggests that with respect to dual agency, divided loyalties, breaches of patient trust, and interference with the patient–physician relationship, we do not now have ways to prevent or mitigate these problems. Peeno is also concerned with patient autonomy, informed consent, whether capitation is inherently unethical in view of its goals and results (i.e., the withholding or denying of care), and whether as a society we can "really talk about rationing health care when executives and stockholders reap such hefty rewards from the business of rationing" (1996). Finally, with reference to claims by managed care, Peeno questions whether we, indeed, have limited resources. Her view is that, as a matter of fact, we have too many resources compared to the rest of the world. She notes that when the rest of the world talks about limited resources, they mean real scarcity, such as lack of medicine, equipment, and the basic necessities for medicine such as hot water. "When we talk about 'scarcity' we use it as leverage for some economic gain or justification" (1996). Furthermore, Peeno observes that "we always speak of the rationing of care, and never of rationing compensation," and she asks why we are concerned about a glut of physicians but not a glut of health care administrators and executives, whose "increasingly obscene incomes" outstrip the incomes of physicians (1996).

On the matter of cost savings and cost containment, Peeno argues that we have been seduced by the obsession with efficiency and that we must question how alleged cost savings are attained. As a health care executive, she states, "I am able to achieve significant cost reduction by choosing my members carefully, limiting their coverage, denying them access even to the covered benefits, contracting with a network of less-costly providers, etc." (1996). But there are also costs that we do not measure, such as the individual and societal costs from excluding certain members from any health benefits, the costs to families who may be destroyed by out-of-pocket expenses above their insurance, the physical and emotional toll on families and communities when necessary treatment is unavailable because a plan refuses to pay, and the erosion of trust that occurs when physicians become agents of a plan driven by economic motives. Last, Peeno expresses concern that character and competence become irrelevant when one's mission is independent of these traits. "When my performance is measured in numbers and quotas," she contends, "my job and character are severed" (1996). She is worried about the disconnection of conscience from conduct, about depersonalization of patients, and about instrumentalist thinking, in which means-based approaches predominate, for example, "the professional act of caring for a patient becomes a means to keep one's numbers 'in line'; a means to increase one's bonus or the profit of a company; a means to keep one's job, etc.; patient care is no longer an end to itself" (1996).

Peeno, finally, recommends a number of ethical corrections for managed care, including greater transparency regarding criteria for approvals of protocols, training, preservation of the doctor–patient relationship through professional codes and support for good clinical care, tracking and reviewing of "medical necessity" denials, and disclosure of financial arrangements. In Peeno's judgment, the ethical conflicts in health care present emotional, psychological, and communication challenges in the midst of differing desires, interests, and perspectives. What is needed is a set of ethical theories that can help clarify, deepen, and strengthen our understanding of such conflicts while protecting patients and their families from harm. In the end, Peeno observes that managed care has evolved with little significant and effective ethical challenge, leaving serious questions to be addressed. For example, "Are we willing to tolerate a system of access and resource allocation which depends upon constraints of professionals in order to achieve its results? If we object to the micromanagement of plans by the government, why do we allow, without examination, the micromanagement of physicians by managed care plans? Are we really making cost-cutting changes for some 'greater good?' Is any 'greater good' so great that it justifies ethical transgressions to achieve it?"

Michael Makover (1998) argues that managed care and ethical care are incompatible for some of the same reasons provided by Peeno: It forces doctors to serve two masters, it is fee splitting, it puts patients at risk, it imposes cookbook care instead of care tailored to individual patient needs, it promises comprehensive care but denies it arbitrarily, it subverts informed consent, and it destroys the doctor–patient relationship. Makover (1998) maintains that every American should have the right to basic, decent health care, but he does not believe that we must all have the same level of health care. Thus, at the heart of the health care debate is the distribution issue: Who gets what? According to Makover (1998), at present, the rich have all the health care possible at relatively insignificant cost to them; the middle class have mediocre to barely adequate care at too high a cost; and the poor have Medicaid and Medicare, which provide poor to barely adequate care. The uninsured have the emergency room or a clinic.

The third and final physician to be considered here is Raymond Scalettar (1999), who suggests that although managed care has educated physicians on the economics of health care, the crux of the conflict concerns distributive justice in which health care is oriented toward the group rather than the individual. He asserts that many physicians cannot abandon their covenant to be ethical healers in exchange for "the greatest good for the greatest number," and he poses a number of the questions raised by Peeno and Makover: Is for-profit care justifiable when plans are continuing to transfer increased risk and cost to patients and employers? Should shareholders of publicly traded companies be part of the group of competing stakeholders at a time of enormous economic constraints? Do we need a new paradigm for health care in America?

ALTERNATIVE PERSPECTIVES ON MANAGED CARE

Makover (1998) and George Anders (1996) offer two differing perspectives on managed care. On the one hand, Makover (1998) recommends the elimination of managed care, whereas Anders (1996) recommends strategies for operating more effectively within a managed care system. More specifically, the principles underlying Makover's (1998) position include universal coverage and portability; ethical control of excess care and treatment; patients' responsibility for choosing the level of care for which they are willing to pay; means testing so premiums, not prices of services, are set for each person; and a new commitment to the poor and the isolated. From these principles, Makover (1998) recommends Medical Savings Accounts, supplemented by catastrophic insurance with high deductibles. The key notion is patient responsibility and physician independence, with citizens unable to afford Medical Savings Accounts being subsidized in proportion to their need. Makover (1998) concludes that the elimination of managed care, Medicare, Medicaid, and for-profit hospitals would restore sanity and simplicity to the financing and delivery of health care to all Americans.

Anders (1996) argues that "the theoretical appeal of managed care remains immense: a well-planned system that will steer patients to the appropriate level of care whether they are healthy or sick, instead of leaving them to grope randomly for medical help in a crisis" (p. 245). What is needed, in his view, is a way to incorporate better judgment into the system. This entails power sharing beyond an HMO's headquarters; important roles for consumers, doctors, employers, and regulators; and more cooperative but assertive approaches to the health care system.

More specifically, Anders (1996) offers 10 steps that he believes will improve managed care. For example, consumers need to make the managed care system more responsive by becoming informed, by asking questions, and by becoming partners with their doctors and health plans in making medical decisions. Doctors need to accept the emphasis on cost-effective medicine but also need to challenge managed care rules without fear. Doctors, employers, regulators, and HMOs need to combine forces to develop guidelines that people can trust. This means, among other things, that "leadership in outcomes research and the development of treatment guidelines will need to come from outside the HMO industry" (p. 250). Regulators need to patrol the ways that HMOs pay doctors. Anders (1996) argues that the system of capitation, incentives, and risk-sharing, as well as the HMOs' argument that their contracts with doctors and hospitals are proprietary business dealings, ignores the public interest in ensuring the provision of health care to all. Finally, HMOs need to be made accountable for their mistakes through statutory and regulatory change or reinterpretation. The Employee Retirement Income Security Act, for instance, has led to HMOs avoiding state-court jurisdiction when members sue and to federal courts generally ruling "that the pension law exempts both corporate employers and health plans from being sued for negligence" (Anders, 1996, p. 255).

Anders concludes that HMOs deserve credit for focusing on health care costs and for introducing efficient business methods into medicine. But they also deserve lower marks for gaps in care when patients most need their services. "And away from Wall Street, HMOs' success at earning big profits for middlemen — and outfitting executives with 75-foot yachts, Rolls Royces, and other trappings of luxury — will be seen as uncomfortable hypocrisy for an industry that publicly preaches the virtues of austerity" (1996, p. 262). In the end, Anders (1996) hopes that doctors will "figure out how to run a cost-effective medical system without abandoning compassion — just as corporate executives figured out how to satisfy shareholders without ripping apart businesses so drastically" (p. 262).

This excursion through managed care has demonstrated the complexity of the American health care system. Moral, economic, and political issues abound, with no easy answers in sight. However, we believe that the articulation and application of our model of moral agency and citizenship to this policy arena in a later chapter may prove useful in providing practical perspectives and approaches to what is widely understood as one of the most vexing ethical policy debates of our time.

REFERENCES

Adolino, J. R., and C. H. Blake. 2001. *Comparing Public Policies: Issues and Choices in Six Industrialized Countries*. Washington, D.C.: CQ Press.

Anderlik, M. R. 2001. *The Ethics of Managed Care*. Bloomington: Indiana University Press.

Anders, G. 1996. *Health against Wealth: HMOs and the Breakdown of Medical Trust*. Boston: Houghton Mifflin.

Gervais, K. G. et al. 1999. *Ethical Challenges in Managed Care*. Washington, D.C.: Georgetown University Press.

Makover, M. E. 1998. *Mismanaged Care: How Corporate Medicine Jeopardizes Your Health*. Amherst, NY: Prometheus.

Morreim, E. H. 1995. *Balancing Act: The New Medical Ethics of Medicine's New Economics*. Washington, D.C.: Georgetown University Press.

Peeno, L. 1996. Managed Care Ethics: The Close View. Testimony for U. S. House of Representatives, Committee on Commerce, Subcommittee on Health and Environment.

———. 1997. The Menace of Managed Care: A Guide to How Avoidance, Denial and Control Can Result in Patient Harm. Testimony for U. S. House of Representatives, Committee on Commerce, Subcommittee on Health and Environment.

Scalettar, R. L. 1999. *Managed Care: A Work in Progress*. Washington, D.C.: Woodstock Theological Center.

Spencer, E. M. et al. 2000. *Organization Ethics in Health Care*. New York: Oxford University Press.

Wong, K. L. 1998. *Medicine and the Marketplace: The Moral Dimensions of Managed Care*. Notre Dame, IN: University of Notre Dame Press.

6 The Legal Profession

Similar to the fields of medicine and education, the legal profession differs from but maintains some of the characteristics of both private enterprise and public service. Attorneys in the United States and in many other countries may belong to private law firms or serve as independent agents. However, much of the legal system, including public defenders, prosecutors at all governmental levels, and judges, belongs to the public sector. The success of the system depends on both its private and public aspects, sometimes in cooperation with and sometimes in competition with each other. The legal profession, as a whole, is therefore neither fully public nor fully private.

There are other reasons to accord a special status to the legal profession, even in its private aspect. First, attorneys provide a service that is essential for every private citizen. All people need appropriate legal representation that they, except in rare cases, cannot provide for themselves. Legal conflicts inevitably occur among citizens, and they often pit the weak against the powerful. Without an effective legal system, the rights of all citizens would be unequal. Those rights would be especially jeopardized when individuals are in conflict with the government. Proper representation in such cases can mean the difference between life and death and is often the difference between incarceration and freedom.

A second reason for the special status of the legal profession is that, without it, the state cannot support its legal structure. Without a sound legal system, the state cannot survive, let alone provide equitable treatment to citizens regardless of wealth, social standing, or minority status. The legal system, although not the entirety of the state, is surely a necessary condition of its existence, and the legal profession is essential to the legal system.

The vital social importance of a profession demands that its practitioners subscribe to special ethical commitments. In the medical profession, for example, the Hippocratic oath expresses the ethical commitments of doctors, and the code of the American Society for Public Administration (2004) expresses the importance of ethics in the public service. Similarly, attorneys, both nationally and in their individual states, are subject to ethics codes.

One might therefore reasonably ask whether the legal profession is inherently ethical in ways that would serve as guidelines for the ethically concerned private citizen. To respond, one must address two related questions: Are legal professionals moral agents? Are legal professionals, as moral agents, ideal moral exemplars for the private citizen? We will answer the first question with a qualified "Yes," but we will answer the second question negatively.

THE CLIENT'S INTEREST AND THE INTERESTS OF JUSTICE

Private citizens hire attorneys for defense against both other private citizens and governments. One might therefore infer that attorneys are, like auto mechanics, plumbers, or accountants, agents of private individuals with no special professional obligation to the society as a whole except to provide the services contractually agreed on. The attorney might therefore be understood as essentially a business operator with a specialized skill to be used in behalf of a paying customer.

The notion that the attorney is an agent of the client is suggested in authoritative documents concerning legal ethics, such as the *American Lawyer's Code of Conduct, Public Discussion Draft* of The Roscoe Pound Institute and the Association of Trial Lawyers of America (1980). That document states, "It is clear that the lawyer for a private party is and should be an officer of the court only in the sense of serving the court as a zealous, partisan advocate of one side of the case before it." Furthermore, the document maintains, "A lawyer shall use all legal means that are consistent with the retainer agreement, and reasonably available, to advance the client's interest as the client perceives them." The latter statement may be interpreted to suggest that the lawyer is not even an ethical agent because he or she must pursue the client's ends by any means that do not entail violations of the law.

The following examples in the aforementioned draft appear to fortify the claim that attorneys are required to suspend all morality in pursuit of their client's interests.

> 3(e). A lawyer is conducting the defense of a criminal prosecution. The judge calls the lawyer to the bench and asks her whether the defendant is guilty. The lawyer knows that the defendant is guilty, and reasonably believes that an equivocal answer will be taken by the judge as an admission of guilt. The lawyer assures the judge that the defendant is innocent. The lawyer has not committed a disciplinary violation.

> 3(f). The same facts as in 3(e), but the lawyer replies to the judge, "I'm sorry, Your Honor, but it would be improper for me to answer that question." The lawyer has committed a disciplinary violation.

Paragraph 3(e) suggests that it would be acceptable for an attorney to lie to protect the client, and 3(f) implies that, in some cases, the lie would be obligatory. It would appear, then, that the role of an attorney is not that of a moral agent but that of an agent of an individual client. (Roscoe Pound Institute/Association of Trial Lawyers of America, 1980)

The situation of the attorney is, however, more complex than that of a mere representative of a client. The expectation that an attorney is to advocate strongly for his or her client must be understood in the broader context in which attorneys function. The lawyer presents the client's case as effectively as possible, but not merely because of a business arrangement between attorney and client or because the lawyer's reputation rests on his or her success in fulfilling the client's wishes. There are morally significant justifications for such advocacy.

First, the attorney has a moral responsibility to ensure that the morally founded rights of the client are protected. A public defender, trying his or her last case before retirement and therefore with no material interest at stake, is fully morally obligated to defend the client's rights. That public defender is under the same moral obligation as a private attorney defending a billionaire in a highly publicized murder trial. While functioning as an agent of the client, the attorney simultaneously functions as an agent of the moral principles that guarantee all people equal rights. Although business concerns and reputation may provide the attorney with additional private, self-interested motivation to support the client's case, the mere moral responsibility to avail the client of all of his or her rights under the law is sufficient reason for vigorous advocacy. The importance of that reason is expressed in the Roscoe Pound Institute / Association of Trial Lawyers of America Draft:

> The assistance of counsel thus relates significantly to justice under law, in the sense of equal protection of the laws. Leaving each person to his or her own resources alone, without the assistance of counsel in comprehending and coping with the complexities of the legal system, would produce gross disparities in justice under law.

> All these basic rights, individually and together, express the high value placed by our constitutional democracy on the dignity of the individual. Before any person is significantly affected by society in his or her person, relationships, or property, our system requires that certain processes be duly followed — processes to which competent, independent, and zealous lawyers are essential. And if it be observed that the stated ideal is too frequently denied in fact, our response must be that standards for lawyers be so drafted and enforced as to strive to make that ideal a consistent reality (Roscoe Pound Institute / Association of Trial Lawyers of America, 1980).

There is also a second moral reason, based more on the interests of justice to the society than those of the individual client, to justify strong advocacy. The adversary system is intended to promote justice through advocacy. The intent of the system is fully articulated in the code:

> In addition, the adversary system provides the best method we have been able to devise to determine truth in cases in which the facts are in dispute. First, we assign to an advocate on each side of a case the responsibility to ferret out all of the facts, law, and policy considerations relevant to that side. The opposing positions, each expressed as fully and as effectively as possible, are then presented before an impartial judge and/or jury for resolution. Each advocate's position is also subject to searching challenge by an adversary, through cross examination and rebuttal. Thus, the partisanship of the advocates has two important effects—it encourages thoroughness and accuracy in the development of each side of the case, and it permits the judge and jury to remain aloof from partisan involvement until a decision

must actually be made. (Roscoe Pound Institute / Association of Trial Lawyers).

It might therefore be argued that, although the attorney is most directly an agent of the client, the attorney's ultimate principal is justice itself. The system of advocacy, in which the attorney plays an essential role, is intended to discover the truth so that proper judgments may be rendered.

Arthur Applbaum (1999) examines the degree to which attorneys can legitimately appeal to their roles as advocates within the justice system to validate any measures taken in defense of their clients. He argues that, although the role of an attorney entails some behavior that might otherwise be objectionable, there are limits that even the pursuit of legal justice within the system cannot morally permit. First, Applbaum argues that in addition to any role that attorneys play within the legal system, *qua* attorneys, they are also persons and citizens. The status of both person and citizen does not preclude all lawyerly advocacy but "penetrates" the role of advocate to the extent of limiting the moral license of which the attorney can avail himself or herself in defense of a client (1999, p. 109). Furthermore, Applbaum argues, although participation in the legal system, with its conventions and internal criteria of evaluation, may justify some behavior that would not be acceptable outside the system, there are "preconventional" descriptions of their actions that the role of attorney cannot obliterate. Even if a lie is redefined as something else (e.g., staunch defense of a client's rights), under legal conventions, it is still a lie (Applbaum, 1999, p. 109). Legal conventions are not an impenetrable defense against all immoral activity.

Whether or not one agrees with Applbaum concerning the justification for unbridled legal advocacy, one may still recognize the conflict that attorneys, as advocates, must confront. Their obligations under the legal system may contradict their obligations as citizens or persons. For example, in an aforementioned case, the legal conventions may require that an attorney lie when a judge asks him whether his client is guilty. That lie may be obligatory for the attorney under legal requirements but not for a moral person or citizen.

Still, it might be argued that a moral citizen has a responsibility to perform his or her professional functions well, if they contribute to the social order. Under such a premise, the attorney, who tells a lie but only when functioning in his or her capacity of protecting the rights of the individual, is both a good lawyer and a good citizen. The apparent conflict between that attorney's moral responsibility within the legal sphere and his or her moral responsibility as a citizen may be only superficial. In functioning as a good attorney defending one's client's interests, one is behaving as a good citizen, albeit as a citizen who is also a lawyer.

Whether we interpret the conflict as superficial or substantial, one fact remains: In either case, the attorney could still function as a moral agent, either by fulfilling the lawyerly responsibility to the client or by fulfilling the responsibility of the profession in its unique capacity of promoting legal justice. Nevertheless, the attorney is not an exemplar for the private citizen because the moral nature of the attorney's work is not readily evident to the common citizen. In representing his or her client, the attorney may well be motivated by moral principle, but the behavior that the attorney must display is often difficult for the common citizen to understand. Principled strong defense of human rights under the law may resemble unprincipled support of a guilty client's attempt to avoid justice or, worse yet, the attorney's own professional advancement. The common citizen has little means of distinguishing the moral from the immoral motivation merely by observing the attorney's actions. Whereas other members of the legal profession may fully recognize the morality in a lawyer's pursuit of justice for both his or her client and for society in general, the legally untrained populace lacks such powers of recognition. Moreover, the pursuit of justice by the attorney may be beyond anyone's recognition; there are cases in which not even the most perceptive legal expert can tell whether an attorney is pursuing justice or not. Because the attorney is morally responsible to his or her client, who also pays him or her, several motivations coincide and make it difficult to determine whether the moral motive is primary or even operative.

MORAL OBLIGATIONS COMMON TO THE LEGAL PROFESSION

Even the purely moral motives of the attorney are so numerous as to cause confusion. Vincent Luizzi (1993) lists the following as "candidates for a lawyer's obligation" (p. 132–133):

1. To promote justice
2. To engage in *pro bono* activities
3. To educate the lay about the legal system
4. To improve the legal system
5. To improve the penal system
6. To make legal services available
7. To uphold the rule of law
8. To protect the right of the state or its citizens
9. To resolve controversy or conflicts
10. To further the goals of the state
11. To further the goals of society
12. To provide leadership when possible
13. To simplify the law
14. To amass large sums of money that it might "trickle down" to the needy in society

Luizzi does not argue that all entries on the list are true obligations, only that they are reasonable possibilities. With respect to the first entry, as we have seen, although attorneys may be fully committed to the promotion of justice, their activities are so ambiguous that no one would know whether they are promoting justice, the client's interest, or their own. The same ambiguity exists regarding entries 4, 5, 7, and 8, in which terms and phrases such as "improve," "uphold the rule of law," and "protect the rights" indicate activities that could be interpreted as client-serving or self-serving as well as morally founded. Improving a system, upholding the rule of law, and protecting rights may all benefit clients as well as society. Entry 6 may seem altruistic on its face, but in making his or her own legal services available, the attorney is promoting himself or herself as well as his or her clients or the legal system as a whole. He or she would not be in business if he or she did not provide services. Entries 10, 11, and 12 can also be interpreted in ways that make them difficult to distinguish from mere advocacy for one's client. The last entry, which may be included facetiously, is hardly recognizable as a moral obligation.

Entries 3 and 13 appear to entail activities that are distinguishable from self-interest or the pursuit of a specific client's interest. Using public forums to educate people about the law and suggesting ways to simplify the law take time, effort, and expertise when unrelated to individual cases or clients. To the extent that attorneys engage in these activities, they can be seen as exemplifying moral agency. However, they are not activities that attorneys, on the whole, spend much time on, and they are not the primary, essential activities of the profession.

Among the most clearly altruistic activities are those that are *pro bono*, as indicated in entry 2. Unfortunately, Geoffrey Hazard (1978), laments, "So far as concerns legal assistance to the poor, charitable services by practicing lawyers, is now mostly a matter of tokenism" (p. 88). However active attorneys may be in this respect, the profession is uniquely suited to perform this function and thus to exhibit moral agency. But *pro bono* activities, even when they are diligently performed, are understood as charitable acts incumbent on attorneys aside from their normal professional duties. The legal profession does not depend on *pro bono* activities to justify its existence as public administration depends on the public good to justify its existence.

With respect to time and resources, the attorney's *pro bono* activities can interfere with his or her professional obligations as well as complement them. One must not make the facile assumption that an attorney is morally obligated to defend the impoverished just as diligently as one would defend a wealthy, paying client. In an ideal world, equal defense may be possible, but in reality, it may be too much to ask. For example, let us suppose that an attorney has two clients, both with only a very slight chance of acquittal in criminal cases. To defend either client to the limit would require large sums of money that the attorney's law firm cannot afford to pay in the case of a likely losing cause. But the wealthy client has virtually unlimited funds that he or she is willing to expend to cover all costs. The firm is obligated to defend the wealthy client to the best of its ability, but equal defense of the impoverished client and any other impoverished client who might seek assistance would be impossible. The moral aspects of *pro bono* work are more ambiguous than they might seem on the surface.

The public defender is a possible alternative to reliance on private attorneys and private firms to serve the poor. Unfortunately, however, the use of public defenders does not equalize legal services for the rich and the poor. Public defenders do not have the financial resources of private firms, especially when the private firms defend people who are willing to spend vast amounts of their own fortunes. Furthermore, the low pay of the public defender tends to discourage the best-qualified attorneys from choosing public defense as a career.

It may be argued that the public defender is, with all of the limitations of the office, a moral agent. The argument has merit in that the public defender dedicates himself or herself to the cause of helping the poor. But it would not necessarily follow that, if the profession of the public defender instantiates moral agency, the legal profession itself instantiates moral agency. The public defender is a moral agent because he or she is a public agent with a public charge rather than because of his or her participation in the legal profession. The public defender is, in that capacity, a public agent as much as an attorney. The possible confusion between the responsibilities of an attorney, *qua* attorney and *qua* public agent, will be seen also in the cases of the government attorney and the judge.

THE LEGAL PROFESSION AND PUBLIC SERVICE

Government attorneys constitute a special class that might function as moral exemplars as well as moral agents. Because government attorneys more directly represent the public interest, their commitment to social justice is the evident, paramount consideration motivating their actions.

Because of their special status, government attorneys must follow more restrictive rules than private attorneys. For example, prosecutors in criminal cases are obligated to provide the defense attorneys with any factual information that they might need to defend their clients, even if they do not request it. In contrast, defense attorneys may withhold evidence that is potentially useful to the prosecution and may in some circumstances be morally bound to withhold such evidence. In another instance of contrast between prosecution and defense, if a prosecutor is convinced that a client is not receiving adequate defense, the prosecutor is required to inform the defendant that his or her best interests may not be well served. The defense is under no requirement to inform the government that their prosecutors are not making the best possible case against his or her client.

One might conclude, therefore, that government attorneys constitute at least one class of legal professionals who would qualify as exemplary moral agents. But the distinction between the government attorney and the private attorney is significant. The government attorney's moral agency is more closely related to his status as a government agent than to his status as an attorney. The exemption of private attorneys, who constitute the bulk of the profession, from the restrictions on the government attorney indicates that such restrictions are not essential to the profession itself. If they were essential, they would apply to virtually the entire profession. Government attorneys are under more restrictive moral obligations because they represent the government, whereas the private attorney represents the profession more broadly. It follows, then, that insofar as government attorneys could be understood as exemplary moral agents, they have much in common with the public administrator. Moreover, in their capacity as representatives of the public, they may be *de facto* public administrators.

Much the same can be said of judges as of government attorneys, though the functions of judges are vastly different from those of government attorneys. The judge must ensure fair, orderly trials and must issue verdicts. The judge acts as a moral agent in both respects, because they are intended to impose justice.

One might argue that the judge's status as a moral agent is compromised because he or she must occasionally subjugate his or her own moral beliefs to the laws that he or she must uphold. Judges may have private beliefs on abortion, capital punishment, environmental concerns, or civil disobedience, but they must administer the law even if it is in conflict with those beliefs. In failing to support firmly held moral commitments, the judge might be understood as behaving unlike a moral agent, who would stand on principle. However, the judges' setting aside of those principles does not necessarily indicate a failure of moral agency. The judge may decide that his or her moral commitment to the upholding of the law, as written, is higher than his or her commitment to the values that he or she privately holds. Ironically, one may have moral reasons for rejecting one's own moral values.

Such a rejection is not a wholesale dismissal of one's moral values. The judge's decision does not eschew morality in favor of legality. The judge's commitment to the law is, itself, a moral commitment. Therefore, the judge is in a state of conflict because at least one of his or her moral values, his or her respect for the law, is at odds with others. In the case of such a moral dilemma, one does not reject morality but only chooses one moral value over others. Such moral dilemmas are hardly restricted to the judiciary. Public administrators also have them, as, for example, when they have to make budgetary decisions to cut programs. They may favor the programs over fiscal restraint but be forced, by the public will, to forgo them.

A strong case can be made for the judge as moral exemplar, but the case must recognize some limiting factors. First, the activities of a judge are hardly similar to those of the common citizen. Most citizens do not have the responsibility of imposing the law — only that of following it. One might argue that this limitation is not unique in a way that disqualifies the judge as a moral exemplar. Because every profession is special in some way and is thus different from the activities of the citizenry, as a whole, no profession would function as moral exemplar. Nevertheless, the judge's activities are so far removed from those of most citizens that the judge's exemplarship would be of limited value.

Perhaps more significant, the judge's moral exemplarship derives from the same source as that of the government attorney. The judge's moral agency derives from his or her position as a servant of the public. As such, the judge can be included, together with public administrators, as a professional ultimately responsible to the society. The judge is a moral agent more because he or she is a public agent than because he or she is in the legal profession.

CIVIL LAW

Until now, we have concerned ourselves most with cases of criminal law, in which the interests of the individual and justice, as interpreted by the state, are in conflict. But there are moral aspects of civil law that are distinct from those that occur in criminal cases. We might discover the roots of moral agency in civil justice.

Whereas criminal cases pit the state against an individual or group, civil cases pit private citizens against each other. In civil cases, by and large, the profound issues of the rights of the individual against the state are absent, but some other interesting issues emerge. To exemplify them, let us use an imaginary case against a computer company as an example. In this case, an individual sues the company because he or she suffers from eyestrain as a result of looking at the computer company's monitors. The monitors are not defective and are no different from the monitors of other computer manufacturers, but the suit is based on the effectiveness of the company's advertising. The customer maintains that the advertising was so irresistible that he or she was induced into buying the computer and using it to excess, with eyestrain as the result.

The customer seeks the services of an attorney, who regards the case as frivolous, dishonest, and morally ludicrous. If the attorney is utterly self-serving, he or she may encourage the client to pursue the case merely because of the fee that he or she will earn, win or lose. But this attorney is not as egocentric and greedy. Nevertheless, he or she believes that the client has a case that might conclude in a manner that satisfies him or her. He or she considers the case winnable on legal if not moral grounds because he or she has discovered a poorly written consumer law that he or she can abuse. Furthermore, even if the client does not win the case outright, the attorney can cause enough trouble and expense for the computer company that it will likely settle out of court just to bring the matter to conclusion.

Should attorneys take cases that they consider morally weak but winnable? If the case were a criminal case, the attorney would be obligated to make the strongest possible defense of the client. Furthermore, in a criminal case, the client and the attorney have no choice to drop the issue: The state has brought the charges and the defendant is inextricably caught in the legal apparatus. But in a civil case, the plaintiff does not have to sue. Should the attorney recommend the pursuit of the client's self-interest at the expense of an innocent party? Should the attorney refuse, because of his or her own moral convictions, to pursue a case that his or her client can win?

An attorney functioning as a moral agent would seem obligated to refuse to defend a plaintiff whose case he or she believes to be morally unfounded. In making a choice against taking such a potentially successful and possibly lucrative case, the attorney would have the opportunity to function as a moral agent. Nevertheless, the attorney's moral agency would not follow from his or her profession itself, as would the moral agency of a public administrator. Another attorney may adopt the principle, equally compatible with the legal profession, that he or she will, regardless of his or her own moral convictions, defend any client to the fullest extent allowed under the law. The legal profession therefore permits moral agency in such cases but does not require it. As a consequence, the legal profession does not express moral agency as an essential or necessary aspect.

Conflicts between client interest and morality are not restricted to cases in which the attorney represents the plaintiff. An attorney may be asked, in a civil suit, to represent defendants that he or she considers to have a legal but morally questionable case. In such instances, the attorney cannot merely advise the client to drop the matter. Nevertheless, if the attorney is a moral agent, concerned with the morality of a cause rather than merely its chance of success, he or she might find himself or herself inclined to leave the case to another attorney, who does not share his or her moral commitments. He or she would thus refuse to let his or her expertise be used for purposes that he or she considers immoral. Still, his or her stance on principle cannot be seen as essential to the legal profession. People, even when they are immoral, have legitimate legal rights. Such people will not be accorded the defense to which they are entitled if every attorney, standing on moral principle, refuses to take their cases. Furthermore, the laws that may be used to defend such cases would be refused a test of their adequacy. It is, therefore, not only permissible but perhaps even legally essential that some attorneys defend morally indefensible but legally viable cases.

ATTORNEYS COMMITTED TO CAUSES

The last possible candidate to be considered in searching for evidence of moral agency in the legal profession is the attorney who seeks to use the law to promote a moral cause. On the one hand, one might argue that not all attorneys commit themselves to causes, so the morally committed attorney is not central to the profession itself. However, the morally committed attorney may argue that, although most professionals may not recognize the centrality of morality to their profession, they are mistaken. The morally committed attorney might argue that morality is "what the profession is all about," that morality is at the heart of the profession, and that all other aspects are ancillary. He or she might argue that although many attorneys may not agree that morality is so central to the profession, they should. (1978, p. 89)

Hazard, in discussing attorneys for unpopular causes — though, for our purposes, their unpopularity is insignificant — states that the theory that a lawyer has an obligation to a cause "submerges the lawyer's responsibility to a cause into the purposes of his client." The cause–client conflict can be illustrated in a hypothetical example in which an attorney defends a client accused of drug possession. The attorney takes the case because he or she is committed to reforming the drug laws. If he or she lets the case be driven by his or her cause, he or she would argue that the client is innocent on the basis of the inconsistency of the laws with the state or national constitution. It might even be to his or her advantage to lose the initial trial to bring the matter to a higher court so that the constitutionality of the laws can be examined. However, the client's interest might be better served by arguing that the state lacked sufficient evidence that he or she ever possessed a drug. The attorney's cause might interfere with his or her responsibility to his client. His or her advocacy of this cause must therefore be subordinated to the interests of the client.

CONCLUSION

We began this chapter with two questions: Are legal professionals moral agents? Are legal professionals, as moral agents, ideal moral exemplars for the private citizen? We are now in the position to answer them.

Attorneys have opportunities to express moral agency in several ways. They can be moral agents, for example, in their choice of whom to represent, their choice of a cause to represent, and the degree to which they sacrifice their resources for the sake of justice. Nevertheless, there remains at least one factor that complicates the moral agency of the attorney: his or her commitment to the personal interests of his or her client. That commitment, essential to the profession, can conflict with other moral values. To the extent that the client's interest overrules those other values, the attorney will not serve as a moral exemplar in a way that is obvious and useful to the public citizen. Even when the commitment to the client is grounded in morality, it will not be seen as such to the public citizen unschooled in legal subtlety. Moreover, the behavior of an attorney acting as a moral agent may be impossible to distinguish from that of an attorney acting solely in his or her client's interest or even in his or her own interest.

The public defender, the government attorney, and the judge may be seen as better moral exemplars than the private attorney. But their difference from the private attorney weakens, rather than supports, the case for the legal profession as the ideal source of moral exemplarship. To the extent that the public defender, government attorney, and judge function as moral agents, with justice as their cause, they act as agents of the state. Their moral agency is therefore a function of their status as public agents rather than as members of the legal profession.

Our conclusion that the legal profession does not serve as an ideal source of moral exemplarship does not disparage the profession. Members of the profession can and often must act as moral agents. We maintain only that moral agency is not central to the legal profession per se. Our conclusion does not suggest that individual members of the profession cannot or do not choose to be moral agents. Moreover, we maintain that moral agency is central to legal professionals, such as prosecutors and judges, acting as *de facto* public administrators.

REFERENCES

American Society for Public Administration Code of Ethics. 2001. Center for the Study of Ethics in the Professions, Illinois Institute of Technology. Available at: http://www.aspanet.org/scriptcontent/index_codeofethics.cfm. Accessed 2004.

Applbaum, A. I. 1999. *Ethics for Adversaries*. Princeton, NJ: Princeton University Press.
Hazard, G. C. 1978. *Ethics in the Practice of Law*. New Haven: Yale University Press.
Luizzi, V. L. 1993. *A Case for Legal Ethics*. Albany: State University of New York Press.
Roscoe Pound Institute and the Association of Trial Lawyers of America Code of Ethics.
    American Lawyer's Code of Conduct, Public Discussion Draft. 1980. Available
    at: http://www.iit.edu/departments/csep/codes/coe/american_lawyers.html.

7 Higher Education

American higher education has never been cloistered or secluded from society. The land grant movement, federal support for research — particularly in defense and health-university–business partnerships, and intercollegiate athletics exemplify the symbiotic relationships and tensions between universities and their environments. Both public and private universities depend on external support and are expected to respond to external interests in particular and to the public interest in general. In this regard, they are similar to governmental agencies. Both sets of institutions attempt to balance the challenges and opportunities of a market-driven, pluralistic environment while at the same time sharing the goal of shaping citizens and encouraging their civic roles and responsibilities in a democracy.

On one level, as A. Bartlett Giamatti (1981) observes, governmental and educational institutions serve the same public interest and public trust, defining issues in terms of commonalities rather than constituencies. On another level, we would argue, universities and governmental agencies are enmeshed in networks of multiple stakeholders with clashing values and conflicting priorities. On both levels, public service and higher education entail a multiplicity of skills, approaches, and perspectives as each strives to fulfill its obligations as a calling as well as a profession.

In this context, an open secret, at least to some in and around higher education, is that it is neither so pure nor pristine as popular imagery would have us believe. Athletic scandals, discriminatory admissions policies, sexual and other forms of exploitation, and questionable research and business practices, for example, litter the landscape of American higher education (Wilcox and Ebbs, 1992). Coupled with confusion about the mission, values, and role and responsibility of higher education as a corporate enterprise, these issues have raised serious questions in the minds of many scholars and others.

However, at least until recently, traditional higher education has enjoyed a monopoly over the credentialing of millions of students and professionals. Ironically, despite its ivory tower image, it has controlled their career development and their professional prospects. It truly has held the keys to the kingdom. Today, however, traditional higher education faces new challenges from private and for-profit competitors, stimulated by the growth of information technology and the changing demographic profile of higher education's clientele (Cantor, 2000).

In this chapter, we consider the tortuous path that American higher education follows as it seeks to honor its transcendent ideals of truth, knowledge, and the life of the mind while simultaneously participating in the cultural imperatives of professionalism, careerism, and commercialism. The dynamics of this symbiosis are daunting in their complexity but must be understood, especially if we are to apprehend the moral role and responsibility of higher education in the constellation of institutions and professions in the United States.

The university is the source of information, knowledge, and credentials, but it also is expected, at least by some, to promote and protect other values, such as citizenship and moral agency. Many Americans, particularly the professoriate and the literati, more generally, are troubled by what they perceive as the loss of ideals and values in the academy amid the relentless emphasis on careerism and commercial relationships. Others worry about various aspects of contemporary careerism and commercialization but believe that, with some adjustments, they can be set right. We share a number of the concerns of both groups but maintain that the practical or vocational perspective on education is part of the story of America, the belief in the nexus between education and upward mobility, assimilation, and economic success.

In our view, interest in careers is not some recent or inexplicable anomaly to which academics are immune. Instead, the question is which careers are valued and by whom. Professors in the humanities, for example, are as career-oriented as other groups, but their careers happen to lack the perceived practical value appreciated by others, including the general public, and thus, to these academics, careerism and commercialization are to be condemned. Other members of the academy, such as scientists, economists, and accountants, tend to see things differently and thus find the growth in university–business and university–government relationships quite appropriate, promising, and even profitable. Therefore, we must acknowledge that in these respects, as well as in others, the academy is a diverse and perplexing place, the contradictions and conflicts of which encompass myriad challenges, including the development of moral agency and citizenship.

ETHICS IN THE ACADEMY: LEVEL 1

Ethics in higher education can be understood on at least two levels: the general principles and obligations applicable to colleges and universities, and the particular issues that arise from the relationships that colleges and universities have with their many stakeholders. On the first level, consider, for example, the obligations of academics everywhere: teaching, research, and service to a department, institution, and profession (Shils, 1983). Although the combination and configuration of these obligations may vary from one institution or one class of institutions to another, their essential nature defines the disposition of most of the professoriate. Higher education is expected to advance and transmit knowledge, to perform important functions for society, and to certify the credentials of those who complete required courses of study. Whether for employment, graduate or professional school, or citizenship, higher education serves as the gatekeeper that, in turn, implies nurturance of ethical values, democratic responsibility, and global awareness (Smith and Reynolds, 1990).

Equally implicated in higher education are character and the ability to exercise ethical judgment (Kadish, 1991). According to Mortimer Kadish (1991), what distinguishes higher education is its bearing on the complex questions of ethical judgment. The university does not educate for a specific set of ethical judgments, but it does address questions of ethics and shapes the conclusions that reflective students will reach. Although basic character traits are formed long before students arrive at the university, the university, ideally, fosters the exercise of ethical judgment by presenting students with a context for the use of those traits, along with knowledge of their consequences. Kadish (1991) dismisses the common assumptions that ethics consists in compliance with rules and that higher education is irrelevant to ethical judgments because we are all egoistic and self-interested. He maintains that who we are and what we are to want — our self-interest — are never entirely settled, and that what the self wants must be formed within a social context.

James Laney (1990) distinguishes between thin and thick theories of the academy's moral responsibility. Thin theory refers to law, obedience, and duty. It omits most of human personality and the untidy reality of lives filled with dread and aspiration. Neat and clean, thin theory ignores the particularity, the details, of individuals. Thick theory, in contrast, focuses on what is good rather than what is right — on virtue, character, and tradition, instead of law, obedience, and duty. In Laney's (1990) opinion, however, most people have a thin view of the moral life of the academy, which leaves the academy with a functional, not a moral, identity. Notions of stewardship, of higher education as a calling, have given way to an academic pecking order committed to money, power, and achievement of personal and institutional interests. Credentials and careers are paramount, and what is vital is a rededication to substantive moral discourse, a new reward system, and faculty involved in the life of the community.

We see, then, in both Kadish (1991) and Laney (1990) suggestions that the ideal of higher education as a kind of moral city on the hill may not be universally shared or admired. However, their positions are neither mere nostalgia nor sentimentality. Neither these observers nor many others who have addressed the moral dimensions of higher education are naïve or utopian in their descriptions and prescriptions concerning colleges and universities today. They fully recognize that our systems of higher education are both in and of the world, with all its uncertainty, perplexity, and general messiness. Thus, they seek what we refer to as a revival or introduction of a clarity and proportionality in American higher education, or what Kadish (1991) calls "coherence" between campus and society.

The concept of coherence between campus and society is or should be central to ethics in higher education. What is especially important is the balance between purely academic tendencies and more practical or professional impulses. Moreover, higher education is itself a profession, replete with ethical challenges, obligations, and responsibilities. Thus, in this connection, a salient feature is the convergence of these concerns in moral agency, partnerships with government and business, and intercollegiate athletics.

ETHICS IN THE ACADEMY: LEVEL 2

Similar to other systems and institutions, higher education is rife with moral challenges that must be engaged, managed, and mediated in the context of its own values, goals, and relationships. Moral agency entails involvement in those challenges, not withdrawal from worldly affairs for the sake of moral purity. The fundamental task for higher education is to create and sustain Kadish's (1991) coherence between campus and society as well as the capacity to be self-reflective and to apply to itself the critical analytical skills that it purports to develop in its students as it struggles with determining the proper relationship between scholarship and society.

Edward Long (1992) is concerned with this relationship as he explores higher education's role as a moral enterprise. Using Noam Chomsky as an exemplar of the moral interlocutor, Long (1992) cites Chomsky's criticism of the New Mandarins, those academicians who pose as experts but who ask no questions about the moral consequences of the policies that they have helped to shape. Whether one agrees with Chomsky's politics, he may serve as a model of the critical intellectual who raises important issues regarding the uses to which university-generated knowledge is put, issues that are generally absent from professorial dialogue and debate. Long's (1992) point here is that the ends to which knowledge is put or will be put not only must be included in such dialogue and debate but also should be at the very heart of educational policy, the touchstone for determining education's role in society. "Educated citizens of a free society," he argues, "cannot be trained merely to offer society technical expertise — whether in the form of scientific know-how or operational skills — while not being imbued with the imaginative capacity to push persistently for justice and community in human affairs" (p. 167).

In Long's (1992) view, the first obligation of higher education to society is to provide perceptive analyses of how public policies are shaped and to define the role of the educational enterprise in relation to that process. Second, higher education must bring its own values and commitments into the open, abandoning the confusion between neutrality and objectivity. Scholarly fairness is a crucial moral value, but it does not depend on a simplistic neutrality or a refusal to deal with value questions. Long (1992) argues that the question about the academy's role in society is often phrased as "Should colleges or universities take stands on social and political matters?" But he suggests this formulation instead: "How can institutions of higher learning render the most appropriate and constructive contribution to achieving greater social justice and a more enriched public life?" The academy must be socially concerned, but in ways that are indigenous to its nature and compatible with its mandate.

This position is essentially in keeping with the views expressed by Derek Bok (1982) in his discussion of the social responsibilities of the university. First, he notes the increased contacts between the university and the outside world, which includes enlarged research, enhanced incomes, and greater prestige and excitement. Second, he points out that research subjects are clearly influenced by the opportunities available to obtain governmental and corporate resources; that scholars who consult develop subtle dependencies on their patrons that, in turn, tend to curb dissent from official policies or advocacy of positions that might offend their patrons or jeopardize their own interests; and that professors become more "pragmatic" or "realistic" as well as more conventional, cautious, and less critical. "As the research university has grown in influence," Bok (1982) claims, "a measure of scholarly independence has been lost" (p. 26). Thus, in Kadish's (1991) terms, coherence between campus and society has been breached.

In Bok's (1982) judgment, "The function of the university is not to define and enforce proper moral and political standards for the society." Rather, "The function of the university is to engage in teaching and research of the highest attainable quality," or to remain within the boundaries of its own expertise (p. 35). Otherwise, "It runs intolerable risks of making unwise decisions, diminishing the quality of its faculty, and exposing itself to continuous pressures from all the groups and factions that may wish to impose their own political convictions on the university's work" (p. 35). Finally, Bok (1982) suggests that, although universities should respond to social needs, the problem is to decide what kind of response is appropriate. In this regard, he broaches three questions that must be considered. First, how important is the social need, and how likely is it that the university will succeed in doing something about it? Second, will the action requested interfere with the freedom of individual professors and students, especially their freedom to form their own beliefs and express their opinions as they choose? Third, what effect will the desired initiative have on the operation of the university as a whole?

Long (1992) and Bok (1982) limn the contours of academic moral agency and provide a context in which particular moral issues can be considered. In both analyses, the challenges of moral agency in higher education are apparent, as each explores the values, knowledge, and expertise embedded in individual and institutional responsibilities and relationships. Although the scope and intensity of moral problems such as secrecy in research, issues of patents and royalties, and risks to human subjects are greater in some institutions than in others, moral dilemmas and temptations envelop all of higher education, despite its diversity or complexity. As Clark Kerr (2001) argues, the ivory tower has become an arm of the state and of industry, which in turn raises many ethical and political issues for the academy as a whole.

UNIVERSITY–GOVERNMENT PARTNERSHIPS

University partnerships with government are a well-mined field of study. In regard to the federal government, for example, we are told that federal influence on American higher education is enduring and pervasive, particularly in land-grant institutions, student loans, research and development, and tax policies (Gladieux and King, 1999). Today, two types of spending — direct aid to students and research and development — exceed outlays of states, industry, and other donors. Although states retain fundamental responsibility for higher education, primarily through support of public systems, the federal role is to provide particular kinds of support to meet perceived national objectives. In this regard, no distinction is drawn between public and private institutions.

A major federal priority is financing campus-based research, which by 1995 amounted to more than $13 billion. Although federal funding is significant, it is concentrated on a relatively small number of institutions, mostly major research universities. According to the National Science Foundation, 100 doctorate-granting institutions receive more than 80 percent of federal research and development dollars. Moreover, for most of the last half century, these resources were dedicated to defense-related science and technology. Until recently, however, the country's research enterprises were reorienting their activities toward projects that promise benefits to the American economy and quality of life. Economic security and competitiveness, rather than military preparedness, were the rationales for many research budgets, with biomedical research being the fastest-growing sector of federal research support. The pattern began to change, however, after September 11, 2001, as the federal research emphasis shifted to homeland defense.

Many moral issues are nested within this congeries of policies, priorities, and programs. For example, consider pork barrel science, in which millions of dollars are earmarked for academic science without competition and merit review. Proponents of peer review argue that it ensures the highest-quality research, whereas opponents claim that it is an "old boys" network that precludes many worthwhile projects and discriminates against younger faculty, women, and minorities. On yet a different level, congressional earmarking is partly a reaction to the heavy concentration of research and development spending on a relatively few institutions and partly a response to the deterioration and obsolescence of scientific equipment and facilities — the infrastructure that universities are expected to maintain. Thus, as with most moral questions, the issues surrounding federal support of university research and development are perplexing and complex.

Pork barrel science is not the end of it, however. In recent years, the university research establishment has been confronted with controversy concerning a number of ethical and legal breaches, including fraud, improper cost-recovery procedures on grants and contracts, and violations of protocols related to the use of human subjects and treatment of laboratory animals. In light of tight federal budgets and skepticism about academic research practices, it is likely that this litany of issues will continue to be on the federal research and development agenda.

Besides research-related moral issues, we must consider the impact of partnerships with government on internal institutional functioning, including the ability of universities to establish and maintain some level of coherence between society and themselves. First, however, we need to acknowledge Kerr's (2001) observation that despite their pride in their autonomy, American universities are what they are because of their response to pressures from their environments as much as their own preferences and priorities. Higher education reacted to the federal stimulus with what Kerr (2001) describes as fidelity and alacrity to national needs and committed itself to the service of technology development and transfer. As a result, we have in this country today the federal grant university, namely, the first-tier research institution that willingly succumbed to the federal embrace.

Among the issues that Kerr (2001) identifies as problematic in relation to university–government partnerships are the balance between the wishes of individual scholars and those of their institutions, the connection between merit and politics, and the respective value of science and the humanities. In Kerr's (2001) view, one particular issue concerns the substantial reduction of the university's control over its own destiny in the face of individual faculty members negotiating federal research contracts with particular agencies and bypassing established internal review processes. The university's authority structure is vitiated, with chairs, deans, and presidents becoming *pro forma* signatories to the brokered agreements, and faculty loyalty is invested in the federal agency, which becomes their new alma mater.

Kerr (2001) also argues that federal support has added a new dimension to the eternal intrauniversity struggles related to the sciences versus the humanities. Given the reward system in many institutions, scientists with federal research contracts are often promoted faster, get more staff and space, earn more income through summer employment and consulting, have easier access to travel funds, and enjoy more status both in and out of the university. The question, in Kerr's opinion, is what is appropriate to each field in each period, and the answer is that each should receive support in accordance with its current potentialities. There are no timeless priorities, although inequities favoring such fields as law, medicine, and agriculture are embedded in the academy.

Finally, after touching on other issues such as the devaluation in large universities of undergraduate teaching, induced partly by federal research support; the potential for interference with academic integrity that comes with research opportunities; and the increasing balkanization of the university, Kerr (2001) concludes with some comments on the need to devise an ethical system for the university of the future. The last code of ethics, he notes, was formulated in 1915 by the American Association of University Professors. Focusing on internal ethical problems concerning trustees, presidents, and faculties, it ignored the university's external relations, which by contemporary standards were scant indeed. Today, in contrast, the university's ethical problems are found more in the flow of contacts between the academic and the outside world and have never been so abundant or perplexing. It is time for a new debate on the ethical position of what Kerr (2001) calls the postmodern university.

UNIVERSITY–BUSINESS PARTNERSHIPS

Commercialization in higher education has a long history (Bok, 2003). For decades, universities have been able to sell the right to use their discoveries; corporations have sponsored courses delivered via cable television and, more recently, the Internet; corporate logos have adorned athletic uniforms; and the names of universities can be found on caps, sweatshirts, and coffee mugs. Perhaps, even more telling morally, in our view, is the practice of many universities allowing the marketing of credit cards on campus. Some universities collect millions of dollars from credit card companies in return for permission to hawk their cards on campus — a practice that raises serious questions concerning university complicity in acquiring resources at the expense of young, inexperienced students. The same can be said of cell phone and other vendors. But what is new, according to Bok (2003), is the unprecedented size and scope of commercial practices involving the academy, reflected in a variety of ways, including faculty members with titles such as Yahoo! Professor of Computer Science or K-Mart Professor of Marketing.

A number of explanations have been offered for the growth of commercialization on American campuses. Humanities faculties claim that the university lacks purpose and has no clear mission beyond a vague commitment to undefined excellence. In contrast, some faculties, such as scientists, are very clear about their purpose and mission. Commercialization, Bok (2003) argues, has, in fact, taken hold mostly in schools of business and medicine, where many of the most lucrative consulting and entrepreneurial opportunities are to be found.

Another explanation is that businessmen and lawyers on boards of trustees wish "to 'commodify' education and research, reduce the faculty to the status of employees, and ultimately, make the university serve the interests of corporate America" (Bok, 2003, p. 6). Bok's (2003) response to this explanation is, first, to acknowledge the undeniable influence of the private economy on higher education, as reflected, for example, in the "opulence of business schools" compared "with the shabbiness of most schools of education and social work" or in the "generous compensation offered to professors of management and economics, compared to that paid to colleagues in literature and philosophy" (pp. 6–7). But Bok (2003) dismisses the ascription of commercialization to a corporate plot and argues that the growing complexity of higher education requires trustees with fund-raising and administrative skills. "Business executives and corporate lawyers simply seemed better suited to the changing needs of the university" (Bok, 2003, p. 7).

Yet another explanation for the growth of commercial activity in the academy comes from professors of higher education who assert that the "recent wave of entrepreneurial behavior is a response to the reductions in government support for higher education that began in the 1970s. Bok (2003, p. 8) however, believes that, although government cutbacks may have been the impetus to greater commercialization of universities in other countries, they are not the whole story in the United States. There have been reductions in government support in the past without bursts of profit-seeking ventures; private universities have been as entrepreneurial as public ones, "even though few of them had much state funding to lose," and most have enjoyed increases in their endowments; and biomedical and business faculties have been among the most entrepreneurial despite increases in federal research support and few, if any, cutbacks, respectively. Therefore, declining appropriations are only part of the explanation for the rise of entrepreneurial activity on American campuses.

In Bok's (2003) judgment, what also helps to account for the contemporary increase in commercialization in higher education is the endless need for money to satisfy faculty and student ambitions, to cover the relentless rises in the cost of books and journals as well as technology and scientific equipment, and to stay at the cutting edge of discovery and invention. Bok (2003) suggests that "universities share one characteristic with compulsive gamblers and exiled royalty: there is never enough money to satisfy their desires" (p. 9). Moreover, this need for money is chronic, not the result of periodic budget reductions. Clearly, then, commercialization has multiple causes: financial cutbacks, post-1980s entrepreneurial impulses, ambiguous academic values, and the "rapid growth of money-making opportunities provided by a more technologically sophisticated, knowledge-based economy" (Bok, 2003, p. 15).

In the general context, then, of the commercialization of the academy, let us consider university–business partnerships, in particular. According to Norman Bowie (1990), corporations receive three advantages from such partnerships: access to information, access to potential commercial products, and access to creative faculty and students. In return, universities enjoy several advantages as well: money, support for graduate students and postdoctoral fellows, scientific equipment, and the opportunity to add to the state of knowledge — one of their primary purposes. At the same time, however, these partnerships tend to result in more applied, as opposed to basic, research, which does not receive universal approval. Bowie (1990) argues that the mission of state-supported institutions includes a strong public-interest component that may justify university–business partnerships as a means to meet a university's responsibility to the larger community.

The major issues in university–business partnerships center on confidentiality or secrecy in research, ownership of patents, and potential conflicts of interest for both the institution and the faculty. In university–business partnerships, research is often required to be kept confidential, which means, among other things, that the business sponsor must give its permission before the results can be published. As a number of observers have noted, this practice is inconsistent with the principle of freely contributing to the store of knowledge. However, the business sponsor may bring moral and economic arguments to bear to support the protection of trade secrets. First, the corporation has a property right in the formula, pattern, device, or compilation of information protected as a trade secret. Second, trade secrets are necessary to protect American industry from foreign competitors. Third, trade secrets are necessary if American firms are to invest in basic research.

These arguments have been contested, however, from the university perspective. In Bowie's (1990) view, for example, the university should turn a deaf ear to the first two claims. Knowledge takes priority over the right of a corporation to its intellectual property, and the university should not surrender its central values to help business solve its problems with foreign competitors. With respect to the third claim, the anti-free-rider argument applies, as increasing research is one of the university's core functions.

In regard to the ownership of patents, most university–business contracts provide exclusive rights to the industry sponsor of the research. Some critics, however, think that the university should retain ownership of all patents, as collaboration in withholding an invention from the market would be a violation of its central mission. If universities owned patents, corporations could still make money through various profit-sharing arrangements with researchers and universities themselves. In any event, these are complicated matters that carry justifications and counter-justifications and that require flexibility on both sides.

The third major issue is the potential for conflicts of interest related to individual faculty members, the university, or both. The answers to these concerns are not obvious. For example, should a university take an equity position in a company of which one of its faculty members is a principal stockholder or officer? Should a university allow faculty members to affiliate with a biotechnology firm? What are the permissible limits related to faculty consulting, especially with sponsors in the areas of sponsored research? Each of these questions, as well as a host of others, requires careful ethical, legal, and financial analysis if reasonable resolutions are to be attained.

INTERCOLLEGIATE ATHLETICS

Like university–government and university–business partnerships, intercollegiate athletics is a well-researched topic. But there the similarities end, for although these partnerships are replete with moral ambiguities and moral complexities, the moral position of intercollegiate athletics appears to be clear: Intercollegiate athletics is difficult, if not impossible, to justify on moral grounds alone, despite the magical thinking associated with its finances, effects on institutional morale, and academic stature. However, regardless of its dubious moral as well as financial and institutional status, intercollegiate athletics, as many have suggested, is virtually impossible to change. Sport as spectacle is deeply embedded in American culture and would be too costly to reform (Kliever, 1990).

The diversity of American higher education noted earlier extends to intercollegiate athletics. As Bok (2003) observes, although moral conflicts and dilemmas exist at all levels, it is chiefly the high-pressure basketball and football programs in Division I of the National Collegiate Athletics Association that seriously contravene academic principles. Compromised admission and performance standards, rampant student-athlete exploitation, competition for bowl games and tournaments, television revenues, luxury boxes, corporate logos, and millionaire coaches are among the signature features of modern big-time intercollegiate athletics. Collusion, corruption, and cynicism are the order of the day.

Thus, from a moral perspective, we must ask how this commercialization and professionalization of intercollegiate athletics are justified. Bok (2003) discusses and dismisses five standard justifications: that intercollegiate athletics provides-character building, that it is a path to a college education for poor minority youths, that a winning team can attract more and better students, that winning teams raise morale and school spirit, and that winning teams can generate more donations from alumni.

With respect to character building, according to Bok (2003), there is little proof of such salutary effects, especially as athletes have a narrower experience and report less growth than other students. In regard to educational opportunities for minority youths, the dismal graduation rate of minority athletes is well known. In reference to the alleged connection between a winning team and increased numbers and quality of students, the evidence is shaky. As Bok (2003) argues, "High-visibility sports offer a dubious strategy for improving the quality of the student body, even for schools with the most successful teams" (p. 48). The fourth justification — that winning teams raise morale and school spirit — is equally questionable. "In fact," Bok (2003) notes, "Surveys at selective universities show that athletics are one of the aspects of their college young alumni would most like to see de-emphasized" (p. 49). Finally, the putative link between winning teams and donations is also groundless, with increases in donations tending to go to the athletic program (Zimbalist, 1999). Therefore, Bok (2003) concludes, "When universities view their athletic teams not only as a means of making money, but also as the mechanism for improving the status of the entire institution, the pressure to win grows very intense indeed. The single most likely outcome is that academic standards will be a major casualty of the process" (p. 51).

In spite of the egregious and unethical practices in intercollegiate athletics, the prospects for change, according to seasoned observers, are dim. Proposals galore have been made to deemphasize professional athletic standards at the collegiate level; to reduce the resources of athletic programs such as coaching staffs, recruiting budgets, and time for practice, conditioning, and road trips; to educate boards of governance about the effects of intercollegiate athletics on academic standards; and to alter athletic scholarships to reduce the leverage of coaches in their control of athletes. A major obstacle to implementation of these proposals, however, is that universities, despite their lofty ideals, are entranced by the illusory promise of profits and are, therefore, not above sacrificing academic values to achieve their financial goals. Second, intercollegiate athletics are part of the university's hidden curriculum — those activities outside the established courses and programs that also convey to both internal and external constituencies what the institution values. Thus, as Kliever (1990) asks, "How can we expect a university's athletic program to change for the better if the operative morality of its academic programs and extracurricular activities does not rise above narrow self-centeredness and cutthroat competition?" (p. 117).

The answer, of course, is that we cannot. But even piecemeal reforms would be better than none, and as Bok (2003) suggests, presidents cannot claim to be powerless to act if they are unwilling even to consider such reforms as sharing revenues more equally among Division I schools to reduce the financial incentive to corrupt the system and erode academic standards. In the end, then, what may be needed to confront this pretense called intercollegiate athletics is to raise the moral question again and again, until at least incremental reform thinking begins to take hold. For example, we might begin by asking why institutions of higher education should operate farm systems for the National Football League and the National Basketball Association (Kliever, 1990).

CONCLUSION

American higher education's struggle for coherence between campus and society is clearly not new. The challenges presented to institutions of higher learning by our commercial culture have deep historical roots. But given the scope and variety of external expectations, pressures, and relationships that confront colleges and universities today, their capacity to achieve clarity, proportionality, and balance is sorely strained. Inquiry into ultimate purposes, explorations of meaning, and independent thought — the stuff of the liberal arts — is confronted with a curious compound of anti-intellectualism and moralism. Theory is denigrated, expressions of ideals or values evoke snickers, and interest in learning for its own sake is greeted with incredulity. At the same time, however, trust in higher education erodes in the face of athletic scandals, institutional excesses, and other unseemly, if not illegal or immoral, behavior. Like all ideologies, the ideology of commercialism purports to provide answers to life's important questions but inevitably fails, leaving in its wake complexities and confusions on both the individual and institutional level as well as the illusory desire for material certainty and stability. In our view, however, the liberal arts, professional education, and interinstitutional relationships are neither contradictory nor mutually exclusive. Rather, they can complement and support each other, provided there is reasonable consensus on our underlying moral structure, ambitions, and aspirations.

In theory, the university is a source of moral exemplars, but theory and reality do not always correspond. The size, diversity, complexity, and conflicting interests of higher education have altered the nature of the profession. Unlike the administrator of a social services agency, an environmental protection agency, or even a federal or state education agency, university personnel answer increasingly to their own interests and to institutional interests rather than to those of society or its moral values. Under cover of academic freedom, professors jealously guard their independence from supervision, citizens' expectations, or any obligation to moral agency and moral exemplarship.

Higher education, therefore, needs an active moral structure if it is to balance basic versus applied research, the overt versus the hidden curriculum, and civic development versus economic success. Only in this way can higher education move toward coherence not only between itself and society but between the individual and the institution as well, for individual coherence is the necessary precondition for institutional coherence. However, although necessary, coherence is not sufficient. There also must be consistency and conviction. Unfortunately, in higher education, as in other institutions, there is palpable incoherence between expressed values and observed behavior. Whether it produces enough discomfort to provide an incentive for change, however, is another matter.

Students of organizational culture often argue that members of organizations at all levels tend to respond to proposals for change with skepticism and even resistance. This behavior is no less true in the academy. Higher education practitioners, whether faculty or administrators, are no more enamored of change than are corporate managers or public administrators. Similar to corporate managers and public administrators, professors, deans, vice presidents, and even presidents vigorously protect their individual and institutional interests, their slice of the status quo, unless they perceive some personal benefit in proposals for change. This is entirely understandable, but it leaves us with this question: Where in the academy is there sufficient discomfort with the status quo to mount an effort to initiate changes in university–government partnerships, university–business partnerships, and even intercollegiate athletics?

Such an effort would, first, require a clarity, consistency, and conviction about academic values, as well as the energy to promote them, in the vortex of the academy's internal and external stakeholders. Second, it would require sufficient discomfort and passion to go beyond cosmetic proposals, self-interested compromises and accommodations, and what often passes for realism. Third, it would require leadership by both faculty and administrators. Above all, finally, it would require a moral framework combined with a model of what Howard Gardner and colleagues (2001) call good work: to achieve even modest change in established expectations and behavior. In chapter nine, we offer such a framework and discussion of the good work model in the humble hope that they will provide both an incentive for change and a strategy to attain it.

REFERENCES

Bok, D. 1982. *Beyond the Ivory Tower: Social Responsibilities of the Modern University.* Cambridge, MA: Harvard University Press.

———. 2003. *Universities in the Marketplace: The Commercialization of Higher Education.* Princeton, NJ: Princeton University Press.

Bowie, N. E. 1990. Business–University Partnerships. In *Morality, Responsibility, and the University: Studies in Academic Ethics*, ed. S. M. Cahn, pp. 195–217. Philadelphia: Temple University Press.

Cantor, J. A. 2000. *Higher Education Outside of the Academy.* San Francisco: Jossey-Bass.

Gardner, H. et al. 2001. *Good Work: When Excellence and Ethics Meet.* New York: Basic Books.

Giamatti. A. B. 1981. *The University and the Public Interest.* New York: Atheneum.

Gladieux, L. E., and J. E. King. 1999. The Federal Government and Higher Education. In *American Higher Education in the Twenty-First Century: Social, Political, and Economic Challenges*, eds. P. G. Altbach, R. O. Berdahl, and P. J. Gumport, pp. 152–182. Baltimore, MD: The Johns Hopkins University Press.

Kadish, M. R. 1991. *Toward an Ethic of Higher Education.* Stanford, CA: Stanford University Press.

Kerr, C. 2001. *The Uses of the University*, 5th ed. Cambridge, MA: Harvard University Press.

Kliever, L. D. 1990. Ethical Issues in Intercollegiate Athletics. In *Ethics and Higher Education*, ed. W. W. May, pp. 103–118. New York: Macmillan.

Laney, J. T. 1990. Through Thick and Thin: Two Ways of Talking about the Academy and Moral Responsibility. In *Ethics and Higher Education*, ed. W. W. May, pp. 49–66. New York: Macmillan.

Long, E. L. 1992. *Higher Education as a Moral Enterprise*. Washington, D.C.: Georgetown University Press.

Shils, E. 1983. *The Academic Ethic*. Chicago: University of Chicago Press.

Smith, D. C., and C. H. Reynolds. 1990. Institutional Culture and Ethics. In *Ethics and Higher Education*, ed. W. W. May, pp. 21–31. New York: Macmillan.

Wilcox, J. R., and S. L. Ebbs. 1992. *The Leadership Compass: Values and Ethics in Higher Education*. Washington, D.C.: George Washington University.

www.eng.utah.edu/~mshah/student.html.

Zimbalist, A. 1999. *Unpaid Professionals: Commercialization and Conflict in Big-Time College Sports*. Princeton, NJ: Princeton University Press.

8 Unifying Ethical Theory

In this chapter, we examine the theoretical framework in which the moral agent operates. We begin with an examination of the traditional ethical theories of ethical relativism, teleology, deontology, intuitionism, and virtue theory. After rejecting the first as antithetical to the concept of moral agency, we present a unified ethic, which combines the nonrelativistic theories into a complex whole. The aspect of the whole that we consider most applicable to the citizen is the Kantian notion of the kingdom of ends. We explore that concept and its relation to some of the dominant contemporary theories of social value, including communutarianism, individualism, and Rawlsianism.

TRADITIONAL ETHICAL THEORIES

In any endeavor, motivation and effectiveness are both essential, and morality is no exception. Many people wish to act as moral agents but have little understanding of how to think about morality, let alone choose the most appropriate course of action. Moral philosophy has not demonstrated any significant measurable success in teaching people to want to be moral, but it can provide an understanding of moral thinking for those already inclined to act morally. We summarize classes of philosophical moral theories in this section as a preparation for application of moral thinking to problems faced by moral agents both as professionals and as citizens. We have examined these theories more extensively in two other works (Garofalo and Geuras, 1999; Geuras and Garofalo, 2002), but we present our analysis in more condensed form here.

Ethical Relativism

Ethical relativism is the denial of any universal moral standard. The ethical relativist would deny that there is any single moral standard applicable to all people at all times and that, therefore, morality is entirely culturally determined. Initially, ethical relativism seems plausible, because there are so many different ethical systems in the world, and it would seem inappropriate to designate one as correct while discrediting all of the others as wrong. But on closer examination, ethical relativism itself has problems. If the relativist is correct, there is no universally valid reason to justify or disclaim any moral practice. The relativist's position may seem strong with respect to issues such as capital punishment, abortion, and even polygamy, on which there is substantial disagreement. However, a consistent relativism would have to deny that there is any valid reason to condemn even willful murder for money as immoral. To justify such a condemnation, the relativist would have to provide a good reason that would be acceptable on rational grounds. But if the reason is acceptable on rational grounds, it would be objectively valid and would therefore constitute a universal standard to justify moral action. The relativist must reject the notion of valid rational moral justification to deny the existence of a universally valid standard.

Without such a standard, the relativist would have to argue that, aside from mere social customs, which vary from group to group, there is no objectively valid reason why Mohandas Gandhi should be considered a morally better person than Joseph Stalin or Jack the Ripper. To establish their own moral superiority — if the notion of moral superiority makes any sense at all for a relativist — the latter two individuals could merely proclaim that in their societies of like-minded people, they live up to their own standards in an exemplary manner, whereas Gandhi, by their chosen standards, was a scoundrel.

A thoroughgoing relativist could ensure his or her own perfection. He or she could declare himself or herself to be a society of one and choose, as his or her own standard, the proposition "Whatever I do is right, by definition." He or she could also broaden his or her society to include others who worship him or her enough to accept the proposition.

Ethical relativism would render all claims to moral validity meaningless by denying any universal meaning to moral judgments. A word or concept whose meaning shifts from group to group or individual to individual would have no common meaning and therefore no practical meaning in general usage. The reduction of morality to meaninglessness is espoused by A. J. Ayer (2001), Charles Stevenson (1937), and others in the logical positivist movement. It is evident that the moral agent cannot be an ethical relativist, because the moral agent is motivated by a sense of moral obligation that the relativist would render devoid of significance.

The moral agent must therefore assume the perspective of the ethical absolutist rather than the ethical relativist. The ethical absolutist believes that there is a universally valid moral standard that ought to motivate all people. That standard would constitute the proper motive for the moral agent. Unfortunately, there is no universal agreement on the standard. Different absolutists believe in different standards.

There are innumerable possible standards in which the absolutist might believe, but they can be generally classified under four groups: teleological ethical theories, deontological ethical theories, virtue theories, and intuitionist theories. We maintain that out of all of them, taken as a whole, a unified ethical approach, which we call the unified ethic, can emerge.

TELEOLOGICAL ETHICAL THEORIES

Teleological ethical theories maintain that the end result, or *telos*, of an action determines its moral worth. Teleological theories therefore entail that the proper end justifies whatever means are required to attain it. Teleological theories are also called "consequentialist theories" because of their emphasis on the consequences that follow from the actions.

Utilitarianism, the belief that an act is moral's good to the degree that it promotes happiness, is the predominant teleological theory and is defended by such philosophers as Jeremy Bentham (1996) and John Stuart Mill (1907). To answer the question "What is the morally correct action?" the utilitarian would consider all of the likely consequences of all of the alternative possible actions and choose the course of action that would produce the greatest total happiness. The happiness in question is not the egocentric happiness of the person performing the action, or even the happiness of the majority, but the total happiness, all things considered. The happiness of the majority may not be the greatest total happiness. For example, taxation to fund programs that assist the poorest 2% of the society may not increase the happiness of the majority, most of whom would receive no benefit but pay more in taxes. Nevertheless, the great relief to the few impoverished might outweigh the minimal inconvenience of the majority.

According to the utilitarian, the commonly accepted rules of morality, such as "Do not steal," "Do not lie," and "Do not murder," are properly revered because they generally promote the greatest happiness. The utilitarian maintains that such rules are not absolute and inviolable but that they serve the truly absolute good of happiness. As a consequence, although the rules are extremely good guidelines and should seldom be disobeyed, exceptions can occur when breaking the rule would promote more happiness than would strict adherence. For example, if a world leader would jeopardize a peace process by revealing its details, he or she may have to lie to protect international security. Such a lie, according to the utilitarian, would be warranted. Utilitarians differ among themselves concerning when, in what circumstances, and how often the rules can be broken, but their differences on such matters should not concern us here.

The definition of happiness is another matter of dispute among utilitarians. The concept is very elusive, and different utilitarians define it differently. Bentham, for example, attempts to define happiness quantitatively by means of a numerical calculus of pleasure and pain. Mill finds such a procedure insufficient to account for "quality," which he considers unmeasurable, in happiness. For Mill, some kinds of happiness are not greater in amount, but merely better. He argues for his position by maintaining that it would be better to be a dissatisfied human being, who recognizes happiness of a higher order, than a fully satisfied pig, whose happiness is without depth or culturally significant content.

Perhaps the most significant problem for the utilitarian arises from the justification for breaking a moral rule to promote the greatest happiness. Most people would agree that lying is often done to promote the greater good, as was the case of the head of state who lied to preserve world peace, but there are some rules that we are loath to break, even if to do so would promote greatest happiness. For example, suppose that it can be shown that the world would be a happier place if penalties for drug usage were so severe as to virtually banish it. If so, would it be morally acceptable to impose the death penalty for marijuana use? Even if such punishment would promote the utilitarian greatest happiness, the question of its fairness would remain. And so would the broader question "Should all other values, including fairness and justice, be sacrificed to secure general happiness?" John Rawls (2001), among many others, thinks not.

Teleology, in the form of utilitarianism, has both strengths and weaknesses. Its strength is in its down-to-earth recognition that people value happiness and generally consider the promotion of happiness to be good. Its potential weakness is its sacrifice of all other values and principles in the name of happiness. Strengths and weaknesses of theories may be argued indefinitely, but virtually all significant theories have valuable insights. The teleological theorist's insight is his or her recognition of the moral importance of the question "What are the full consequences of all possible alternative actions?"

Deontological Ethical Theories

Whereas teleological ethical theories argue that the consequence of an action gives it moral significance, deontological ethical theories consider an act morally good or bad in itself, regardless of its consequences. The deontologist would argue that if an act is morally good, it remains so even if its consequences are unfortunate, and if an act is morally bad, fortunate consequences will not remove its immorality. Most deontological theorists, including Immanuel Kant (1989), the dominant figure in deontological theory if not in modern ethics as a whole, regard the morality of the act to depend on the principle that motivates it.

For Kant, the most important factor in all principles, whether they occur in science, politics, mathematics, or morality, is consistency. The nature of principle as a universal rule demands consistency. For example, suppose that we were to promote an alleged rule "Never smoke in a building" but honored the rule on some occasions while arbitrarily ignoring it on others. One would rightly object that the alleged rule was, for us, not really a rule at all; to be a genuine rule or principle, it must be consistent.

Some rules, according to Kant, can never be rendered consistent and therefore must be dismissed. Let us consider the possible rule "Always lie." Such a rule cannot be rendered fully consistent. Suppose one were asked a question, such as "Are you a Canadian citizen?" in a society that observed the rule. How could one lie? If one told the truth, one would not lie. But if one answered the question falsely, no one would be deceived because he or she would expect a false answer. The ancient liar paradox "Everything that I say (including this statement) is a lie" exhibits the inherent contradiction in universal lying.

The rule "Stealing is acceptable" would also contradict itself. If stealing were an acceptable form of behavior, property rights would cease to exist, and nothing could be stolen. Stealing is taking the property of another, but in a society that observed the rule in question, there would be no property to steal.

For the utilitarians, happiness was the ultimate human value, and therefore the nature of a human being was that of a happiness seeker. For Kant, consistency is the ultimate human value, and therefore he regarded the nature of a human being as that of a rational being. Rationality is the basis on which people recognize logical consistency and inconsistency.

Kant regards the Golden Rule, "Do unto others as you would have them do unto you," as a flawed expression of the concept of consistency. The Golden Rule is flawed in its formulation because, if abused, it could countenance the imposition of one's own preferences on others. If one is a lobster fisherman, one may well wish to promulgate the rule, to which oneself will consistently adhere, that everyone ought to eat lobster once a day. The lobsterman would therefore do unto others as he or she would have them do unto him or her: require the consumption of lobster. Clearly, the Golden Rule was not intended for such use.

Kant considers all formulations of the notion of consistency to be flawed, but he offers three that he considers most helpful. The first can be stated as "Act according to a rule that you could will to be a universal law." Lying and stealing could never be so willed, because, as we have seen, they could never become consistent universal rules. Nor would one likely render "Wanton killing is acceptable" a universal law, for fear of being a murder victim.

But one might ask, "What if someone doesn't value his life but likes to murder?" Or "What about the aforementioned lobsterman?" These people are willing to make their rules universal laws but are not moral.

Kant recognizes the flaw in his first formulation and therefore provides a second formulation for cases that defy the first. The second formulation recognizes the rational nature of human beings as the source of their moral decisions and thus as the constituting factor in their moral worth. As a consequence, the second formulation can be stated as "Treat all rational beings as ends in themselves and not entirely as means." Consistency requires that if any rational being, including oneself, is an end in itself, then all rational beings must be ends in themselves. One cannot therefore, like the lobsterman, consider himself or herself as inherently valuable while reducing others as means to his or her own financial advancement. Moreover, all rational beings, as moral choosers, are inherently valuable, according to Kant, so even the person who rejects the value of his or her own life is wrong to do so.

But the second formulation is imperfect also, because it fails to enlighten cases in which treating one person as an end in itself entails treating another as a means. Consider, for example, the case of a family protecting a Jewish guest hiding from the authorities in Nazi Germany. If a German soldier asks the family members whether a Jewish person is in residence, the family would seem to defy the second formulation in any case. By lying to the officer, they fail to treat the soldier as an end in himself, but by telling the truth and sacrificing the life of the guest, they fail to treat the guest as an end in himself. Such cases require Kant to propose a third formulation.

In the third formulation, which plays a prominent role in our analysis, Kant seeks a grand comprehensive consistency among all the values of all people. According to this formulation, each person should act as a legislator in a kingdom of ends. The kingdom of ends is an ideal society, presumably comprising all of humanity, in which all peoples' desires, aspirations, and values form a coherent consistent whole in which all mutually support each other. The legislator in a kingdom of ends acts according to principles that would promote and perpetuate such a condition.

The third formulation cannot be applied with formulaic rigidity. In applying this formulation, one must often speculate concerning the nature of an ideal world, what principles would apply within it, and what course of action would contribute to its realization. But the retreat from rigidity and its replacement by informed judgment saves Kant from the charge of inflexibility that is often leveled at his first formulation.

The inclusion of the third formulation, with its flexibility, is also important as a reminder that all of the formulations are only imperfect attempts to put the concept of consistency into words that apply to human behavior. Some interpretations of Kant misinterpret the formulations as unexceptionable regulations or stipulations. Instead, we interpret them as general ideals to be used as guiding principles in deciding moral issues. We compare them to the ideals in the U.S. Constitution, especially the Bill of Rights, which provides the framework and rationale for judicial judgment without providing a formula from which all decisions can be deduced. The disagreement among Supreme Court justices evidences the flexibility of the document. Kant's formulations should be understood in the same way, as providing the rational structure of moral decision making without necessarily implying specific conclusions.

Kant may be criticized for concentrating too exclusively on the rational aspects of human nature as the foundation of his moral system. Even if that criticism is valid, Kant can still be understood as providing analysis of one important aspect of morality, though he may have overlooked others. Kant contributes an understanding of the importance of the question "What universal consistent principles best apply?" in examining moral issues. His three formulations of the categorical imperative provide a degree of clarity in responding to that question.

INTUITIONIST THEORIES

It would be folly to disregard moral feelings entirely in moral thinking. On the contrary, philosophers often judge the validity of moral theories on the basis of feelings. We would rightly reject any theory, even if it seemed unassailably logical, that recommended monstrous behavior such as wanton mass murder. One would sooner question one's own reasoning powers or even reject the authority of reason itself than accept such a conclusion.

Intuitionism pays deference to our moral feelings. Intuitionists, G. E. Moore (1912) being the most prominent of them, believe that human beings have a moral sense that enables them to determine whether an act is good or bad morally. Moore compares this moral sense, or intuition, to color perception. We know that an object has a particular color by observing it. If our senses are functioning properly, we do not infer the color of the object; we simply see it. The intuitionist believes that the moral sense functions in a similar manner. When we contemplate an action, our moral sense informs us, albeit fallibly and more or less clearly, in the manner of the five familiar senses, of its moral property.

The fallibility, imprecision, and absence of unanimity of the moral sensitivities present a problem for the intuitionist. Color perception is admittedly fallible and imprecise also, but it is at least empirical and can be verified by multiple observations by different people from different positions. People agree in their moral intuitions most of the time and on most issues but disagree vastly on numerous important matters such as capital punishment and abortion. The intuitions, if they even exist at all, are much more controversial and perhaps more subjective than the empirical senses.

Nevertheless, the intuitionist makes a strong case that we cannot ignore our feelings in analyzing a moral issue. The intuitionist's problem may not be his or her use of intuition but his or her exclusive reliance on it. We add the intuitionist's question "How do I feel about this action?" to our list, which already includes those from the teleologist and the deontologist.

VIRTUE THEORY

Virtue theory, of which Aristotle (1985), Alisdair MacIntyre (1981), and Thomas Lynch and Cynthia Lynch (1999) are advocates, evaluates the character traits that an action displays rather than the action itself. The Encyclopedia of Philosophy gives the following extended definition of virtue theory:

> Virtue theory is the view that the foundation of morality is the development of good character traits, or virtues. A person is good, then, if he has virtues and lacks vices. Typical virtues include courage, temperance, justice, prudence, fortitude, liberality, and truthfulness. Some virtue theorists mention as many as 100 virtuous character traits, which contribute to making someone a good person. Virtue theory places special emphasis on moral education, since virtuous character traits are developed in one's youth; adults, therefore, are responsible for instilling virtues in the young. The failure to properly develop virtuous character traits will result in the agent acquiring vices, or bad character traits instead. Vices include cowardice, insensibility, injustice, and vanity.

At first glance, virtue theory may seem free of the "ends-justify-the-means" aspect of teleology, the cold appeal to rational rules of the stricter interpretations of Kantiansm, and the apparent subjectivity of intuitionism. But, on closer analysis, virtue theory may be more closely tied to one or all of those theories than one might initially suppose. It may not be coincidental that the traits that the virtue theorist appraises highly, such as courage, honesty, and generosity, are the very traits that would likely produce behavior of which the teleologist, deontologist, and intuitionist would approve. Honesty, courage, and generosity are traits that the utilitarian would prize as beneficial to society. They are also traits that are characteristic of people who obey the principles that a Kantian would promote. The intuitionist would undoubtedly "feel good" about them, also.

The problem for the virtue theorist is to answer the question "Why are some traits considered good and others bad?" The traits cannot be considered moral or immoral for arbitrary reasons. But when one attempts to answer the question, one finds himself or herself answering on teleological, deontological, or intuitionist grounds. One must wonder, therefore, whether virtue theory is distinct from the others at all.

Despite that problem, the virtue theorist contributes a fourth query to our list of morally relevant questions. The virtue theorist reminds us to ask of an action, "What character traits does it evidence and promote in both the person performing the action and in other people?"

THE UNITY OF THE ABSOLUTIST THEORIES

Each of the major ethical theories makes a strong case for a different aspect of ethics. Their problems lie in their exclusivity; the defenders of each theory maintain not that their theory accounts for an important part of ethics but that their theory includes all of ethics. We adopt the assumption that ethics, like human beings in general, is multifaceted yet unified into one organism. The utilitarian is correct in regarding human happiness as very valuable but is on much weaker ground in asserting that happiness is the only thing that is valuable. Principle is also valuable, as the Kantian maintains, but like happiness, it is not the totality of ethics. The virtue theorist's character traits are also among the valuable entities of the world. Human moral sensitivities or intuitions must also be given a substantial say in determining any other things that are valuable.

There is a noteworthy concurrence among the conclusions of the four theories concerning the decisions that one should make in most cases. Most often, the action that produces the most happiness, when all things are considered, will also follow principle, promote good character, and conform to one's feelings concerning what is right. Much is made of the cases in which the theories would differ, but one cannot ignore the near uniformity in most instances. That uniformity would suggest that the theories might be inherently connected.

Interconnections emerge as one examines the theories closely. Although the utilitarian, the dominant teleologist, considers principles to be subordinate to the promotion of happiness, teleology itself rests on a principle: One always ought to promote the greatest happiness. The deontologist believes in the supremacy of principles, but those that have no possible relevance to human happiness are insignificant. One could formulate the principle "One must always use the same foot in the first step of an ascent," but to elevate such a rule to the status of a moral dictate would be ludicrous. A principle can have moral content only if it affects people positively. Kant implicitly recognized that a moral principle must have influence on people in his second formulation, which asks us to treat people as ends in themselves. But treating people as ends in themselves requires promoting their happiness. Moral principle and happiness appear to be inseparable. Our intuitions, also, have confirmed their implicit indivisibility. In considering the rule "One must always use the same foot in the first step of an ascent," no reasonable intuitions would inform us that it was a moral principle. With respect to virtue theory, when we consider people's character traits, we find praiseworthy both those that promote happiness and those that display principle, especially because, as we have already noted, principle and happiness so often coincide.

UNIFYING ETHICAL THEORIES IN THE DECISION-MAKING PROCESS

All of the traditional theories that we have considered make valuable contributions to the moral decision-making process. Each theory emphasized an important question, which we can formulate as follows:

- Teleology: What are the full consequences of all possible alternative actions?
- Deontology: What universal consistent principles best apply?
- Intuitionism: How do I feel about this action?
- Virtue theory: What character traits does it evidence and promote in both the person performing the action and other people?

From those questions, we may infer four ethical recommendations for the moral agent:

- Teleology: Act to produce the greatest happiness as a consequence.
- Deontology: Act according to the proper principle, and be consistent in applying it.
- Intuitionism: Act according to your inner sense of what is right or wrong.
- Virtue theory: Act as a person of good character, and set a good moral example for others to follow.

We have noted that consideration of the above four questions and recommendations will usually lead to the same conclusions regarding moral behavior. However, the challenging question arises when they appear to lead to conflicting conclusions. It is easy to think of cases in which strict obedience to the principle "Do not lie" would conflict with promotion of the greatest happiness of a society or even the entire world. The Nazis, under Adolf Hitler, probably would have taken over the world if no one, including foreign intelligence services, ever lied to them.

Such cases are most troublesome if one interprets the theories as providing exclusive and uncompromising dictates rather than recommendations to be taken in concert with others. But rather than emphasize the conflict, one might do better to examine ways in which the apparent contradictions can be reconciled. In the above case, for example, one might argue for a middle-ground rationale that would result in reasonable moral behavior. The teleologist might argue that lying is, indeed, a risky business and ought to be avoided if at all possible. The lie, even for a good purpose, weakens social credibility in a way that is harmful in the long run. Even the "good lie" damages the liar because it lessens the taboo associated with lying and increases his or her likelihood of lying in the future and, thus, would tend to degrade one's character. The deontologist may soften his or her own position in a parallel manner by noting that rules apply only in proper context and that the normal rules do not apply in such an unnatural situation. Moreover, he or she may argue that the rule that best applies (Sullivan, 1991) is not "Do not lie" but "Protect innocent life" or "Prevent injustice."

There is flexibility in all of the theories if they are not interpreted as "last word" or "only word" theories. When the theories' recommendations appear to conflict, judgment, perhaps in the form of intuition, must be used. People of good judgment will usually agree, as they likely would in the above case. Only the extreme ideologue would sacrifice the world to a Nazi regime merely to cling to the principle that one ought not to lie.

Nevertheless, there will be cases in which honorable people of good will finally disagree, as they do in contemporary society on issues such as abortion and capital punishment. Some moral questions simply have no clear and unambiguous answers. In such cases, one cannot be faulted on moral grounds for using one's best, impartial, detached judgment. One may not always have the right answers, but one can reach one's own reasonable moral conclusions.

THE CITIZENSHIP OF THE MORAL AGENT

In one respect, the public administrator is a model for all moral agents because, as we have seen, moral agency is a part of the profession of public administration. There is, however, also a special commonality between the public administrator and the private citizen. The concept of citizenship entails participation in the public life of a community and promotion of the social good. One might characterize the role of citizen as that of a political office holder who is to act in behalf of the society, as the public administrator acts in behalf of the society. Also, similar to the ideal public administrator, the ideal private citizen, who does not stand for election, has no constituency except the public good. The private citizen does not have to please other groups to maintain the status of citizen. Therefore, the private citizen and public administrator have morality, embodied in the social good, as the principals of their moral agency.

Let us distinguish between formal and informal citizenship. The formal citizen is recognized as having the legal rights of citizenship, such as the right to vote in a democracy and freedom from restrictions under which aliens must live. However, one need not be a formal citizen to be a part of a society. A moral agent, whether a citizen or not, can be a contributor to a society; moreover, moral agency would suggest not only that one can contribute to the society in which one lives but that, morally, one must be such a contributor. When we use the term "citizen," we intend it in the more inclusive informal sense.

When one speaks of citizenship in the informal sense, there is considerable ambiguity in defining the society or societies of which one is a citizen. Most proximately, one is a citizen of one's community. The term "resident" is usually used to designate a member of a city or town, but like "citizen," resident has a formal, legalistic meaning and an informal, more inclusive meaning. In their informal senses, citizenship in a community is synonymous with residency. Stated in either terminology, an individual has a moral responsibility to his or her immediate community. Most people belong to numerous communities, some defined geographically, some professionally, and some socially. Common ideological, religious, or ethnic ties also bind people together in communities, as may numerous other uniting factors.

One also is a citizen of larger politically defined entities such as states and nations. Although the social ties that connect people to states and nations are much weaker than those in communities, the obligations that one has to such politically defined entities are substantial. One depends on them for protection, social order, utilities, and innumerable other benefits. As a consequence, one has moral duties to such entities, in addition to the legal requirements such as payment of taxes and service on a jury. Such moral obligations include contributing to the needy members of the community, participating in civic organizations, and lending assistance in emergencies. A good citizen will also demonstrate respect for the society, even when its aims conflict with his or her own. In cases of such conflict, he or she will, insofar as it is reasonable, accept some laws and regulations with which he or she does not agree and that cost him or her financially rather than fighting them both within the law and in defiance of it. For example, a tire manufacturer should be willing to lower his or her company's profits to comply with clean air restrictions. Socrates' commitment to his society of Athens was so strong that he obeyed its laws even when they were used to bring about his death. Although some would consider Socrates' actions extreme, all civic-minded people should be willing to sacrifice some portion of their own self-interest for the sake of the society as a whole.

However, informal citizenship extends beyond national boundaries. The tendency toward globalism makes one's inclusion in a larger citizenry increasingly evident. Although people have special moral responsibilities to communities, states, and nations, they cannot ignore their international responsibilities or their international citizenship. Often these citizenships coincide, but they sometimes appear to overlap. When they do, the moral agent is challenged to balance his or her responsibilities to find ultimate resolution. That resolution, however, cannot be decided by the designation of any one of those communities as the real or defining one. If such a designation were in effect, conflicts would be removed because the designated community would be the citizen's ultimate authority. If, for example, one were to designate the proximate community as ultimate, the citizen would be required to sacrifice national interests whenever they conflicted with those of his or her town, social group, or church. But if the nation were the designated ultimate, nationalism and jingoistic patriotism would justify brutality for world domination. However, if world citizenship were ultimate, one's responsibility to one's own country — or city, in the case of Socrates — would virtually disappear. There is no evident single community to which one's total loyalty belongs.

The moral agent recognizes a more encompassing authority, which provides the context in which conflicts among communities can be resolved. Because the moral agent recognizes morality itself as a principal, he or she must appeal to it in order to clarify his or her moral obligations in such conflicts. One might metaphorically consider the moral agent as a citizen of the moral realm. With respect to such a realm, we may return to Kant, whose concept of the kingdom of ends suddenly has acquired a new relevance.

THE KANTIAN LEGISLATOR IN THE KINGDOM OF ENDS AND THE MORAL AGENT

The concept of the Kantian kingdom of ends is applicable to our notion of persons as moral agents. As we have seen, the moral agent, although recognizing his or her responsibility to the community and the nation, as a citizen, also has a broader and more fundamental responsibility to morality as a principal. But morality means nothing without a social context. Behavior is morally significant only because of its potential effect on conscious beings. The kingdom of ends supplies such a context and provides a structure, as Kant has outlined it, for moral guidance. When one acts as a legislator in a kingdom of ends, one moves the society in which he or she lives toward an ideal society in which he or she and all of humanity ought to live. Therefore, the actions of the person acting as legislator in the kingdom of ends harmonize concern for the flesh-and-blood people about him or her with the ideals that belong to humanity as a whole. The person thus becomes a moral agent and a complete human being. But the notion of such a moral agent/legislator needs clarification, and to provide it, we attempt to give first a more general, and then a more specific account, of how such a person would behave.

The legislator of a kingdom of ends, like any legislator, must consider the society with which he or she is charged as his or her highest concern. He or she must not think of himself or herself as the beneficiary of his or her actions but only as a member of a society, all of whose members are of equal importance as ends in themselves. One of the chief characteristics, therefore, of the legislator is impartiality. He or she must not privilege himself or herself, persons with whom he or she has a special personal relationship, or groups of which he or she is a member. It is this concept of impartiality that John Rawls attempts to capture in the notion of action under a veil of ignorance.

The Kantian legislator's decisions must take into account the reasons for which people are ends in themselves. Paramount among those reasons is the status of the person as a rational being, capable of making his or her own choices and recognizing his or her responsibility for them. Therefore, the Kantian legislator cannot act in a manner that limits human freedom. The Kantian legislator cannot act despotically by imposing his or her own beliefs by force on others.

Nevertheless, the Kantian legislator, on the basis of that same rational freedom, has the right — and moreover the responsibility — to appeal to the rational nature of other members of the society to convince them of the moral values that he or she considers valid. We can therefore infer that the Kantian moral agent attempts to institute a vision of the ideal by means of rational dialogue with other rational human beings.

But there are cases in which rational dialogue fails to prevent monstrous actions. The point at which the moral agent should use more coercive force is difficult to determine and is case specific. We therefore consider the matter later, when we move beyond a general description of the qualities of the moral agent toward application of the notion of moral agency to specific issues.

If human beings are intrinsically valuable because of their rationality, then they must respect moral principles. One could not be considered rational if one were not logically consistent, and as Kant has demonstrated, logical consistency is inherent in the nature of principles, per se. The legislator in the kingdom of ends must therefore consider his or her actions as instances of principle in action rather than as individual, isolated events.

We are now in a position to provide a brief summary of the Kantian legislator and as a moral agent in the kingdom of ends. The Kantian legislator and moral agent treats people as ends in themselves rather than as means, recognizes their rational autonomy, and regards them as subject to principles that they are rational enough to accept. He or she is also committed to the ideal of a society of equal moral legislators and takes action to promote that ideal.

There would seem to be a possible oversight in Kant's view, however. Although according the status of end in itself to rational beings, he appears to deny the intrinsic value of animals. He (1989) argues that people should treat animals kindly, but only because habitual cruelty to animals may develop a tendency to abuse human beings, whom Kant considers truly important. However, although Kant does not consider animals to be rational and therefore does not consider them intrinsically valuable on the same grounds on which he considers human beings to be, he never gives conclusive reasons to preclude any other sources of intrinsic value but rationality. One might argue that consciousness, awareness of pain, capacity for altruistic feelings, or some other trait may bestow intrinsic value. We are inclined to suppose that some such reasons can be given and that, therefore, the moral agent would consider at least some animate beings other than human beings to have value in themselves. We would therefore include, among the moral agent's traits, the characteristic of being humane.

THE UNIFIED ETHIC, COMMUNITARIANISM, AND INDIVIDUALISM

The terms "communitarianism" and "individualism" are easier to express in general terms than to define because advocates of each position define them in their own ways, some of which run for several paragraphs. (Bell, 1993, p. 13–15).

The following definitions from the *Oxford Dictionary of Philosophy* (1996) suffice for our purposes:

> Communitarianism: A model of political organization that stresses ties of affection, kinship, and a sense of common purpose and tradition, as opposed to the meager morality of contractual ties entered into between a loose conglomeration of individuals. (p. 70)

> Individualism: The view that the single person is the basic unit of political analysis, with social wholes being merely logical constructions, or ways of talking about numbers of such individuals and the relations among them. (p. 191)

In general, communitarians, including Charles Taylor (1999) and Alysdair MacIntyre (1981), and Amitai Etzioni (1995), believe that the individual's rights are subordinate to the greater good of the society, whereas individualists, including John Rawls (2001) and Robert Nozick (1974), believe that the rights of the individual are primary.

We can further divide both communitarianism and individualism into extreme and moderate positions. Extreme communitarians believe that individual rights do not exist and that the good of a group is the only legitimate moral aim. Marxism can be seen as an extreme communitarianism. Moderate communitarians, such as Taylor and McIntyre, and Etzioni, believe in individual rights but maintain that they should be sacrificed for the good of the entire group. Extreme individualists, such as Nozick (1974), believe that only individual rights exist and that the individual has no moral obligation to any social group. Moderate individualists, such as Rawls, believe that the interests of the society should be sacrificed to preserve individual rights but that the social good is also a legitimate value.

Our position is opposed to extreme communitarianism. As legislator in the kingdom of ends, the individual has the free moral right and responsibility to make moral decisions. Moral agency would not be possible without both the right to make moral decisions and the responsibility to act on them.

Our position is also opposed to extreme individualism. A legislator in a kingdom of ends must consider the interests of other members of the society, who are also ends in themselves. Second, legislators in any kingdom or society must consider the interests of the society as a whole. Moreover, the kingdom of ends, which the legislator must promote, is a social order in which all ends for a coherent whole.

We are therefore somewhere between moderate communitarianism and moderate individualism. We share with the individualist the notion that the individual must make moral decisions based on his or her own moral lights. In making those decisions, the moral agent, as legislator in the kingdom of ends, must consider teleological utilitarian considerations as well as considerations of character and intuitive moral insights. But whatever reasons he or she uses to justify his or her actions, they must emanate from his or her moral insights, which he or she has the right, as an individual, to make. But we share with the communitarian the belief that the individual is under a moral obligation to serve the society, which he or she will, ideally, convert into a kingdom of ends.

The line between communitarianism and individualism is difficult to draw, as different writers define the two concepts in slightly different ways. Rather than anoint one demarcation and clearly locate our view as one or the other, we will note how our position concurs and disagrees with each. Like the individualist, we argue that the individual is the source of his or her own morally responsible actions. However, we do not maintain that the individual is the sole source of morality. If each individual were free to choose his or her own moral system, and if all systems were equally valid, relativism would result. In our perspective, each individual would use his or her best judgment in trying to find the correct moral action, but it is to be discovered rather than invented. What is morally correct does not depend on what one considers to be moral. What one considers to be moral should depend on what, in fact, is moral.

Our position shares an important feature with the communitarian position. The legislator in a kingdom of ends cannot make decisions independent of his or her community. The moral agent belongs to a community in that there are other people to whom the moral agent is morally responsible. As legislator in a kingdom of ends, the ends of others in the community are to be considered paramount. Unlike some communitarians, such as Alisdair McIntyre, however, we argue that the community ultimately includes the entire population of the earth rather than only one distinct cultural group.

There is also another important sense in which our position bears resemblance to communitarianism. The kingdom of ends is the ideal community that defines moral action for the moral agent. That community defines him or her much as the smaller society defines a person for the communitarian.

RAWLS AND THE UNIFIED ETHIC

Our position, because of its Kantian influence, might be considered comparable to the theory of Rawls (2001), whose position is often considered Kantian. However, there are significant differences between our position and his. Rawls considers justice in society to result from a hypothetical decision, made under a "veil of ignorance," concerning the choice of a social structure.

When someone acts under a Rawlsian veil of ignorance, he or she makes decisions for a society as if without knowledge of the person or group whose interest he or she represents and therefore without knowledge of how his or her decisions will affect them specifically. As a consequence, without considering the effect of his or her action on whom he or she represents, he or she will choose the actions that treat the members of the society most justly. According to Rawls, he or she will be especially concerned with promoting the interests of the least advantaged group because those whom he or she represents may be within it. He or she would fear more the prospect of being a member of that group that is harmed by an act or policy than by the prospect of being a member of an advantaged group that loses a portion of its benefits. Thus, the person acting under a veil of ignorance is likely to promote equality in society as much as possible.

The notion of the veil of ignorance captures an important part of the notion of the legislator in the kingdom of ends within the context of the unified ethic. Like the Kantian legislator, the representative under the veil of ignorance makes impartial decisions for an entire society comprising equal individuals. But Rawls's analysis omits some other important Kantian elements that we consider significant.

The decisions made under the veil of ignorance assume an "original position," in which no objective moral values are assumed:

> Immediately the question arises as to how the fair terms of cooperation are specified. For example: Are they specified by an authority distinct from the persons cooperating, say, by God's law? Or are these terms recognized by everyone as fair by reference to a moral order of values,[14] say, by rational intuition, or by reference to what some have viewed as "natural law." Or are they settled by an agreement reached by free and equal citizens engaged in cooperation, and made in view of what they regard as their reciprocal advantage (2001, pp. 14–15) or good?,

> Justice as fairness adopts a form of the last answer: The fair terms of social cooperation are to given by an agreement entered into by those engaged in it (2001, p. 15).

[14] This order I assume to be viewed as objective in some form of moral realism.

In contrast, our position asserts the reality of moral values that are not merely accepted by convention. Although it may be possible, though in our opinion mistaken, to interpret the Kantian kingdom of ends as sharing values on the basis of agreement alone rather than on the basis of a belief in their objective validity, the context of the unified ethic precludes such an interpretation. We understand the Kantian perspective as a deontological aspect of a moral complex whole that recognizes the validity of other aspects including teleology and virtue theory, all of which recognize a moral reality. Furthermore, there is a hint of self-interest in the suggestion in the quotation that the cooperation is for reciprocal advantage.

That hint of self-interest also enters into the decisions that people make in the hypothetical veil of ignorance. Under that veil, representatives make decisions in ignorance of the groups that they represent. They therefore make fair decisions that are not specifically intended to give advantage to any group, and they therefore choose to institute systems that ensure basic rights for all and that preserve the best interests of the least advantaged because "Only in this way . . . can they act responsibly as trustees: that is, effectively protect the fundamental interests of the person each represents: and, at the same time make sure to avoid possibilities the realization of which would be altogether intolerable" (2001, p. 102).

But choices on the basis of self-interest, as impartial as they may seem under a veil of ignorance, are still not moral actions. The Kantian legislator in the kingdom of ends would not replace moral motives with egocentricity contrived to result in justice.

More than merely being impartial, the Kantian legislator reveres human beings as ends in themselves. The Kantian does not merely act out of concern about the possible ramifications of his or her action for him or her but out of respect for other people. The Kantian legislator acts out of respect for the interests of others of status and significance equal to his or her own, whereas the Rawlsian acts under the fear that the interests that he or she damages may be his or her own.

The Rawlsian veil of ignorance, furthermore, is explicitly devoid of nearly all moral judgment. The original position is one in which people refuse to consider any values but those that are commonly accepted by the entire social structure. Therefore, one's moral beliefs that are not universally shared by all members of the society, such as beliefs about abortion, capital punishment, free speech, the rights of animals, or any other such moral issue are left out of the decisions made under the veil of ignorance. Rawls treats moral beliefs as if they were merely aspects that define different factions, such as social status or professional affiliation (p. 60). The moral agency of someone choosing under the veil of ignorance would be limited to recognition of a very few principals commonly agreed on by all members of the society. Moreover, the Rawlsian moral agent would act not out of personal moral commitment but out of commitment to a social agreement. There must be more to the moral fiber of the legislator, who makes decisions on all moral matters rather than on those universally accepted by convention, in the Kantian kingdom of ends.

We argue that neither the physical, existent community nor the individual is the source of morality. Either of those options would suggest relativism. The first would entail a relativism of conformity to community customs, and the second would entail a chaotic free-for-all in which everyone chooses whatever values strike his or her fancy. The moral agent as legislator in a kingdom of ends is motivated by the responsibility to serve morality and, in doing so, to serve the human community.

Aside from the question of whether societies are more significant than individuals or individuals are more significant than societies, another, more important issue remains. Regardless of communitarian or individualist views, we have responsibilities regarding members of societies distinct from our own. If we had no such responsibilities, we would have no duty to help needy members of other societies and would have moral license to treat them in any way that we chose, no matter how monstrous. We could even kill or torture them wantonly. Regardless of whether the source of morality lies in the community, the self, or some other entity, our responsibilities extend to all human beings. Membership in a society or a specific relation to another individual may entail additional moral obligations, but we must treat all human beings in an at least minimally moral manner. The notion of the legislator in the kingdom of ends acknowledges, more evidently than either the communitarian or individualist views, that responsibility to all of humanity.

One might still ask what the source of morality might be if neither the individual nor the society create it. Our answer is implicit in our analysis of the unified ethic. As we have seen, teleologists, deontologists, virtue theorists, and intuitionists all claim their favorite sources. We argue that morality is a complex entity with all four aspects. A scoop of ice cream can be described by its flavor, its ingredients, its chemical make-up, or its molecular structures. None of those descriptions is the object in its entirety, but accounts of different aspects.

The concept of the legislator in the kingdom of ends, although a part of the Kantian deontological theory, can be used in relation to all aspects. In addition to its Kantian roots, it displays teleological concerns (Auxter, 1982) in that the legislator must consider the happiness of the residents of the society in making decisions affecting them. The decisions of the ideal legislator, in that they are of moral intent, would display the favored moral traits of the virtue theorist. Moreover, the legislator's decisions would consider the effect of legislation on the moral character of the members of the society. The moral intuitions would also, one would suppose, generally concur with the legislator's ideal principles.

REFERENCES

Aristotle. 1985. *Nicomachean Ethics*, trans. T. Irwin. Indianapolis, IN: Hackett.

Auxter, T. 1982. *Kant's Moral Teleology.* Macon, GA: Mercer University Press.

Ayer, A. J. 2001. *Language, Truth and Logic*. London: Penguin, 2001.

Bell, D. 1993. *Communtarianism and Its Critics*. Oxford: Clarendon Press.

Bentham, J. 1996. *An Introduction to the Principles of Morals and Legislation*, ed. J. H. Burns and H. L. A. Hart. Oxford: Clarendon Press.

Etzioni, A. 1995. *New Communitarian Thinking*. Charlottesville: University of Virginia Press.

Garofalo, C., and D. Geuras. 1999. *Ethics in the Public Service: The Moral Mind at Work*. Washington, D.C.: Georgetown University Press.

Geuras, D., and C. Garofalo. 2002. *Practical Ethics in Public Administration*. Vienna, VA: Management Concepts.

Kant, I. 1989. *Fundamental Principles of the Metaphysics of Morals*. T.K. Abbot, trans. New York: MacMillan.

Lynch, T. D., and C. E. Lynch. 1991. Applying Spiritual Wisdom. *Global Virtue Ethics Review* 1(1):71–87.

MacIntyre, A. 1981. *After Virtue*. Notre Dame, IN: Notre Dame University Press.

Mill, J. S. 1907. *Utilitarianism*. London: Longmans.

Moore, G. E. 1912.   London: Oxford University Press.

Nozick, R. 1974. *Anarchy, State, and Utopia*. New York: Basic Books.

Oxford Dictionary of Philosophy. 1996. ed. S. Blackburn. New York: Oxford University Press.

Rawls, J. 2001. *Justice as Fairness: A Restatement*. Cambridge, MA: Belknap.

Stevenson, C. 1937. The Emotive Meaning of Ethical Terms. *Mind*. 14–31.

Sullivan, R. J. 1991. *Immanuel Kant's Moral Theory*. Cambridge: Cambridge University Press.

Taylor, C. 1999. Conditions of an Unforced Consensus on Human Rights. In *The East Asian Challenge for Human Rights*, eds. J. R. Bauer and D. Bell. New York: Cambridge University Press.

The Internet Encyclopedia of Philosophy. Available at: http://www.utm.edu/research/iep.

9 Applying the Unified Ethic to Moral Agency

In the previous chapter, we examined the unified ethic and the legislator in the kingdom of ends as the theoretical framework of the moral agent. In this chapter, we use that framework to reconsider moral agency in citizenship, business, law, medicine, and higher education with a view toward developing the notion of the ideal moral agent in all of those areas. We will use the exemplarship of the public administrator, as discussed in Chapters 2 and 3, to model those ideals.

THE MORAL AGENT AS MORALLY RESPONSIBLE CITIZEN

Now that we have a general concept of the moral agent, we must apply it to issues of social significance if we are to make the concept "real" (i.e., to give it a more specific characterization). The nature of that more specific account partially depends on the area of moral agency, be it citizenship, business, law, medicine, or education. We begin with the area of citizenship and proceed to the professions. In Chapter 3, we discussed moral and ethical breakdowns in public administration to more fully understand that contrary condition of the public administrator as moral agent. We divided those breakdowns into two general categories: insufficient commitment to moral values and overcommitment to moral values. We here adopt the same approach with respect to the moral agent as citizen in a kingdom of ends. We let the concept of the moral agent develop from an account of the common failures of moral agency.

INSUFFICIENT COMMITMENT TO MORAL VALUES

Most people are generally moral with respect to their own families, friends, community, and social groups. If one does not behave morally with those closest to him or her, he or she would not likely qualify as a moral agent. There are exceptions, however. Presidents Franklin Roosevelt and John Kennedy may have been morally lacking at a personal level while morally committed to grander social values. But even such people, who engage in occasional unseemly behavior, are generally moral and ethical most of the time. There is no evidence that the human race is fundamentally lacking in morality toward their immediate associates.

It is harder to be optimistic regarding the human tendency to disregard matters a few steps removed from one's own personal concerns. Although many people hold views concerning the environment, globalism, capital punishment, and other social issues, few people participate actively in advancing their moral beliefs. Moral agents at the macro level are few, though opinions are many. The grand issues are left largely to the professionals, usually in public agencies. But there are two problems with the "let the government do it" attitude. First, it replaces moral action with paid professional activity. Second, rather than using the public administrator as a model, the attitude substitutes the public agent's actions for one's own. No government except a completely totalitarian regime could ever fully replace the moral agency of individuals, and if it could, the remainder of humanity would be bereft of social morality.

The few private citizens who engage in moral agency often meet resistance from their fellow citizens. One reason for such resistance may be a resentment that some people hold against those who morally exceed them. Occasionally, good Samaritans who turn in lost valuables are derided as fools by those who would have chosen a more selfish option. A second reason may be the reluctance that people have to recognize their own responsibilities. The socially active moral agent has a way of reminding people of what they ought to be doing but are not.

Among those who are not active in pursuing moral goals, there may also be a sentiment condemning the socially active as busybodies or as people who refuse to "mind their own business." The moral agent is difficult for those without a sense of moral agency to understand; they may take the attitude that if something does not affect one directly or at least in some evident indirect way, no intervention is warranted. But it is an essential aspect of moral agency to involve oneself in issues on the basis of purely moral consideration, regardless of personal self-interest. The moral agent views such involvement as morally obligatory.

The moral agent as legislator in a kingdom of ends does not avoid important social issues because they are "someone else's business" or not of immediate personal concern. The moral agent for whom morality itself is a motive actively pursues the social good as he or she understands it. As a member of a kingdom of ends, a universal ideal society, the moral agent's commitment is not confined within national borders, though one must recognize a special obligation to the political structure that unites him or her with others in a national community. In the sense that the moral agent recognizes moral value as a motive in itself, all moral agents are social activists.

But social activism has pitfalls. Sometimes, people use their activism as a platform for personal recognition, political power, or other personal advantage in a manner similar to that of the public administrator who elevates himself or herself over the social value that he or she overtly promotes. Certainly Huey Long believed strongly in the social justice of the causes that he or she promoted. Equally certainly, he used those causes to promote a political career in a manner that may have harmed the state of Louisiana in some respects, even while helping it in other ways. The same confusion of moral values and personal advancement can occur at the level of community service as well as at the level of national politics and anywhere in between. The moral agent's commitment must be one of detachment from egocentric interests.

The attitude of "I want to make a difference" constitutes another form of unwarranted intrusion of the self into the area of moral commitment. Some people engage in actions that they consider moral to leave a legacy, be important, or merely feel useful. They may be on a search for "meaning" in their lives. It has been said, though perhaps falsely, of several U.S. presidents, including Lyndon Johnson, Bill Clinton, and Richard Nixon, that they were absorbed with how history, in the form of academic historians, would describe them. Such prideful motives may seem harmless, even if less than purely moral, because they would still likely produce beneficial results. However, those motives, which much of humanity shares, may sometimes distract someone from performing the best action to perform the most conspicuous action. One must keep in mind the quote often attributed to Indira Gandhi, "My grandfather once told me that there are two kinds of people: those who work and those who take the credit. He told me to try to be in the first group; there was less competition there" (Indira Gandhi Quotes, http://www.thinkexist.com/english/author/x/author_3141_1.htm. Accessed April 9, 2005.)

Another form of insufficient commitment to a cause is analogous to the public administrator's elevation of the organization over the social good. Social activism is often most effective when conducted through the coordinated efforts of groups such as the National Association for the Advancement of Colored People, the American Civil Liberties Union, or the Christian Coalition. But the groups often take on a significance of their own and inspire a loyalty to the organization that may in some cases rival their loyalty to the cause. The phenomenon is easily noticeable at the level of national party politics, when the demands of party loyalty and unity stifle dissent, but all organizations, no matter how sincerely they were founded, can assume the status of ends in themselves.

OVERCOMMITMENT TO SPECIFIC VALUES

It is not possible to be overly committed to moral agency when it is properly understood. Because moral agency is commitment to those things to which one ought to be committed, there can be no excess of moral agency. But there can be an excessive commitment to one value or set of values in a manner that causes undue conflict with other values. Anthony Downs's (1967) concept of zealotry, which he intended to apply to the public administrator, is also a potential corruptor of moral agency.

CONFLICTS AMONG MORAL VALUES

In public administration, we noted that conflicts can occur among organizations. Such conflicts opposed the values that one organization intended to advance to those of another organization. The organizational conflict expressed a competition among the underlying values for supremacy, when a balancing of them was more appropriate.

Sincere, conscientious moral agents can also conflict because they lack a comprehensive perspective in which values form a coherent, unified whole. In Kantian terms, those moral agents fail to consider the entire kingdom of ends but focus on individual values out of proportion to others. The kingdom of ends is a condition under which values form a consistent structure rather than a competition among themselves.

Contemporary society is a conglomeration of values pitted against each other: environmental concerns versus business interests; Rawlsian economic equality versus utilitarian productivity; free market versus regulation by the public; right to life versus right to choose; the rights of the individual to pursue his or her own interests freely versus the interests of the society as a whole. The entire list is too large to specify all. Virtually all of the values that socially active citizens champion have merit. The problem for such activists is twofold. They must advance their cause and thus avoid undercommitment but, at the same time, they must respect other values in the kingdom of ends and thus avoid overcommitment to a single value or subset of them. Such an overcommitment can lead easily to extremism.

The logging industry has been the source of much environmental damage, including the destruction of valuable timberland, cutting down of old-growth forest, and removal of habitat for endangered species. Such corporate behavior, which may be dismissed as pure self-interest and pursuit of profit, is often defended as producing needed products. Laissez-faire capitalists often support wanton environmental destruction on the basis of the blessings that the free market provides. Such defenses, although hardly convincing, nevertheless contain an element of validity. The exercise of free enterprise has been remarkably productive throughout history and is probably worthy of protection. The products of the logging industry, from paper to relatively well-insulating building materials, are of significant benefit to society. The free-market defenders of the right of the logging industry to pursue profit while materially benefiting society are not entirely without merit. The problem is not that their beliefs are unfounded on any legitimate value but that they fail to consider all of the values essential to social well being, including the protection of natural habitats. The failure is a lack of inclusiveness in consideration of competing values and mechanisms to resolve complex disputes.

Some environmentalists are guilty of the same sin. They properly recognize the dangers of unbridled materialism and have observed the damage that uncontrolled logging has done. They also realize that laws and regulations are unlikely to remove all environmental abuses. But the more radical among the environmental movement have used tactics such as tree spiking that endanger the lives of loggers. Other less violent forms of protest, such as tree sitting, not only endanger the lives of the protesters themselves but also appear to aim at the virtual cessation of all logging activities.

The legislator in the kingdom of ends would adopt neither of the extreme positions but would examine the entire moral landscape to arrive at a unified, balanced policy. The best policy would be one in which the logging industry was regulated in a way that would perpetuate the forests rather than destroy them and would recognize society's debt to both the environmentalists and the logging industry for their collaboration in improving society.

We do not argue here that all conflicts should end in compromise. We speak specifically of cases in which there is a conflict of legitimate moral values. Some cases require not collaboration but outright refutation of one side's perspective. If a chemical insecticide can be shown to cause cancer, it should be banned despite its utility in producing better crops, assisting farmers, promoting the chemical industry, or improving the stock market.

Some legitimate, conscientious moral conflicts cannot end in compromise for another reason: There is simply no middle position. Those who, on moral grounds, oppose all capital punishment or abortion cannot be reconciled with those who believe that those practices should be allowed. In such cases, some people win and some people lose with respect to public policy. The losing party may still claim the morally valid position and, perhaps from the standpoint of omniscience, may be correct. But as legislator in a kingdom of ends, in which all values are rendered consistent, one must not impose his or her perspective on the rest of society. The Kantian legislator recognizes all people as autonomous ends in themselves, but the individual who imposes his or her perspective on others would not accord such recognition on them. The moral agent must recognize that respect for moral autonomy is itself a moral value and must be defended as well as any other. The moral zealot tends to see the value that he or she champions, as the only possible valid ones and therefore is given to extreme action. But the Kantian legislator respects the conflict between his or her own values and those of autonomous other people, whom he or she must convince rationally, if at all possible. If he or she uses other means, he or she does not treat them as rational beings and therefore implicitly denies their status as autonomous ends in themselves. Extremist antiabortionists, environmental saboteurs, and violent antiglobalists are recent examples of insufficient respect for that autonomy.

The moral agent who must accept the freedom of a society to opt for a policy that he or she considers morally wrong is in a position similar to that of the aforementioned judge who must follow laws with which he or she disagrees. In a conflict between one's own moral convictions and the duly chosen policies of the society, the moral agent, like the judge, should generally defer to the social will.

However, there are exceptional cases. Sometimes people lose their reason and should have it imposed on them. Such cases are rare, but they must be acknowledged. Slavery in the United Sates and genocide in Germany are simply morally unacceptable, and the moral agent would fight them even if society could not be rationally convinced of their monstrousness. The moral agent must have the perspicuity and judgment to determine when relentless total opposition is required.

The public administrator, in his or her treatment of the moral dilemmas discussed in Chapter 3, can serve as the exemplar of moral agency in cases of conflict between one's own values and those chosen by a society of autonomous people. In functioning as Taylor's (1982) strong evaluator in such cases, the public administrator, in a publicly observable structure, demonstrates how such cases should be approached.

There will always be the cases that are on the blurry line that separates justified rebellion against socially instituted immorality from acceptance of the social order. Was the abolitionist John Brown justified in murdering people to free slaves? Were the Roman senators justified in assassinating Caesar? No moral theory can hope to successfully address every case, but it can at best provide the framework in which the moral agent must function.

There is one class of cases in which the legislator in the kingdom of ends might not betray his or her own moral values for those of the society: the case in which the society does not acknowledge the autonomous will of the individual. In cases in which society acknowledges this autonomy, the moral agent who disagrees with society on a moral issue is in a dilemma that opposes his or her personal value against his or her recognition of the sanctity of the autonomous wills of his or her fellows. But when a society is structured in a manner that denies that autonomy, the dilemma is removed. Moreover, the moral agent should oppose any such social or political structure precisely because it is fundamentally immoral. If the society is one's own, rebellion or revolution may be in order.

Nations that behave as moral agents must confront the question of how to behave toward other nations that do not treat their citizens as ends in themselves. The Kantian quest for a kingdom of ends would entail that at least some action, if possible, should be taken to oppose such despotic systems that deny human dignity. However, no nation has an absolute right to impose its will on another without engaging in political or military domination, which, itself, denies autonomy to the residents of the morally questionable nation to be reformed. The United States has faced such dilemmas with respect to the apartheid regime in South Africa, the Idi Amin dictatorship in Uganda, and the brutal regime of Saddam Hussein in Iraq. There is no single policy that will apply to all such cases, but once again, the reasoning of Taylor's strong evaluator is needed. The public administrator's exemplarship is especially warranted in such cases because he or she is part of the government that must make the decision concerning how to respond.

The moral agent, as Kantian legislator, regards the entirety of humanity as his or her domain of moral responsibility. He or she does not restrict his or her concerns to the matters that immediately affect him or her, his or her community, or even his or her nation, but includes them all within a comprehensive moral perspective — a kingdom of ends. He or she is therefore an agent of morality itself rather than of an individual, locale, or political entity. His or her own professional or business interests are fundamentally influenced by his or her comprehensive view because it is the source of their significance. He or she welcomes reasonable, morally founded restraints and regulations on his or her activities because they remove the competitive pressure to cross the lines of moral rectitude. As a consumer, he or she is willing to favor the products of corporations that display moral responsibility, even at substantial cost. He or she invests only in such corporations, even if they seem less likely to produce the greatest income. But more important than any of his or her actions is the dominance of morality among all of his or her concerns. Moral agency is an entire life perspective.

David K. Hart (1992) divides moral action into moral episodes and moral processes, but moral agency goes beyond both. He divides moral episodes, or moral incidents, into the subcategories of moral crisis and moral confrontation. Moral crises are cases in which the individual who acts rightly is endangered, and moral confrontations are cases of risk below the level of endangerment. Surely, moral agency includes performance of moral action in such cases but does not await potential difficulty to assert itself. The moral agent's vision of the kingdom of ends, together with all that it entails, is present as the context of all of his or her actions.

Hart comes closer to the concept of the moral agent in describing moral processes. His first class of moral processes is the moral project, in which one attempts to improve the moral quality of individual or organizational lives, and his second class is moral work, which refers to the intentional decision to think and act in virtuous ways. His first class, although characteristic of the moral agent, nevertheless falls short. Like the moral episode, the moral project is undertaken as a discrete and temporally defined set of activities within one's life, but for the moral agent, moral activity is a lifelong disposition that cannot be divided into individual projects. The second class is also characteristic of the moral agent but is also unduly limited. When Hart speaks of an intentional decision, he restricts his moral process to an event (i.e., a decision that can be delineated within specific temporal borders within one's life). For the moral agent, morality defines one's life as the motivating force for and the context of all of his or her behavior.

CLARIFICATION OF THE ROLE OF THE MORAL AGENT AS MORAL EXEMPLAR

Hart and others have discussed the role of the public administrator as a moral exemplar extensively. In general, we agree with the conclusion of Hart (1992) that the public administrator has the responsibility to be a moral exemplar, but we would add to his position by complementing it. We offer, in the language of parliamentary procedure, friendly amendments.

Hart (1992), Cooper (1992), and Frank Sherwood (1992) emphasize the role of the public administrator as a moral exemplar for other public administrators. The authors give examples of and praise public administrators such as George Hartzog and George C. Marshall as models for other public administrators to follow. However, we would broaden the responsibility of the public administrator to the point of serving as an exemplar for the entire citizenry. The other authors do not deny that responsibility but emphasize exemplarship directed to other public administrators.

We would distinguish between the public administrator's having greater reason than the private citizen to be a moral exemplar and the public administrator's having greater reason than the private citizen to be moral. We maintain that the responsibility to be moral applies totally to everyone. No one has an exemption from morality. The public administrator would not be a moral exemplar for the private citizen unless they were both under the same moral charge. One can be an example only for another engaged in the same general activity. We, therefore, maintain that the private citizen, as well as the public administrator, must be a moral agent and acknowledge the kingdom of ends as the guide and context of behavior. The public administrator, however, has greater reason to function as the exemplar, because of the nature of the profession of public administration. Because moral agency is essential to the profession of the public administrator, he or she is in a better position than most citizens to exhibit the morality that all citizens should display.

We would also disagree with Hart, who believes that the public administrator acquires an increased level of responsibility to be of good character because of an oath:

> Today, we have lost the significance of what it means to swear an oath. In its most basic expression, it means that public servants have a greater obligation than those in the private sector to be men and women of good character, prepared at all times to sacrifice personal gain for the public interest. (1992, pp. 25–26)

As moral agents, all people have the responsibility to be men and women of good character. The contrasting position is that some people, excepting those who are disadvantaged in specific ways, are not obligated to be of good character. That position is absurd because it is a tautology that people ought to be good rather than bad. The public administrator's oath is merely the overt acknowledgment that he or she recognizes the responsibility to be moral in professional activities.

We also differ with those who would consider the concentration on virtue as that which the moral agent should exemplify. We agree that virtue is one of the aspects of the moral whole included in our unified ethic, but virtue is not the whole story. A person making a moral decision needs more than just an admonition to be virtuous to decide what to do in a morally ambiguous case. The possession of moral virtue does not guarantee that one will make the best choice in a difficult situation. Moreover, as we have noted earlier in discussing virtue theory, there must be some grounds on which one decides whether particular traits are virtues or vices, both in general and in specific instances. The consummate moral exemplar must not only display virtue but also be able to make the best moral choices and give the best reasons for making them. We accept much of the recent emphasis on virtue in moral exemplarship, but we maintain that the moral exemplar must exhibit the entire spectrum of moral agency rather than virtue alone. The moral exemplar must, as legislator in a kingdom of ends, interpret his or her entire world as a moral structure, which forms the context for all significant actions.

TRANSFORMATION AND RECONFIGURATION

The challenge of shifting institutions and professions from moral inertia or indifference to active moral agency and citizenship can be framed as a version of the is–ought problem, as a matter of coherence and consistency, or as an issue of values alignment. However framed, it presents a persistent problem of articulating and advocating ideals, goals, and aspirations that can contribute to the creation of a more rational and responsible moral order. Although morality is encoded in human nature, our daily struggles with competing obligations, our self-interest, and our confusion make it hard to reify and sustain. The power of the status quo, the press of the immediate, and the complexities of contemporary life all converge to leave us perplexed, anxious, and susceptible to simplistic solutions to very difficult dilemmas. Therefore, a sensible first step in any proposal for change is to acknowledge and understand the nature of the resistance that is likely to ensue. Like public policy, moral agency and citizenship may attract support on the general level, but when it comes to specific propositions and details, that support may quickly fade, thus requiring approaches and strategies designed to engender mutual respect, reciprocity, and trust, particularly in the public service — our engine of change.

In the face of these natural and artificial difficulties, therefore, we have offered the unified ethic, a moral construct that can leaven ideology, sectarianism, self-interest, and nationalism. Combined with transformational as opposed to transactional leadership (Burns, 1978), the unified ethic has the potential to deepen our understanding of global as well as local interdependence and enliven our commitment to a national and international moral order. It can contribute to our efforts to shift from the "is" to the "ought" in the political arena; to develop greater coherence and consistency between our professions, institutions, and citizens; and to align our personal and professional values. It is a framework for viable moral change, particularly in the context of our natural drive to do what Howard Gardner and others (2001) call good work.

According to Gardner, Mihaly Csikszentmihalyi, and William Damon (2001), those who do good work are skilled in one or more professional realms. But rather than merely following money or fame alone, or choosing the path of least resistance when in conflict, they are thoughtful about their responsibilities and the implications of their work. They wish to act responsibly, with respect toward their own goals; their family, friends, and colleagues; their mission or sense of calling; the institutions with which they are affiliated; and the wider world, including people they do not know, future generations, and the entire planet.

Like the rest of us, professionals who do good work are embroiled in the complexities of modern life. Whether they are scientists, physicians, journalists, educators, attorneys, or members of some other profession, they confront the same pressures and dilemmas that produce distress and misalignments of values, in one form or another, in the populace as a whole. No one is immune to ceaseless technological innovations, relentless market forces, and the domestic and global conundrums and conflicts that assail us at every turn. The question is how we can cope effectively with the scope and speed of change in our personal and professional lives. How can we maintain our integrity and do good work in the face of the moral dilemmas and temptations that arise in the endless variety of circumstances that confront human beings across the world?

Consider, for example, the physician in a health maintenance organization whose standards of care conflict with those of the management, or an attorney in a multinational organization who is told that a bribe will be necessary to do business in another country, or a teacher who is required to teach to a state-mandated test. According to Gardner and his colleagues, at such times, thoughtful practitioners should weigh three basic issues: the mission or defining features of their profession, the standards or best practices of their profession, and their identity or personal integrity and values. Each realm of work has a central mission that reflects a basic societal need. A physician's mission is to heal the sick, an attorney's to pursue justice, a teacher's to share knowledge and prepare students for the future. We would add to the list the public administrator whose central mission, we have argued, is service to the commonweal as a moral agent and an exemplary citizen. In any event, practitioners should be able to state the core mission of their fields, and a way to clarify this sense of mission is to ask: "Why should society reward the kind of work that I do with status and certain privileges?" (Gardner, 2001, p. 10).

With respect to standards or best practices, Gardner and colleagues suggest that each profession prescribes criteria of performance, some permanent and some changing with time and place. The important question is which members of the profession best realize the calling and why. In one's identity, which consists of a person's convictions about who he or she is and what matters most as a worker, a citizen, or a human being, a central element is moral and is encapsulated in the issue of what lines one will not cross and why. Finally, in the face of the pressures on professions today, Gardner and colleagues recommend that good workers expand their domain by clarifying the values on which it is based, bringing new knowledge to bear on its central task and instituting better procedures to serve its purposes. But if expanding or reconfiguring one's domain is not enough or is not feasible, then taking a personal stand may be required, particularly when one's integrity is at stake or one's values are no longer aligned with one's position. This is a decision that, in the end, only the individual involved is qualified to make.

Transformational leadership of the moral exemplar and reconfiguration of one's personal domain are effected when the moral agent regards himself or herself as a legislator in the kingdom of ends. The recognition of one's citizenship in the kingdom of ends is transformational in that it reconfigures one's orientation from self-centered to morality-centered. Whereas Hart and Cooper appear intent on leading public administration in that direction, the transformation must be broader in that it applies to all citizens and deeper in that it extends to the nature of humanity itself rather than the confines of a profession. The public administrator may be better equipped than most to bring about the reconfiguration, but it should apply to all citizens.

MORAL AGENCY IN BUSINESS

The transformation and reconfiguration would appear to be difficult to effect in business but might be facilitated if one could provide some analysis of how the moral agent in private business would act. The concept of the moral agent as legislator in the kingdom of ends serves as the context for the analysis.

By our definition, the moral agent is motivated by morality. It follows, therefore, that the moral agent in business would dedicate his or her professional life to an enterprise of significant value to humanity. The moral agent chooses the profession by means of which his or her talents could be of greatest benefit. Nearly all enterprises can be understood to have some positive effect on society. The value of producing healthful food, publishing good literature, and developing medicines is beyond question, but even the manufacturing of products that may be seen as frivolous, such as nose rings or automobile bumper stickers, nevertheless pleases some people and, perhaps more important, provides employment.

Kant (1949, p. 40) argues that it is morally unacceptable to let one's talents lie fallow merely to enjoy a leisurely, pleasant, indolent life. A legislator in a kingdom of ends would never promulgate the rule "Don't be concerned to benefit others when you are capable of doing so," because it would deny the very notion of a kingdom of ends as a society in which people's values cohere. The Kantian legislator would, instead, promote the rule "Benefit others to the extent that you are capable of doing so." This reasoning, carried to its logical conclusion, would entail that people choose the profession that permits their talents to best serve society. If such a rule were to be followed, the most capable people would devote themselves to professions that provide the greatest means by which society can be improved. The least capable would spend their time on nose rings.

The Kantian admonition to engage in the professional activity that would most benefit society would have the ironic consequence that the people with the most commitment to moral agency in business may forgo business itself in favor of other means of employment. Those who would use their talents most productively to promote the social best interest may, if endowed with the appropriate abilities, choose to serve the public in medicine, law, or public service. Those three professions are among the most important social benefactors and would, in turn, become, together with society as a whole, the beneficiaries of the Kantian admonition. It is not surprising that the areas that we discussed as the most likely sources of moral exemplarship, with public service as the first among them, should also attract the best exemplars of moral agency.

Some people, however, will continue to find their best means of contributing within the private sector, where moral agents are sorely needed. For the moral agent, in the public or the private sector, professional activities not only are means of employment and remuneration but also must be justified on the basis of their contribution to the social good. But a serious problem arises for the moral agent who concludes that the field in which he or she is working produces more harm than good.

USE OF FOREIGN, LOW-WAGE LABOR

The use of foreign labor presents a major intractable moral issue for corporations in wealthy nations such as the United States. The location of factories in countries in which labor is cheap enables the corporations to produce less expensive products, which at least in theory should benefit consumers. At the same time, the corporation employs people who would otherwise be unemployed or working for less money than the corporation can pay.

However, the practice of using foreign labor has its drawbacks. Exportation of jobs reduces opportunities for domestic laborers, and as we have noted, one has a special, albeit not always overriding, responsibility to one's country. Both domestic employment and the nation's tax revenues suffer. Furthermore, the wages paid to foreign workers are often so meager that they barely improve the condition of an impoverished people.

There is not a "one suits all" moral solution to the problem. It is a moral dilemma in that there are moral reasons both for employing foreign labor and for use of domestic labor. But although there is no universal, clear solution, the concept of the kingdom of ends provides a means of approaching the problem.

A legislator in a kingdom of ends would not legislate an absolute rule forbidding the use of foreign labor. A particular nation's legislator who has no concern for anyone beyond his or her national borders might favor such a rule. But a legislator in a kingdom of ends, although recognizing deference for his or her own country, would acknowledge that moral responsibility is global and that people in foreign lands have needs that must be met. However, that same concern for people in foreign lands dictates that they must not be compensated so poorly as to provide only minimal relief from their economic deprivation. A corporation under the governance of moral agents, who would be legislators in a kingdom of ends, would sacrifice profits to ensure that foreign workers are not exploited but are compensated in a manner that substantially improves their lot. In a purely capitalistic society, the laws of supply and demand determine the cost of all things, but people are not things to the legislator in a kingdom of ends. They are, instead, ends in themselves.

A company bent on exploitation might argue that paying more than the least possible for labor would be counterproductive. If a corporation behaved in the altruistic manner of a legislator in a kingdom of ends, it would sell its products at a less competitive price than other more exploitive companies and might therefore have to shut down its foreign factories or perhaps even cease production. The workers would then be without jobs, consumers would pay higher prices, and fewer products would be offered to the general public.

One must acknowledge that the exploitive corporations' arguments have logical merit. If one corporation is directed by legislators in a kingdom of ends while another exploits, the moral corporation and all of its beneficiaries would be disadvantaged. Laws might be passed to avoid the advantage that the immoral corporation might have over the moral one, but it would be difficult to imagine how such laws would be formulated. Moreover, unscrupulous people can usually find ways around laws. But aside from any laws that might be passed, our concern is with morality rather than legality, so our question is "Should the moral corporation lower its wages to compete with the immoral corporation?"

The consumer must enter into the equation. People must show morality themselves if they expect morality from their institutions, both private and public. Citizens must, as we have noted, also be legislators in the kingdom of ends. The moral corporation could spend some of its advertising funds to inform the consumer of the morality of its policies so that moral consumers would favor products produced morally rather than immorally. In providing such information, the corporation would also educate the public concerning both the plight of people in impoverished nations and the responsibility of more advantaged societies to them.

The case, whose complexity we could barely outline, demonstrates the interrelationship between morality in business and morality in citizenship. A moral society is possible only if citizens behave as moral agents. If citizens followed the exemplarship of the public administrator in moral agency, they would force even self-interested private businesses to behave in a manner consistent with morality.

We appear to have reached the "chicken and egg" stage: Which comes first, the moral agency of the citizen or the moral agency of the corporation? Although there is no universal answer to the question, we maintain that in most cases, including the issue of wages for foreign workers, the primary responsibility rests with the corporations. First, there are fewer corporations than citizens. It is easier for a small number of citizens who control corporations to agree to behave morally than for an entire populace to behave morally *en masse*. Second, and perhaps more important, the corporations have expertise in their businesses and are therefore better informed concerning morally relevant issues such as the economic conditions in impoverished nations. The corporation is in a much better position to educate the public than the public is to educate the corporation. The process can begin when the corporation treats its workers fairly and explains its policies to the public, which should then understand why it should pay higher prices for the sake of morality. Although such an approach entails economic risks, a corporation of moral agents would take them.

SHOULD TOBACCO COMPANIES EXIST?

When tobacco was first produced, there were no serious concerns about any health risks arising from the use of an apparently innocent plant. Over the centuries, the tobacco industry employed countless people and benefited countless others by stimulating local economies and providing a tax base. The increasing, and now indisputable, evidence that tobacco causes cancer, however, has placed the entire industry and those who benefit from it under threat. Private individuals have won huge amounts through lawsuits against and settlements with tobacco companies. Communities have passed ordinances to discourage smoking, and some have virtually banned it. If the product is so harmful, one might ask why it is legally permitted at all.

The prohibition of alcoholic beverages in the United States demonstrates how difficult it is to ban consumption of products that the society deems harmful. The prohibition of all harmful products, including foods high in fat or sugar, would seem to be no more promising or perhaps even desirable than the liquor prohibitions. A ban of tobacco would seem equally unlikely to succeed. Nevertheless, responsible members of the tobacco industry may themselves effect a gradual disappearance of tobacco. When political legislation fails, the moral agent, as legislator in the kingdom of ends, can fill the void.

Let us suppose that a hitherto morally obtuse CEO of a tobacco company undergoes an epiphany and decides to become a moral agent. What is he or she to do? His or her livelihood and that of others depends on a business whose product is potentially lethal. He or she is unlikely to convince the board of directors to shut down the entire business, and if they ever made such a stunning decision, their investors would probably sue them.

The CEO has a moral option. He or she can decide to leave his or her position, whatever the cost, and publicize his or her reasons for doing so. He or she would thus act as a legislator of a kingdom of ends by acting as he or she would have all people in the society act, according to the principle that none should profit by knowingly and systematically harming the society and its people. But if that option is open to him or her, it is also open to all other members of the organization. To follow such moral legislation would indeed entail the demise of the firm. Just as the CEO would risk his or her career, the moral board members would risk the lawsuits and disaffection of investors and employees. The board members would even benefit those objectors by removing from them the moral guilt of participating in an unethical endeavor. Moreover, if the investors and employees acted as legislators in a kingdom of ends, they would voluntarily choose to dissociate themselves from the endeavor.

No one could expect such a felicitous sacrifice of self-interest by all concerned, and a board of moral agents would invite repercussion by any such action. But the repercussions would come from people who choose against morality. When confronted with an option to favor the difficult moral choice or make a concession to immorality, the moral agent sides with morality.

Perhaps a middle ground can be found. The termination of thousands of employees and the financial losses of countless investors are matters of moral concern. One should not easily choose to ruin so many people financially, albeit for a moral cause. Most tobacco companies have large sums of money and interests outside tobacco. A gradual increased diversification may balance health and financial concerns. At the very least, the corporations could cease efforts to recruit new smokers. Moreover, to compensate for a debt to society for past abuses, the corporation could, at its own expense, conduct research on the possible valuable but yet undiscovered beneficial uses of the tobacco plant. If no such uses exist, the lost research money can be considered part of the repayment of the social debt.

The debt to be paid extends beyond national borders. The corporation not only should work toward detachment from its involvement in the smoking industry domestically but also, as citizen of a kingdom of ends, should stop creating health hazards in foreign countries.

To expect such altruism from a corporation may appear to be ludicrously idealistic; however, a moral analysis is not a prediction of human behavior but a description of how people would act if they were ideal. Still, another part of the moral endeavor is the attempt to move people from the imperfect state toward a better, if not perfect, condition. Exemplars are needed to initiate such movement, and the public administrator is, as we have suggested, a fitting exemplar in this and other cases in which companies produce products that, in their net effect, harm society.

Public organizations conduct periodic reviews of their programs to ensure that they continue to serve the public. Some states have "sunset laws" that require such reviews to continue a program in existence. The need for justifying the existence of an organization on the basis of its influence on the public interest is standard procedure in public administration. The moral agent in public service welcomes such reviews and, if his or her organization is shown to have failed the public, promotes the appropriate remedies, even if they include an organizational "death sentence." The seemingly unrealistic ideal for private industry is already in practice in the public service. Here, the moral exemplarship of the public administrator is clearly manifest.

Although it is extremely unlikely that humanity will change overnight into a flesh-and-blood kingdom of ends, incremental change is not only possible but also necessary if improvement is ever to occur. Businesspeople are not likely, at least now, to act *en masse* as moral agents, but the emergence of at least a few can be expected. In all times and in all societies, some people have moral commitments. They become exemplars for the rest. But the well-intended exemplars in business need exemplars of their own. The public administrator, through his or her routine justification of the public value of his or her activities, becomes the "higher-order" exemplar; that is, the exemplar for other exemplars.

THE MORAL EXEMPLARSHIP OF THE PRIVATE EXECUTIVE

There is one aspect of moral agency that the private business can exemplify better than the public agency. Because public agencies are funded for specific purposes, they are generally prohibited from contributing money to charities and other nonprofit agencies. The public agency's own work is its social contribution. The private firm has the opportunity, and therefore the responsibility, to contribute to worthy causes.

Kant speaks of two kinds of duties: perfect duties and imperfect duties. Perfect duties admit no exceptions for any inclination in any instances. (1949, p. 39, note 9.) Imperfect duties indicate generally what a person should do but do not specify the manner in which someone must do it. (1996, p. 153.) Perfect duties are actions that are morally required under specific conditions at specific times, as for example, the duty to tell the truth concerning relevant facts in a murder trial. Imperfect duties are actions of a class that must be performed but not necessarily under any specific conditions or any specific time. The duty to contribute to worthy causes is an imperfect duty, because the contributor chooses at his or her own discretion when and to whom to give. Public administrators in most organizations have less discretion than directors of private firms, so the private company may be better suited to exemplify imperfect duties such as that of contributing to charities.

It would be easy for the director to avoid a decision about contributing because of the potential for betraying the faith of investors with their money. However, although directors of a corporations are to some degree restricted by their legal and moral obligations to investors, one must not assume that investors themselves recognize no moral obligations. The director may, at least to a limited degree, act as the moral conscience of the investors in deciding how they can best perform their imperfect duties. They, as a class, cannot make such a decision.

One might argue, further, that the director has an obligation to make charitable contributions on behalf of investors when he or she is not sure that they would approve, even in some cases in which they may object. If the director, on the basis of sound reasons, believes that contribution in one instance or another is extremely warranted, he or she may make a decision that he or she is certain that they morally should make, even though they might not have chosen it. The director would thus function as a moral exemplar for the investors as well as for the entire organization.

The case of the director suggests that the private businessperson's exemplarship is notably different from that of the public administrator. The public administrator's profession is founded on the public good, and he or she is therefore a moral agent by profession. His or her professional activities are motivated by the public value that his or her agency serves. In essence, the public administrator's moral agency is required professionally and is thus a defined, perfect duty, for the private businessperson's organization is, in most cases, motivated and maintained by profit. The private businessperson, therefore, is not a moral agent on account of his or her profession but only on account of his or her private initiative.

The private businessperson therefore chooses moral exemplarship opportunities that are not professionally required. In contrast to the public administrator, the moral agent in private business decides on the right time to make contributions and the right amount to give, or when and how profits should be sacrificed for social equity. The public administrator is less likely to face such decisions because he or she controls no profit.

In the ideal kingdom of ends, the businessperson, because of his or her greater opportunity to demonstrate obedience to imperfect duty, may serve as the better moral exemplar. However, we are far from the ideal, so the professionally inspired moral agency of the public administrator is most apt in contemporary society. If the public administrator completes the potential of his or her moral exemplarship and inspires greater moral agency in the culture of the private sector, the mantle could then pass from public to private.

MORAL AGENCY AND THE ATTORNEY

In discussing the legal profession in Chapter 6, we noted Applbaum's (1999, p. 109) distinction between the lawyer's role as advocate for a client and the lawyer's role as a citizen. As advocate, the attorney operates under a different set of rules and expectations in defense of the client's interest. The attorney's role as a citizen, concerned with the society, may conflict with the role of advocate. Applbaum maintains that the role of citizen is more fundamental than that of advocate and can "penetrate" it. We go somewhat further than Applbaum and argue that the two roles should be made consistent, with the role of advocate conforming to the role of citizen. Even the role of advocate is, as part of a kingdom of ends, subordinate to and justified by the moral legislation of the moral agent.

There is an evident function for the attorney in the kingdom of ends: the promotion of justice. The attorney defends his or her client to secure justice and should conduct himself or herself in accordance with justice. Dishonesty, unfair attacks on witnesses, manipulation of legal formulations, and other such tactics intended to win cases at any moral cost are unbefitting the moral agent in the legal profession. Although the private defense attorney is not under the more restrictive formal rules of the government attorney, the private attorney is under the same moral aegis.

We do not propose new formal ethical rules for attorneys. They already have enough, and perhaps even too many. But the attorney as moral agent would approach his or her profession with a different understanding from that of the pure advocate. His or her relationship with his or her client would be of a different order. Instead of a bond of mutual self-interest, the moral agent would be bound to the client by principle. In defending the client, the moral agent would defend a principle of justice that applied to the client. For example, in defending a client who may be a victim of racial profiling, the principle of racial equality would bind the attorney to the client. The attorney would be the advocate for the principle, and the client's case would exemplify that principle. It would be the legislation in the kingdom of ends to be analyzed in the debate between defense and prosecution or plaintiff and to be adjudicated by judge or jury.

Vincent Luizzi (1993, pp. 132–133) mentioned 14 possible obligations that a lawyer might genuinely recognize. Of those, we reject the last one, "to amass large sums of money that it might 'trickle down' to the needy in society," but entertain the remaining 13:

1. To promote justice
2. To engage in *pro bono* activities
3. To educate the lay about the legal system
4. To improve the legal system
5. To improve the penal system
6. To make legal services available
7. To uphold the rule of law
8. To protect the right of the state or its citizens
9. To resolve controversy or conflicts
10. To further the goals of the state
11. To further the goals of society
12. To provide leadership when possible
13. To simplify the law

In discussing the above list in Chapter 6, we noted that many of these items can be used as camouflage for self-interest. However, they can also be taken at face value as genuine values that a legislator in a kingdom of ends would pursue. The attorney who is a moral agent would recognize the morally based obligation to them.

ENCOURAGING THE PROCESS OF MORAL AGENCY IN THE HEALTH PROFESSIONS

Moral agency can be either a process or a pivotal personal choice. As we conceive it, moral agency is preferably a process, a quotidian commitment to ethical discovery, discourse, and decision, although moments of critical choice inevitably will arise in the midst of policy and professional activity. In both instances, moral agency is an essential complement to moral judgment.

It is difficult, if not impossible, to imagine the opposite of moral agency in the context of the kingdom of ends the unified ethic, or Rawls' theory of justice. What kinds of compromises, accommodations, and even surrenders, large and small, are required to strip a human being of his or her moral autonomy and his or her capacity to pose the moral question? What kinds of systemic or institutional imperatives sanction such an evisceration? Why are these expectations and behaviors seen as normal? These questions evoke the realities of power, conflict, and competing agendas that members of organizations, professions, and systems experience in their daily struggles to maintain some semblance of integrity, self-respect, and efficacy. They evoke what Dennis Thompson (1985) calls the ethic of neutrality and the ethic of structure.

Consider the health profession, particularly American managed care. Given the complexities of finance, health maintenance organizations, demographic changes, cost containment, quality, and access, even the responsible public official or health care professional may find himself or herself perplexed by the health care landscape in the early-21st-century United States. The average citizen may well be utterly bewildered. Thus, for the public official, the health care professional, and the citizen, two useful points of entry into the complicated and conflicted health care debate may be Richard Rose's (1987) emphasis on a recalcitrant policy environment and Rushworth Kidder's (1995) emphasis on common ground, instead of polemics, in sorting through intimidating policy dilemmas. Both of these approaches assume a level of trust and reciprocity that, admittedly, may not exist in some cases. But whether they exist or not, good-faith efforts are required if the ethical framework embodied in this work is to come to fruition and assist us in meeting at least some of the most formidable moral challenges of our time.

Rose (1987) suggests the substitution of a recalcitrant policy environment for mutual distrust or enmity as the linchpin in political–administrative relations. Rather than elected and appointed officials spending time and energy jockeying for position, influence, or control, they and the public interest would be better served if they focused on the policy problem at hand. Shifting their attention to the conditions that cause, exacerbate, or perpetuate the policy problem, in our view, would begin to transform elected and appointed officials, as well as corporate health care executives and physicians, from ordinary, even pedestrian, policy entrepreneurs to moral agents and public citizens, stewards of the polity. Again, however, such a transformation would require strong and sustained leadership, probably from multiple sources. In any event, targeting the policy environment as the object of ingenuity, energy, and resources may be an effective first step in a comprehensive strategy to confront the American health care dilemma.

The second step involves Kidder's (1995) proposal to try to find common ground in policy disputes. For example, even in as incendiary an issue as abortion, Kidder (1995) identifies values-based common ground between the pro-choice and pro-life camps. Through a brief, imaginary scenario, he suggests that both sides believe that life is sacred, neither supports murder, and each advocates freedom of choice and women's equality. Therefore, he asks where the disagreement is, and he asserts that it lies in the definition of the point at which life begins — a divisive and perhaps unanswerable difference on which civil and informed debate may eventually shed more light than heat — at least at the values level.

The search for common ground is essential to the concept of legislation in a kingdom of ends, which respects all human beings equally. Though one might be thoroughly convinced of the moral correctness of his or her position and recognize people as ends in themselves, as residents of a kingdom of ends, and as legislators in that kingdom, one must respect the free, responsible opinions of others. Within the context of that kingdom, compromise is neither weakness of commitment to one's own principles nor betrayal of them to maintain one's own popular standing but, rather, recognition of the equal moral rights of other members of a society.

So it is, then, that as a modest but important initial step, we envision a series of broad-based national and regional fora, including patients, health care providers, insurance company and public officials, health policy experts, and interested citizens, animated by moral as well as economic and ideological concerns, and focused on the wisdom and justification of the present health care system in comparison to other systems in the advanced democracies. Just as pro-choice and pro-life advocates in the abortion controversy may find common ground, so, too, may health care antagonists reach at least a preliminary agreement on which further concord might be attained in the struggle to resolve the value-laden issues in health care, such as access, profit, and patient, as well as physician, autonomy. It is the recalcitrant policy environment that must be targeted, including the entrenched perspectives and privileges that obstruct original thinking, creative approaches, and viable solutions to one of the largest moral challenges in the contemporary United States.

HIGHER EDUCATION IN THE CONTEXT OF THE KINGDOM OF ENDS

One might argue that American higher education, despite its putative commitment to intellectual and institutional probity, displays the same kind of moral ambiguity and confusion found in the other professions explored in this book. However, those who find the present arrangements salutary may balk at the suggestion that things have gone awry in the academy. Thus, as in the other professional realms we have explored, agreement on higher education's mission and operations has, at least on some level, frayed or even unraveled. Nonetheless, this lack of consensus, let alone unanimity, emphasizes the importance — even urgency — of addressing what some might characterize as higher education's hypocrisy or, at best, moral banality.

However, in all fairness, higher education functions in an extraordinarily complex environment that presents to both administrators and faculty a panoply of perplexing problems. These problems can be organized in binary fashion, with the first set being problematic but probably manageable and the second set being morally dubious, if not bankrupt. For example, the first set of problems includes the partnerships that many universities have entered into with government and industry. These partnerships involve legal issues, research practices, and faculty–university relations. Although these issues and others often raise significant ethical concerns, with proper oversight we suggest that the university is still able to do the good work that is central to its mission.

If these partnerships are merely instances of *quid pro quo*, in which each party seeks some personal or organizational advantage, they would violate Kant's second formulation, which demands that people be treated as ends rather than means. The parties would each be using each other as means, and both would be using the taxpayers, contributors, and stakeholders as means. However, when the partnerships are undertaken to better serve the social good and thus to promote the kingdom of ends, they are morally justified.

On the other hand, Division I intercollegiate athletic programs, as currently organized, managed, and financed, are morally corrosive and belie the claims of integrity and excellence espoused by the higher education establishment. As Derek Bok (2003) points out, the conventional justifications for intercollegiate athletics simply do not stand up to scrutiny. But as he and others also note, confronting the entrenched interests behind intercollegiate sports is neither a simple nor straightforward matter. This, however, in our judgment, does not excuse inaction by administrators and faculty who are troubled by the mystique surrounding athletic programs. What it means is that organization, alliances, dialogue, and strategic measures are required if higher education wishes to achieve and maintain the coherence between campus and community that is so crucial to its future.

Like government, higher education is expected, in some fashion, to serve the public interest and like, government, higher education is in a morally critical but economically dependent position. Government provides the legal and regulatory framework in which the American market economy functions, but government relies on the productivity and prosperity of the market economy for its financial resources. It is a symbiotic relationship characterized by multiple stakeholders with multiple interests. In higher education, the situation is much the same. Colleges and universities are expected to provide the human capital needed by the economy, and in exchange, they expect to receive the financial capital to conduct their operations. This, too, is a symbiotic relationship with multiple stakeholders with multiple interests.

In a sense, universities are like monasteries that sell bread, jellies, and other commodities produced on site. Universities, too, sell their commodities in the form of knowledge, expertise, and even entertainment, and like monasteries, they are in a way in, but not of, the outside world. In the case of both monasteries and universities, therefore, one of the major challenges is to balance their respective versions or visions of the secular and the sacred. Monks and professors pursue their callings, not merely their careers, but those pursuits, particularly in the academy, necessarily entail interaction with the mundane and even the profane. Thus, especially for higher education, the salience of coherence between campus and community is especially high. We submit that the salience of coherence between our moral nature and our moral responsibilities, as reflected in the unified ethic and as manifested in our striving toward a kingdom of ends, is equally high and enduring.

Higher education has an especially important role to play in changing the ethical tenor of society toward that of a kingdom of ends. Academe is especially strongly situated to educate citizens to become moral agents. But its analyses of moral theory and its authority to pass moral judgments on political and social issues are undermined when it tolerates ethical lacunae in its own structure.

In the end, we confront the complex questions of motivation, self-interest, and organizational culture — indeed, the panoply of issues embedded in the processes of professional and institutional life. Chief among these issues is leadership, a well-mined field of study in several disciplines. According to Thomas Sergiovanni (1992), however, leadership is one of social science's greatest disappointments. Despite a half century of work, Sergiovanni (1992) argues, the "result has been a leadership literature that borders on vacuity and a leadership practice that is not leadership at all" (p. 31). In our view, whether true, partially true, or not true at all, Sergiovanni's (1992) observation illustrates the difficulty of defining and developing leadership, linking it to entrenched practices, and connecting it to a practical ethical framework that enriches the leadership conversation and encourages appropriate change.

In this book, we have provided such an ethical framework that, we believe, can ground political, administrative, and professional leadership and stimulate the design of practical proposals for change. None of this effort will be easy, nor should it be. Any proposal for different perspectives and different approaches to established expectations and patterns of behavior needs to be explained and justified. Novelty confers no special privilege or cachet. Therefore, we hope that our work will be considered seriously by professionals of every stripe and that a dialogue concerning the many issues raised here will begin in earnest. The process of civic education and civic engagement, whether for patients, students, clients, managers, or any other group, never ends.

REFERENCES

Applbaum, A. I. 1999. *Ethics for Adversaries*. Princeton, NJ: Princeton University Press.
Bok, D. 2003. *Universities in the Marketplace: The Commercialization of Higher Education*. Princeton, NJ: Princeton University Press.
Burns, J. M. 1978. *Leadership*. New York: Harper & Row.
Cooper, T. L. 1992. Conclusion: Reflecting on Exemplars of Virtue. The Moral Exemplars in Organizational Society. In *Exemplary Public Administrators*, ed. T. L. Cooper. San Francisco: Jossey-Bass.
Downs, A. 1967. *Inside Bureaucracy*. New York: Harper Collins
Gardner, H., Csikszentmihaly, M., and Damon, W. 2001. *Good Work: When Excellence and Ethics Meet*. New York: Basic Books.
Hart, D. K. 1992. The Moral Exemplars in Organizational Society. In *Exemplary Public Administrators*, ed. T. L. Cooper. San Francisco: Jossey-Bass.
Kidder, R. M. 1995. *How Good People Make Tough Choices*. New York: Fireside.
Luizzi, V. L. 1993. *A Case for Legal Ethics*. Albany: State University of New York Press.
Rose, R. 1987. Steering the Ship of State: One Tiller but Two Hands. *British Journal of Political Science*. 17(4):409–433.
Sergiovanni, T. H. 1992. *Moral Leadership: Getting to the Heart of School Improvement*. San Francisco: Jossey-Bass.
Sherwood, F. P. 1992. George B. Hartzog Jr.: Protector of the Parks. The Moral Exemplars in Organizational Society. In *Exemplary Public Administrators*, ed. T. L. Cooper. San Francisco: Jossey-Bass.

http://www.thinkexist.com/English/Author/x/Author_3141_1.htm

Taylor, C. 1982. Responsibility for Self. In *Free Will*, ed. G. Watson. Oxford: Oxford University Press, pp. 111–126.

Thompson, D. F. 1985. The Possibility of Administrative Ethics. *Public Administration Review*. 45:555–561.

10 The Public Agent as Exemplar for the Private Professional: A Dialogue

In recent years, the United States appears to some observers to have become increasingly dichotomous. On the one side are the secular, "blue state" liberals, and on the other are the more religious "red state" conservatives. We strongly suspect that the stereotypes of both groups are erroneous. More likely, most people borrow from both perspectives and fit neatly into neither class. Moreover, we believe that even those on opposite ends of the pole probably share more in common than appearances might indicate.

But whatever the state of the great divide, the ideas in this book, which argue that public administrators are model agents of an objective morality, potentially offend both sides. Conservatives may object to using public administrators as a model for anything, and liberals may shrink from the concept of a universal morality. We would like to allay the misgivings of both by demonstrating that our general position is flexible enough to accommodate both sides and the mass of humanity in between.

We demonstrate the flexibility of our perspective by showing that it can accommodate both liberal and conservative opinions, though with somewhat different consequences for each. Our demonstration will take the form of a dialogue in which Dean Geuras adopts a position that may be regarded as conservative and Charles Garofalo presents a position that may be regarded as liberal.

We agree that the public administrator serves as a model for the citizen, and we also agree that professionals are citizens and that, therefore, the public administrator's model applies strongly to them. Geuras, however, believes that professionals who are not public administrators should not always instantiate the public administrator model. Geuras argues that there are occasions in which the responsibilities of a citizen can conflict with professional responsibilities and privately held moral values. He maintains that in some such cases, though not in all, professional roles and private moral convictions may make a stronger moral claim even than that of the citizen. Charles Garofalo agrees that citizenship roles may conflict with professional roles and private moral convictions but maintains that, when such conflicts occur, the role of citizen makes a stronger moral claim than professional or private moral obligations. Geuras's position is more individualistic and libertarian in that it calls for greater moral independence of the individual from the society. Garofalo, adopting a more communitarian stance, suggests that the moral claims of the society are, in general, supreme.

We will begin by summarizing points of agreement, some of which we have already discussed, to provide the context for the dialogue. Each of us will then give his position on the areas in which they differ. We then offer some final observations concerning the similarities and differences in the positions.

POINTS OF AGREEMENT

We consider all members of the society to be citizens, even if they do not fulfill the legal requirements for citizenship. For our purposes, anyone who participates in the social organism is a citizen in the moral, if not the legal, sense. We therefore maintain that the moral demands of citizenship, as embodied in the public administrator, constitute a strong commitment for everyone to act in a manner that advances the welfare of the society. We therefore maintain that the Athenian doctrine that one should leave his or her society a better place than when one entered it applies to all members of a society. Even those who consider that doctrine overly demanding may at least agree that one must not harm the society.

There are, nevertheless, important differences between the rights or obligations of citizens who are in the public service and those who are in private employment. For example, public organizations cannot spend their own money in charitable contributions, whereas private organizations can. Public organizations cannot make a profit, but private organizations must. Public organizations are required to make all of their financial records open for public inspection, though private organizations are not always required to "open the books." Private and public organizations also differ in their hiring practices. In a private firm, an owner is free to hire a relative or friend, even without an open search, but in most public organizations, strict regulations prevent nepotism and consanguinity.

Private organizations also have the freedom to go out of business almost at will, if the owners decide to close down their venture. There are exceptional cases in which the organization is deprived of that freedom, as, for example, the case of an organization that chooses to cease operations with the sole intent of destroying a union, but for the most part, companies can commit suicide. The leaders of a public organization may retire or quit their jobs, but they cannot say, "I am tired of doing this, so let's just close up the whole shop." Private organizations exist at the pleasure of their owners, but public organizations must meet a public mandate.

Public organizations must justify their existence and their activities on the basis of the public interest. Public organizations are, at least indirectly and in some cases directly, charged by the citizenry to offer goods and services designated as valuable to the society. In contrast, private firms retain a right to make a profit on any product that the society does not explicitly forbid. Moreover, private businesses may even provide goods and services that the society as a whole may find objectionable, such as cigarettes, high-fat and otherwise generally unhealthful foods, soft-core pornography, and full-body tattoos. A state may prohibit sale of products or services deemed especially harmful, such as heroin, or morally unacceptable, such as prostitution. A state may also limit sale of some products such as prescription drugs or alcoholic beverages. Nevertheless, there is a strong presumption on the behalf of the right of an individual or group to provide goods and services for profit, in the absence of sound reasons for prohibition or limitation. That presumption is implicit in deeper rights such as the right to freedom of expression and the right to employment in one's chosen profession.

A public organization cannot, without betraying the public trust, sacrifice the interests of the society for those of the organization. Although, to be realistic, organizations have a tendency to become ends in themselves, as in the case of goal displacement, and in various other ways make self-interested choices, such behavior is considered ethically flawed, though perhaps common and natural. As we noted earlier, a private entrepreneur can openly assert that his or her policies are justified by the need to make a profit, but public organizations can not use such justification for their policies.

Moreover, a private organization may, within the bounds of ethics, take actions that maximize profits rather than the public interest. For example, a diversified industry may choose to invest in a profitable business that makes Halloween costumes rather than in a less profitable business that produces environmentally friendly automobile engines. The private organization can choose self-interest over the social good, but a public agency cannot.

Private firms can also act in a manner that public agencies may deem unacceptable under their public charge. For example, a pharmaceutical company may spend enormous resources to find a cure for a rare but not fatal condition, such as albinism. When the cure is found, it is extremely expensive, so that only wealthy potential parents can afford it and health insurance providers generally do not cover it. The medicine helps very few people, nearly all of whom are wealthy. Public funds are unlikely to be expended on such a medicine, because it would be expensive, needed by only a few, and unless subsidized, available only to the financial elite — a clientele that private companies may welcome. Even if, however, a society were to consider the conquest over albinism to be a goal worthy of vast public resources, there would undoubtedly be other challenges that the company would leave to the private sector, such as finding a potion that, when administered in a prenatal stage, would assure the fetus of "natural" blond hair for at least 80 years.

A private corporation would be within its rights to adopt policies that are better for its employees but worse for the community. For example, a company that supplies automobiles for its employees may decide that hybrid cars may be more environmentally friendly than less expensive conventional cars. The company concludes that it could, by reducing potential salary increases, purchase the more expensive models without harming profits or productivity. Nevertheless, out of obligation to employees, the corporation chooses to sacrifice cleaner air rather than salaries. A public agency would be on weaker moral ground in making such a sacrifice of the very public interest that the agency exists to serve.

Private professionals often have yet stronger moral obligations that conflict with those of citizenship. Earlier, we discussed the obligation of an attorney to defend the rights of his client, even at the expense of the social interest. That obligation finds part of its source, at least in the American tradition, in inalienable human rights, some of which are stipulated in the Bill of Rights of the Constitution of the United States. Those rights are retained even when their exercise is not in the best interests of the society.

Although in most cases, private firms retain more freedom than do public organizations, there are some areas in which the private company or corporation is more restricted than the public agency. Antitrust laws limit the ability of a private firm to overwhelm its competition and thus become a monopoly. There is no requirement that the public organization, which provides service without profit, allow competition. In many cases, competition with a public organization would be extremely unlikely. It is difficult, for example, to imagine a private, for-profit organization competing with the public welfare agency to provide free benefits to the impoverished. The public agency might hire a private firm to assist in areas such as research, delivery of benefits, and actuarial services, but there is no profit to be made in giving money away.

The differences between private and public organizations with respect to their members' obligations to the interests of the society can be divided into two general categories: freedoms that private organizations have but that public organizations lack, and obligations that private organizations have or their members have but that do not encumber public organizations in their pursuit of the public interest. The first category includes the freedoms that private firms have to produce goods and services without having to establish their importance to the public welfare.

The second category is more complex. It includes obligations that private organizations have to their clientele. Those obligations range from the responsibility of a law firm toward the people whom it defends to the duty of a purveyor of pornographic movies toward the privacy of its customers. Public agencies have obligations to their clientele, also, but those obligations are of a different nature. The public agency may be obligated to a specific clientele, such as people living in public housing, but the source of the obligation is the public at large, which has seen fit to fund the agency and its charge. The private firm is obligated directly to its clientele and not through the primary obligation to the society as a whole. In some cases, the private firm's obligation is assumed as a result of a contract or agreement with the client. In other cases, as in the example of the attorney defending a client's right to privacy, the agreement may derive from rights that the client has independent of any agreement and prior to it.

The employee of a private firm also has an obligation to the firm itself. In entering into an employment agreement with a private entity, one assumes a responsibility to the employer that is distinct from any that the employee has as a citizen. The obligation of citizenship existed before the new obligation was assumed. The public employee also has an obligation to his or her employer, but that obligation cannot conflict with any other obligation that the public employee has to the society. The public agent's employer is the society itself.

GEURAS: THE PUBLIC ADMINISTRATOR AS CITIZEN EXEMPLAR MODEL DOES NOT FULLY APPLY TO THE PRIVATE SECTOR

We have argued that the public administrator is a model for the citizen. It might therefore be natural to suppose that, as virtually all members of the society are, in a general sense, citizens, the public administrator's model should apply to everyone. One's professional status, it may be argued, is secondary to his or her citizenship. I argue, however, that the responsibilities of a citizen do not always overrule one's professional responsibilities. There is, I maintain, no universal trump of one type of responsibility over the other.

I distinguish the moral responsibility of the citizen from moral responsibility in general. The responsibilities of citizenship are undoubtedly among the most serious of all. Socrates cited his high esteem for the notion of citizenship as a major reason for refusing to escape Athens to avoid execution. However, as our unified ethic implies, moral values form a very complex whole. Moral dilemmas can occur in which the values of citizenship, and thus one's responsibility to promote a good society, may conflict with other moral values.

Herman Melville's short story "Billy Budd" has been interpreted as pondering the conflict between civil responsibilities and deeper moral claims. Aside from any literary interpretation, however, I argue that such conflicts can exist. Suppose for example, that Jane, a citizen, agrees that capital punishment would reduce the crimes for which it is used as a deterrent. Those crimes may include anything from mass murder to drug possession, but in any case, Jane believes that the imposition of death is effective. We may put aside the question of the actual effectiveness of the penalty for purposes of the example and assume that Jane is factually correct. Nevertheless, although she believes that capital punishment benefits the society, she opposes it on deeper moral grounds. She believes that human life should never be taken under any conditions. Her responsibility to her moral convictions clashes with her responsibility as a citizen to the interests of the society.

A public administrator may also find himself in a citizenship–morality dilemma. Jake, a manager of a public organization, discovers that an older employee, who is becoming increasingly less productive, might, in the public interest, be replaced by a younger, less expensive, and more capable prospect. Jake, however, recognizes a moral responsibility to the employee, as a Kantian end in itself.

Though the cases of Jane and Jake are similar, there is still a difference between them. In both cases, a moral value placed on a human being is in conflict with a social good. In both cases, the obligations of citizenship are under pressure from another obligation. However, Jake's case is different in that he has a stronger obligation to the social interest than Jane. Both have the responsibilities of citizenship that all members of the society share. But Jake has an additional measure of the responsibility to the interests of the society because he works for the state. His professional activities are funded by the society, and he is working under a public charge. He thus has an increased moral burden to serve the interests of the society as a whole. His professional life expresses and represents the interest of the public, but Jane represents only herself and her own moral commitments.

If conflicts between the citizenship role and other moral values can occur, in general, they can also occur with a professional context. We have noted the possible conflicts between the role of citizen and the role of professional in the case of the attorney–client relationship, but similar conflicts can occur between the doctor's citizenship role and his or her relationship with his or her client. The doctor must retain confidentiality with a patient regarding his or her HIV status. The doctor may advise the patient against unprotected sex, but if the patient engages in such activity, the doctor cannot betray confidence with the patient even to protect the client's sexual partners.

Journalists may also find themselves in conflicts between their citizenship and other moral principles. A journalist may, for example, interview a terrorist enemy of the state to give him or her the opportunity to make his or her case to the very public that he or she threatens. The journalist has a responsibility as a citizen to reveal as much information as he or she has concerning the terrorist's location but has a journalistic responsibility to keep such information confidential.

Private corporations also have citizenship–professionalism conflicts. Patent laws are intended to protect the rights of private organizations to profit on items from pharmaceuticals to computer components, which would benefit the general public more if they were more available. Managers may find themselves in the position of choosing between their own rights to profit — to which they are entitled — and the public's best interest.

The conflicts that we have described can be construed in several different ways. In one way, the conflicts may be understood not as moral dilemmas but as cases of moral temptation, in which public interest constitutes morality and private interest constitutes temptation. However, this interpretation does not take into account the moral aspects of the reasons for acting against public interest. The doctor and attorney act out of professional ethics rather than self-interest in protecting the rights of their charges. Even the business executive, in availing his or her company fully of the advantage of patent law, can be seen as fulfilling his or her ethical responsibility to the creative minds that produced the product in question as well as the principle of one's right to the fruits of one's own labor.

Instead of moral temptations, the cases are better understood as moral dilemmas in which both claims have a measure of validity. I do not argue that there is any hard and fast rule that justifies either siding with public interest or subordinating it to some other value. The unified ethic avoids such inflexibility. I argue only that the choice in favor of public interest, that is, the choice in favor of citizenship, is not the only morally defensible option. If so, the exemplarship of the public administrator has exceptions when applied to private professionals.

We have seen that public administrators also can find themselves in moral dilemmas when their private moral convictions conflict with those of their organizations. We recommended the Ethical Conscience Statement for that very situation. On the surface, the dilemmas in the private sector and those in the public sector would appear to be parallel, but they have one asymmetry. In the case of the public agent, both the responsibility of citizenship and the professional responsibility to the public organization can incline the agent in the same direction, whereas the agent's private morality contradicts both. For example, one's private beliefs against abortion may conflict with his or her duty to assist people in having abortions. Insofar as the agent chooses to act in favor of his or her private morality, he or she acts against both his or her profession and his or her citizenship. This is not to say that he or she would be morally wrong to do so. He or she may decide that his or her private moral views in fact outweigh his or her duties as a professional and citizen. Whether one agrees with his or her decision or not, the relevant point is that his or her citizenship and his or her profession are in accord.

The private professional, however, is often in the situation in which his or her professional duties conflict with his or her duties as a citizen. The private professional, such as the doctor protecting patients, the attorney protecting clients, or the CEO protecting the interests of stockholders, would find his or her moral justification in responsibilities to individuals that make demands against his or her citizenship. He or she need not, and perhaps cannot, justify his or her professional responsibilities as deriving from his or her citizenship. They may derive from other compelling moral values.

That source in differing values is at the heart of the difference between the public agent and the private professional. The public agent's professional duties derive from the public charge. That charge may be interpreted narrowly as obeying the stated will of the public, or more broadly as choosing the good in behalf of the public. But in either case, the charge and the funding used to fulfill these duties come from the society seeking its best interests. The private firm, however, derives its moral authority over its own affairs from a different source: the right of an individual to seek his or her own professional goals and moral aims without having to justify them to a government or a social body. As a consequence, the consummate public agent is the consummate public citizen, but the private individual represents his or her own private commitments. Those who are contractually obligated to the private individual assume his or her commitments, at least in part, by virtue of the contract.

It is not surprising that the public administrator should be under a stronger public charge than the private professional. The public administrator is employed by the state to represent its interests, so the public administrator's duties as a citizen conform fully with his or her duties as a professional. Private professionals have the normal duties of all citizens, but their responsibilities to their organizations may be at variance with their social expectations. We have designated the public administrator, rather than the private professional, as the moral agent of the society precisely because of that difference.

I will instantiate the difference with a brief discussion of the Ethics Impact Statement. We believe that such statements should be required in public organizations because their ethical responsibility to the society dominates and justifies their activities. Public agencies must ensure not only that their policies do not injure the public but, moreover, that they must maximize public value.

In many cases, a private organization, such as a law firm, may well choose to adopt an Ethics Impact Statement, as long as its stipulations do not interfere with the firm's designated professional duties. However, an Ethics Impact Statement would seem out of place in some organizations, such as soft-porn movie producers, chewing gum wrapper manufacturers, designers of Halloween masks, or publishers of light comic fiction. If all businesses had to demonstrate the positive ethical effect of their activities to exist, many would be abolished.

Ethics Impact Statements may and perhaps should be embraced by at least some private firms. However, as they would be issued by private organizations, they should express the ethical values of those organizations and the professions that they represent. The Ethics Impact Statements of a law firm, a hospital, an environmental engineering firm, and a newspaper may all be very different from each other. Many of those statements would address some of the dilemmas, which we have mentioned earlier, in which the interests of the society clash with those of clients, patients, or consumers. An Ethics Impact Statement for a public organization would, and should, tend to resolve those clashes on the side of the public interest. In contrast, an Ethics Impact Statement for a private firm may, and perhaps should, have a stronger tendency to sacrifice the public interest for a moral value that the organization is charged to serve (e.g., the rights of the accused in a criminal case).

The competitive environment constitutes another, separate, reason for which Ethics Impact Statements are less appropriate for private organizations than for public organizations. Private organizations, unless they are functionally monopolies, have competition. The implementation of Ethics Impact Statements may, in some cases, damage the ability of a company to compete with other, wealthier organizations. For example, let us suppose that, in an Ethics Impact Statement, a policy is justified because it benefits workers, even though it is harmful to profits and requires that the product be sold at higher prices and lower quality. The well-motivated statement sacrifices the interests of the organization for those of the workers. However, if a competing organization imposes no such statement on itself, it could produce a better product at a lower price and thus run the more idealistic firm out of business.

One might argue that to avoid such competitive imbalance, all organizations should be required to have similar Ethics Impact Statements to accompany their policies. But who would authorize the Ethics Impact Statement, ensure that it is appropriate, implement it, and sanction violations? If a governmental agency were to oversee the document, with the authority to enforce it, the agency could exercise tremendous power over private business, to the extent of nullifying the right of the individual to control his or her own professional aspirations. Such power would perhaps be welcomed by those who consider the state as the source of rights and freedoms but would be unwelcome to those who believe that those rights and freedoms are natural or inalienable.

Problems of government control notwithstanding, the universal implementation of Ethics Impact Statements would still damage the competitive environment. Wealthy corporations would, as in the case of a statement requiring higher pay for workers, be able to sacrifice profits much more easily than smaller, poorer, and newer enterprises. Competition would suffer, and competitive environments could quickly become monopolistic.

Many of the problems that the competitive environment poses for the imposition of Ethics Impact Statements on private firms do not exist in the case of the public agency. Public agencies are, for the most part, not in competition with others that engage in the same activity and supply the same goods and services.

I would, nevertheless, encourage private firms to, when appropriate, use Ethics Impact Statements. But neither I nor a governmental agency has the moral authority to require them, specify their content, or monitor them, nor do I or a governmental agency have the moral authority to determine when they are appropriate.

Even when they are appropriate, the use of Ethics Impact Statements should best be considered supererogatory. Like private voluntary contributions, some ethically praiseworthy acts should be left to the discretion of the agent. The agent should also decide which actions are good, according to his or her own moral discernment, especially when his or her private values may conflict with the interests of the society. The public agency, however, operates under a different set of moral assumptions. It cannot conflict with social interests because it exists to serve them. Moreover, its commitment to them is not supererogatory but required.

In summary, there are three essential factors that render the public administrator's moral agency less than fully applicable to the private firm: the rights of the private individual to determine his or her own future; the requirement that public agencies serve the public interest above all other values, private, self-interested, or moral; and the competitive environment of the private firm as opposed to the noncompetitive environment of the public organization.

My conclusion is not a call for private firms to be unethical or to shun the public interest. But for the reasons that I have mentioned, the ethical framework in which private firms function is different from that of public organizations. The public agent is therefore a much better model of moral agency on behalf of the social interest than is the private firm, whose legitimate designated values may, at least in some instances, conflict with those of the society as a whole. The private firm more fully represents the values inherent to its profession, whereas the public agency represents the values of the state.

I now consider some possible objections to my position.

OBJECTION 1: I HAVE ARGUED THAT THE ROLE OF THE CITIZEN CAN CONFLICT WITH THE ROLE OF THE PRIVATE PROFESSIONAL

In response, one might grant that such a conflict can exist, that the private professional has a right to pursue his or her own interests, and that the government may have no way of legitimately removing that right but argue that I miss the point. The freedom that the private professional has can be used to secure his or her own interests, but if he or she is moral, he or she should use it, instead, for the public interest. The issue of concern is not what rights the private professional may have but what he or she should do.

Reply

I agree that the private professional should not use his or her freedom only to pursue his or her personal interest, but it does not follow that he or she should use it for the public interest. There is often a third option: The private professional may freely choose to make a decision based on morality but not public interest.

For example, let us imagine an attorney who personally believes that pornography is bad for society. He or she believes in a right of free expression, but he or she does not consider that right as legitimately protecting the pornography publisher. More specifically, he or she does not believe that his or her client, to whom he or she was assigned by a court, should be found innocent. Nevertheless, he or she considers his or her moral obligation to his or her client greater than his or her obligation to the public. The attorney therefore acts in accordance with morality, but not public interest, as he or she understands it.

Perhaps the publisher himself or herself believes that pornography is harmful to society and wishes that he or she did not feel compelled to publish such trash. Nevertheless, he or she believes so strongly in the fight of free speech that he or she publishes occasional pornographic works. He or she does so only on the belief that if no one publishes them, their creator's freedom of expression, which he or she considers a basic human right, will be eroded. On Kantian grounds, he or she concludes that his or her denial of the opportunity to publish could not be made a universal law. He or she, therefore, under his or her own moral dictates, acts in a manner that is not in the best interest of the public.

OBJECTION 2: I HAVE ARGUED THAT THE RESPONSIBILITIES OF A CITIZEN TO PROMOTE THE PUBLIC INTEREST MIGHT CLASH WITH ONE'S RESPONSIBILITIES TO HIS OR HER OWN MORAL VALUE SYSTEM

However, the objection might be made that the notion of the public interest can be construed to include all moral values. If someone believes that a practice is moral, it may be argued, he or she necessarily thinks that the act is in the public interest because acting morally is always in the public interest. Therefore, there is no conflict between the public interest and moral action.

Reply

The objection appears to employ a question-begging definition of "public interest." When one uses a question-begging definition, one renders true, by means of a questionable definition, a statement that appears to be a disputable factual claim.* For example, suppose that I make the disputable factual claim that I have never been late to class in all of my years as a professor, but a student supplies counterevidence: She recalls that I was 10 minutes late last week. I reply that I could not have been late, and could never be late, because I am the instructor and class cannot begin until I am present.

Likewise, one might make the apparently factual claim that all moral actions are in the public interest. However, someone conceives of a moral act that is not in the public interest, such as an attorney's passionate defense — based solely on the principle that defendants have a right to the strongest possible representation — of a guilty, incorrigible, and dangerous client. But the defender of the original claim replies that the attorney's act must be in the public interest because all moral actions are necessarily in the public interest. The defender of the claim has rendered the original apparently factual statement "All moral actions are in the public interest" true by definition.

One might argue that, in this case, the attorney's behavior really is in the public interest, however, because the right to legal defense is a public necessity. But if one wishes to do so, one could concoct a scenario in which any moral act can be construed as in the public interest. To avoid such interpretations that are devised to fit cases in a way that would salvage one's position, I will describe cases from the perspective of the agent of an action. I will consider the act, and all of its aspects, as an agent interprets them.

I return to the case of Jane, who opposed capital punishment although she considered it beneficial to the public as a deterrent. I will, however, alter the case somewhat. In this instance, Jane believes that capital punishment deters crime and benefits the society in all ways, but the practice is forbidden by her religion. She believes that God disallows that taking of a human life because it is sacred. For that reason alone, she opposes the practice. She believes that she must place God's will above the public interest because God is more important than the public. She believes that God will not punish others who disagree with her and support the practice because God realizes that "they know not what they do."

One might argue that capital punishment is not in the public interest if God disallows it. However, it is to avoid entanglement in such arguments that I restrict our analysis of the case to the facts as Jane sees them. From her perspective, there exists a conflict between God's will and the will and interests of the society.

But now let us remove the theology. Let us return to something more like the original case, in which Jane maintains on deontological moral grounds rather than religious grounds that capital punishment is wrong though in the best inter-

---

* A fuller discussion of this fallacy can be found in Damer (2004), *Attacking Faulty Reasoning: A Practical Guide to Fallacy Free Arguments* (Belmont, Calif.: Wadsworth).

ests of society. She would not be, at least in any obvious, noncontroversial sense, immoral to act on her moral beliefs.

The case of the military conscientious objector in a time of conscription is another, similar case. Let us suppose that the objector believes that all war is immoral. He or she concedes that a specific war is necessary for defense of the society but believes that his or her moral principles are more important than the society. He or she also agrees that the opponent in the war is a dangerous aggressor who could conquer the entire world. But he or she argues that that someone else's immoral decision to start a war does not justify a second wrong, and he or she is willing to accept all consequences of his or her pacifism. In his or her mind, the case clearly opposes the public interest and morality. He or she believes that the moral person should be willing to sacrifice all, including himself, society, and if necessary, the whole world, to be morally pure.

I can conceive of no way to dismiss all examples such as those of Jane, the pacifist, and the committed defense attorney without using a question-begging definition of "public interest."

OBJECTION 3: I HAVE ARGUED THAT THE PUBLIC ADMINISTRATOR, AS A MORAL EXEMPLAR, MUST ACT MORALLY

I have also argued that the private individual should act morally. If they both should act morally, one might ask, why should they not behave in the identical manner? Why should either one not be the exemplar for the other?

Reply

I believe that they should both act morally, but the context of the moral action is different for the public administrator and the private individual. The public administrator is employed by the public to fulfill its charge. The public administrator is therefore under an obligation, in addition to the general obligation that all citizens share, to serve the public interest. As a consequence, the public administrator must place public interest even higher on the scale of values than the common citizen. Moreover, as an agent of the public, the public administrator must defer to the values expressed by the society, even on some occasions when they differ from his or her own. This is not to say that the public agent cannot disagree with the public at large, but that he or she has a special responsibility to act in behalf of public, even in disagreeing with them. Nor do I deny that there are some occasions in which the public agent should let his or her moral values overrule those of the society, as agents of Nazi Germany or the segregationist south should have resisted their society's demands. I argue, however, that the public administrator has a greater responsibility to act as an agent of the public than does the private individual, especially when his or her legitimate professional responsibilities conflict with the public interest.

I provide one final set of examples. Suppose that the owner of a private firm discovers that one of his or her employees, who is old and infirm, is no longer functioning effectively as a professional. The employer decides, however, out of personal concern for the individual, to continue to employ him or her until he or she retires voluntarily. The employer is willing to sacrifice both profits and a portion of his or her own salary out of simple charity. He or she thus performs an act that Kant would consider an imperfect duty: He or she has a duty to be charitable in general, and he or she chooses this occasion to fulfill that duty. We may consider his or her act to be moral.

Now let us suppose that a second employee loses his effectiveness in the same way as the first. The employer would like to treat the second as charitably as the first, but his or her company cannot afford two charity cases and cannot survive if he or she treats all employees with the same indulgence with which he or she treated the first. He or she recognizes the value in treating all people equally, but in this case, equal treatment of all would entail no charity for anyone. He or she decides to continue to employ only one ineffective employee while reluctantly terminating the others.

Now let us suppose that the owner sells the company and becomes the manager of a public agency. His or her moral beliefs and attitudes remain the same, but he or she now functions in a different context. He or she is an agent of the state, and he or she is charged with the proper use of public funds. He or she discovers, within his or her agency, an ineffective employee similar to the one that he or she retained when he or she owned the company. But in this case, he or she has, in addition to and in conflict with his or her recognition of his or her imperfect charitable duty, a responsibility to ensure that the public is best served. He or she also realizes that, in a public agency, the public demands that all employees be treated equally. In this case, he or she must terminate the employee.

One might object that the manager is in different positions as an owner of a company and as a public employee. In one case, he or she owns the company and can do as he or she sees fit, but in the other, he or she is employed and must do as his or her employers see fit. I agree, and the difference is at the heart of the matter. In a public agency, the public is the owner, and for that reason, the public administrator has a special responsibility to the public that the private individual does not have.

GAROFALO'S RESPONSE

Dean Geuras and I have tried in this book to provide a moral basis for common ground and a common future between public administration and other professions, including health care, law, and higher education. We have argued that by virtue of serving the public interest, the public administrator is necessarily a moral agent and a moral exemplar. We, therefore, agree on the central features of our common purpose and perspective. But we have our differences as well. We differ, for example, on the extent to which our moral perspective — the unified ethic supplemented by the Ethics Impact Statement — applies to private and public enterprises. The important point here is that, in our collaboration, Dean and I deal with the same dilemmas as everyone else. Although we recognize that intellectual conflict in the course of writing a book is different from conflict in the policy arena, we believe that our unified ethic, along with the Ethics Impact Statement, can be of value in both venues. Therefore, in the spirit of shared moral and professional perplexities, we pull back the curtain to reveal our own struggles, to which, we suggest, our ethical perspective applies in practical and significant ways.

On the ideological level, Dean and I paint our respective stances with the broad brush of conservative and liberal. But these labels are descriptive only of general tendencies, rather than firm or absolute positions. For example, Dean is a highly unusual conservative — indeed, a highly unusual American in terms of this book — given his advocacy of bureaucrats as moral agents and moral exemplars for the rest of us, including the private sector. Most Americans — conservative, liberal, and other —will find this notion at least novel, if not strange. Nevertheless, in our work together for more than a decade, we have tried to hone our capacity for responsible and relevant reasoning and our willingness to probe the pieties and platitudes that often characterize what passes for public discourse. In our work on this book, we have attempted to transcend conventional American wisdom about government and governance by penetrating the moral life and circumstances of public administration. It will be the reader, of course, who will decide whether we have succeeded. We simply thought it was important to present our personal perspectives, at least to avoid the appearance or implication of outsized gravitas.

We tried to transcend the conventional categories of conservatism and liberalism as well, to pose moral and political questions honestly, in the context of governance and therefore, necessarily, public administration. For example, in our effort to penetrate the moral life and circumstances of public administration as an independent entity and in relation to other professions, we implicitly asked the central question of how we shall live — a question to which we return in our final chapter. This central question subsumes assumptions about whose ideas and what interests should be privileged in decisions about the distribution of resources, work, wages, nurturance of people, and a host of other intractable policy issues. Our goal in promoting the public administrator as a moral agent and moral exemplar was to provide a moral frame for consideration of these issues, moral benchmarks, and guideposts via the unified ethic, personified by public servants.

On the narrower question of whether an Ethics Impact Statement should be used by private, for-profit organizations, Dean believes that, as profit-seekers in a competitive or at least partially competitive environment, such organizations are exempt from the mandatory application of an Ethics Impact Statement, because he maintains that the private firm derives its moral authority as well as economic status from the right of an individual to seek his or her own professional goals and moral aims independent of government or any other institution. In this context, the teleological may be seen as trumping the deontological.

In contrast, although acknowledging that the state is by no means the source of our rights, I first would note the legal and institutional structure that enables the individual pursuit of professional goals and moral aims. Such pursuits do not occur in a state of nature or even in a social vacuum. Second, I ask that the logic of the competition argument be justified as a trump of the Ethics Impact Statement for private firms. More specifically, I would ask whether private firms and individuals are moral equivalents and why competition trumps morality if competition and morality are equally innate in human nature. It is also fairly easy to imagine an economic system based on cooperation, instead of competition, if one draws on different assumptions about human behavior.

On another level, I also question the logic behind approving the mandatory use of Ethics Impact Statements in the public sector but disapproving of their mandatory use in the private sector. Although these positions may seem plausible, I argue that requiring an Ethics Impact Statement in the public sector may be problematic as well, because ethics, by definition, is voluntary. I also posit that requiring an Ethics Impact Statement in the private sector may be merely analogous to economic and social regulation of business, an established constraint justified on the basis of the larger public good. Finally, in the context of so-called corporate welfare as well as increasing privatization, I suggest that companies and contractors who accept public funds also must accept public responsibility. The policy of profits without principles, including a commitment to moral agency, is not legitimate or justifiable public policy. A company that participates in governance is responsible to the public interest as well as its shareholders.

These differences exemplify our broader positions on rights and responsibilities. As an individualist, Dean tends to emphasize rights over responsibilities. As one who leans toward the communitarian perspective, I place equal value on rights and responsibilities. In my view, rights are exercised in a context, which means that rights carry implications and consequences for both the rights-holder and for others. It also means that the rights-holder is obligated to consider those implications and consequences before exercising the right in question. One need only recall the many tragedies of the commons to realize that it is not possible to create the kingdom of ends, a community founded on reciprocity and reconciliation, if individual autonomy and rights routinely take precedence over shared responsibilities. More concretely, we have all experienced the standard neighborhood nuisances of barking dogs, loud music, and boisterous parties.

On one level, this balance of rights and responsibilities may be a simple matter of common courtesy. I may have a right to speak, but that right is legitimately curtailed if my speaking would disturb others in a theater. On another level, the balance of rights and responsibilities is more complicated if, for example, the rights and responsibilities of institutions are invoked. Here, we can refer to the historic debate in the United States over government regulation of business and industry or private conduct. In a market economy, determining the proper balance between regulation and *laissez faire* is a perennial challenge. Thus, although Dean and I champion the public administrator as a moral agent and moral exemplar, and although we agree that the roles of citizens and professionals may conflict, we disagree on the breadth and depth of the moral claim attached to the public interest, as exemplified by the Ethics Impact Statement. Although

Dean would exempt private companies, including cigarette manufacturers, pornographers, and fast food vendors, from the Ethics Impact Statement on the basis of individual rights, I would seek to ground these rights in broader social responsibilities.

The challenge of determining the appropriate balance between rights and responsibilities is difficult on the individual as well as institutional level. In fact, it is tantamount to determining the nature and content of the public interest. For example, Dean cites the hypothetical cases of Jane and Jake, who, respectively, are grappling with the death penalty and firing an older worker. He suggests that Jane's responsibility to her moral convictions clashes with her responsibility as a citizen to society's interest, and he suggests a similar concern with Jake, who is faced with the decision of whether to replace an older employee. In my opinion, there is a discrepancy in Dean's view of individual rights vis-à-vis citizen responsibilities and of the values to be served by the public administrator.

On the first point, Dean appears to believe that Jane's responsibility to society requires her to support the death penalty. If true, then this juxtaposition of her moral convictions and her social responsibilities presents a false dichotomy. On a deeper level, it may well be that Jane's moral convictions are actually consonant with society's fundamental interest. In Jane's case, it would be entirely plausible for a death-penalty opponent to insist that society does not benefit from state-sanctioned murder and to argue that it is in society's interest not to permit the death penalty.

On the second point — the values to be served by the public administrator — the moral nuances and subtleties of Jake's problem need further reflection. Again, one might ask what the public interest entails and how the public interest would be served by firing the older employee. It would be equally plausible in this situation to assert that the public interest entails treating the older employee as an end in himself and that, therefore, firing the older employee, like the death penalty, is not in the public interest. More specifically, as a public administrator, Jake may need a reminder of what values he is obligated to serve. I maintain that the public administrator is obligated to serve two sets of values: instrumental values such as efficiency, effectiveness, and economy; and moral and constitutional values such as equality, freedom, and justice. When these two sets of values are conflated, dilemmas arise that require both a practical moral framework — the unified ethic — and a method for applying the unified ethic to particular problems — the Ethics Impact Statement.

Moral as well as political resolution of these kinds of questions requires discernment, discretion, and discipline. Such questions typify what public administrators face daily as they seek to meet their responsibilities to the rest of us. Embedded in these responsibilities are moral agency and moral exemplarship, the duty to serve the public interest and to embody the values of a democratic polity. But if public administrators are to act effectively and honorably as moral agents and moral exemplars, they need our trust, regardless of our individual political preferences or interests.

As the readers of this book undoubtedly know, trust in government is often described as either an endangered species or as being on life support. Survey after survey shows that trust in institutions, including government, has plummeted in the last three or four decades. The point I want to make here, however, is that both conservatives and liberals trust government, although selectively. Conservatives, for example, tend to trust national security and law enforcement agencies, whereas liberals tend to put their faith in human and social services agencies. In both cases, there is some level of recognition that public servants are performing functions consistent with our conception of a responsible and humane society. Thus, there is some basis for seeking common ground and a common future. The key in this regard is to create a common moral framework as well as a political vocabulary that will enable us as citizens to engage each other in the public square as we try to grapple with the question of how we shall live.

SUMMARY

In our dialogue, we can identify important areas of agreement. We both accept the unified ethic, we both recognize that there are differences between the public and private environments in which that ethic applies, and we both agree that the public administrator has a special role as a moral exemplar for the citizen. Dean, however, recognizes a limit to the application of that role when it conflicts with personal or professional moral values, whereas Charles applies the role more generally.

The specific differences between us can be reduced to two. First, Dean recognizes a limited right of the individual, in both private life and professional capacity, to act independent of the public interest, and thus independent of the role of citizen. Charles, however, considers actions independent of the public interest to be unacceptable, even when public interest conflicts with professional demands: "The policy of profits without principles, including a commitment to moral agency, is not legitimate or justifiable public policy. A company that participates in governance is responsible to the public interest as well as its shareholders" (p. 161).

However, the difference on this matter, although vast with respect to political theory, essentially dissolves when analyzed from a moral perspective. Although Dean argues that the individual or firm has a right to act selfishly, he nevertheless maintains that, morally, it should not. The disagreement on this issue appears to concern the degree to which government can legitimately require moral behavior rather than the responsibility of individuals of firms to act morally. Moreover, although Charles argues that profits without commitment to moral principles are illegitimate, he does not argue that to be allowed to exist, firms must demonstrate that their products contribute to social morality.

The second area of disagreement regards the conflict between private or professional moral commitments and those demanded by citizenship. Dean argues that such conflicts can exist and that on some occasions, one would be justified in acting in behalf of the private values. Charles argues that if someone is acting morally, he or she necessarily acts in the public interest, because moral behavior is always in the public interest.

But even in this second case, the difference is not as pronounced as it may at first seem. Both Dean and Charles agree on the factors that are included within the moral decision and disagree only on how those factors should be categorized. The agreement and disagreement are exemplified in their analyses of the case of Jane, who believes that capital punishment is an effective deterrent but objects to it because of her moral commitment to the sanctity of life. According to Dean, her concern for the interests of society conflicts with her moral commitment to the sanctity of life. According to Charles, if she believes that the sanctity of life is more important than deterrence, she necessarily believes that the sanctity of life is in the greater public interest because morality is always in the public interest. Curiously, however, both Dean and Charles could recommend the same action on Jane's part. The difference is in whether the act is characterized as a conflict between social interest and private moral values or between two aspects of social interest. There is no evident difference between Dean and Charles, however, concerning what Jane should do.

The difference between Dean and Charles appears to concern theoretical matters pertaining to the authority of government and the definition of the public interest. But when Dean and Charles apply the unified ethic, albeit within their own theoretical frameworks, they make essentially identical moral recommendations with respect to personal and professional behavior.

We therefore conclude the dialogue in harmony. Although Dean's position is conservative and Charles's is liberal, the unified ethic and the notion of the public administrator as moral exemplar can be accommodated to both perspectives with largely the same result. The unified ethic, in its application to the concept of the public administrator as moral exemplar, thus demonstrates the flexibility to adapt to a range of political theoretical perspectives.

We do not wish to minimize the difference, because theoretical matters are important in themselves. Although we both agree that the public administrator has a special role as a moral exemplar, Dean's emphasis is on the word "special," whereas Charles's emphasis is on the word "exemplar." From Dean's more individualistic perspective, the public administrator's exemplarship is special in that it applies to one major factor in the moral life of the individual — his or her citizenship — but not to the entire individual, who may have other personal and professional values. For Dean, people are, first and foremost, individuals and secondarily citizens. For Charles, people are individuals and citizens equally. For Dean, the public administrator is an exemplar for the civic aspects of our moral life; for Charles, those civic aspects define our moral life.

Our differences illustrate to some degree the difficulty of creating common ground and the common good to deal with the intractable but, we hope, potentially resolvable public policy challenges that we face. These differences also illustrate that common ground cannot be created by sheer force of intellectual argument, but morally informed dialogue in pursuit of common ground may modify presuppositions and move contending parties and positions closer together. However, our common acceptance of the unified ethic and the concept of the public administrator as a moral exemplar provide a framework for consideration and debate that may eventually lead to richer understanding, if not reconciliation.

11 Common Ground, Common Future

INTRODUCTION

Reform, under any circumstances, is widely known to be one of the more challenging aspects of governance. The difficulties associated with reform, ranging from the adoption of untested, unwarranted, or even unwise premises; inertia; incentives; uncertainty; speculative benefits and immediate costs; technical and measurement problems; and political–administrative relations, have been amply documented. These difficulties, combined with extravagant claims, exaggeration, and simplistic solutions presented by reformers, can produce many intended and unintended consequences alike. Therefore, reform must be understood for what it actually is — a political act, not merely a technical exercise — and for what it can be expected to accomplish.

In recent years, we have experienced what Donald Kettl (2002) calls the transformation of governance and the global public management revolution (Kettl, 2003). This transformation and revolution, which appear to be permanent fixtures of the global landscape, entail multiple challenges for public administration, including privatization, new public management, and performance measurement as well as multiple issues related to such concerns as accountability, shadow bureaucracy, and organizational cultures. However, the subject of this book — moral agency and citizenship — has generally been omitted from reform proposals and programs, as well as academic analysis and critique. Therefore, our goal in this chapter is to advance the case for the public administrator as a moral agent/moral exemplar in a covenant with citizens. We contend that in the midst of this complexity and uncertainty, there is common ground, a common identity, across the public and private sector that can be sustained by meeting our collective need for moral exemplars and for active citizenship in search of community, or what Kant called "the kingdom of ends."

We do not, however, gloss over the many dilemmas and divisions found in all polities. Ideological, professional, cultural, and other differences cannot be denied or suppressed and are likely to endure regardless of the system in place and the governance patterns in practice. What we do suggest is that the conversation concerning our collective values, aspirations, and assumptions can be enriched via consideration of moral agency and moral citizenship, and that those differences might then be subjected to the kind of moral scrutiny that will lead to their mitigation. In the end, moral agency is to be enacted not only by public administrators but by citizens across the spectrum. This is what common ground and common future means.

It may seem ironic, at least in the American context, that public administrators should be promoted as moral exemplars, in light of public administration's status in the United States. Cynical citizens and high-status professions such as law and medicine are being asked to emulate bureaucrats because bureaucrats embody our fundamental values, our public philosophy, and therefore the common ground across American society. But although Americans tend to see politics and government as self-serving and even corrupt, and although greater legitimacy is ascribed to elected than appointed officials, it is also true that most Americans still hold their political institutions in high regard. More important, for our purposes, public administrators have sworn an oath that, in one form or another, includes the commitment to serve as a professional citizen and moral exemplar. Thus, given the power of their oath and its attendant moral obligations, public administrators, particularly in the midst of global challenge and perplexity, can provide the moral compass and gyroscope needed for direction and stability, continuity and integrity. This chapter aims to show how this might happen.

REQUIREMENTS FOR REFORM

There are three proximate conditions that must be met for moral reform in public administration and society to be achieved: adaptation of the principles of the Blacksburg Manifesto, alteration of political–administrative relations, and investment in change. Admittedly, these conditions pose difficult questions for reform, but our promotion of public administrators as moral agents and moral exemplars is by no means an exercise in mere status-seeking. On the contrary, as we argued earlier, public administration is inherently moral, and therefore our position may be seen simply as a call for transparency in governance — a transparency that acknowledges the moral nature of public administration and the attributes required to practice and share it with all citizens.

ADAPTATION OF THE PRINCIPLES OF THE BLACKSBURG MANIFESTO

According to Gary Wamsley and colleagues (1990), the Blacksburg Manifesto is similar in a number of respects to the 1968 Minnowbrook Conference and George Frederickson's (1980) *The New Public Administration*, which captures the spirit of Minnowbrook. In brief, the Manifesto and Minnowbrook share a commitment to greater social equity, a concern for wider participation, and a desire to move values and norms to the center of administrative theory and practice. However, Manifesto adherents argue, Minnowbrook's focus on individual administrators signaled a failure to address the need to consider social constructs as well. As structuralists or neo-institutionalists, the Manifesto authors emphasize social change from both ends of the structural–individual continuum. The Blacksburg Perspective is an institutionally grounded Minnowbrook, especially in its acceptance of authority as an inescapable aspect of society, its concern with governance in a constitutional system, and its commitment to discovering and revitalizing the public interest.

Just as the Blacksburg Manifesto and Minnowbrook share common ground, so does our position share features with both. We, too, are concerned with governance, the public interest, and civil society. But just as the Blacksburg Manifesto reflects an effort to move beyond Minnowbrook, our position reflects an effort to move beyond Blacksburg by building on the Manifesto's emphasis on values and norms as the heart of public administration. Because we have detailed the nature and purpose of moral agency and citizenship in public administration, both in this volume and in an earlier work, and have acknowledged the value of the Blacksburg Perspective (Garofalo and Geuras, 1999), we will simply summarize our argument: The Blacksburg Manifesto is a significant contribution to normative public administration; however, it lacks an explicit moral foundation. But, as we have also argued (Garofalo and Geuras, 1999), "taken together, the normative goals of the Blacksburg Manifesto and what we will label our integrated objective ethics, can provide a basis for moral agency" (p. 21).

With the Blacksburg Manifesto and our unified ethic as a backdrop, we now turn to the concept of the moral exemplar, drawing from the work of David K. Hart (1992). In "The Moral Exemplar in an Organizational Society" (1992), Hart maintains that "moral exemplars are essential for a good society" (p. 11) and that they "give confidence in public leadership . . . serve as moral guides, and . . . provide a necessary encouragement for individual moral development" (p. 13). Furthermore, Hart identifies the characteristics that distinguish moral exemplars, beginning with the notion that "good moral character must be a constant aspect of the personality of the exemplar. . . . Second, the exemplar must act intentionally and freely; there can be no compulsion involved. Third, the exemplar must be relatively faultless; he or she need not be perfect in *all* things but must always strive for virtue in *most* things. Finally, the actions of the exemplar must bring about real good, even in failure: one's moral actions must never be frivolous" (p. 15).

These are the qualities of the honorable person and the honorable public servant who comes into being through intentional moral action. Although for clarity and consciousness, moral exemplars in public administration ideally ground their decisions and actions in the Blacksburg Manifesto–unified ethic framework, we recognize that moral voices develop and are heard via a variety of traditions and experiences, as exemplified by George C. Marshall, C. Everett Koop, William D. Ruckelshaus, and the other less-celebrated individuals discussed in *Exemplary Public Administrators* (Cooper and Wright, 1992). The important point is the presence of conscience and conviction in service of the public interest.

POLITICAL–ADMINISTRATIVE RELATIONS

The second proximate condition that must be met for moral reform of governance to be achieved is the alteration of political–administrative relations. Our contention, in the spirit of the Blacksburg Manifesto, is that we will have arrived at political maturity when administrators can speak to truth and to power and have their question or objection seen as a second thought rather than an act of sabotage. Therefore, this section explores moral agency and moral citizenship in the context of the hoary politics–administration dichotomy.

Political–administrative relations are at the heart of modern governance. In the context of conventional democratic theory, traditional academic treatments of political–administrative relations tend to focus on bureaucratic discretion, bureaucratic participation in the policy process, and the influence of interest groups on legislative and administrative actors. These treatments also tend to be unidirectional, with administrators identified as the targets of concern, consternation, or reform. The elected official's position is inviolate, sanctioned, and even sacrosanct, whereas the bureaucrat's position is suspect, dubious, and even diabolic. Election or political appointment is assumed to confer a moral status or legitimacy that places the legislator or appointee beyond the pale of criticism. Regardless of the representative nature or size of a politician's electoral strength, it bestows moral and functional superiority over the public administrator. The problem, however, is that several essential questions continue to be unasked, let alone answered. For example, what are the basic goals and consequences of political–administrative relations with respect to the quality of governance? What differences do the variations in political–administrative relations make for the challenges of governance? How will altering political–administrative relations affect governance?

The scholarly literature on political–administrative relations offers a rich and detailed description of institutional circumstances across many countries, individual incentives and advantages, models of bureaucratic behavior, and the skills and strategies associated with one type of arrangement or another — in other words, the vast array of characteristics and conditions constituting this major insiders' game (Aberbach et al., 1981; Smith, 1984; Rose, 1987; Campbell, 1988; Peters, 1995; Dunn, 1997; Svara, 1999; Israel, 2002; Mouritzen and Svara, 2002; Smith and Millick, 2002; Lee, 2002, Wilson and Barker, 2003). Seldom, however, are questions asked about the effect of this game on the quality of governance and the lives of citizens. Although the skill, capacity, and commitment of ministers and high-level civil servants are occasionally invoked as salient issues in reform initiatives as well as established practices, the moral and policy consequences for citizens and for governance of the various permutations of political–administrative relations tend to be absent from the academic literature.

Two exceptions that prove the rule are Richard Rose (1987) and B. Guy Peters (1995). Rose (1987) prefigures Svara's (1999) concept of complementarity by arguing that "the differences between politicians and higher civil servants are not proof of a dilemma, in which a choice is forced between rule by ineffective elected officeholders, or effective but unrepresentative higher civil servants. . . . Differences can be the basis for an exchange, to the mutual advantage of both politicians and civil servants" (p. 410). From a normative standpoint, however, dangers loom, for "the terms of trade in this exchange can be viewed in contrasting ways," including the "village life in Whitehall" perspective. In that instance, politicians and civil servants constitute a single community "maintained by consensus about informal norms, and by the exclusion of awkward outsiders" (p. 410). If those awkward outsiders happen to be citizens, then the potential for abuse in this cozy relationship is painfully obvious.

But an equally significant point that touches on the quality of governance concerns infiltrating or interpenetrating the civil service. In Rose's (1987) view, if politicians are to give effective direction to government, then they need more knowledge of the government for which they are responsible. Seeking such knowledge by infiltrating or interpenetrating civil service ranks "shows a readiness to respect and listen to civil servants, which tends to be lacking in measures that exploit weaknesses . . . or that ignore strengths" (Rose, 1987, p. 424). The aim of this process includes symbiosis, not capture; more nuanced understandings of political energy and administrative equilibrium; and an end to adversarial relations. "Instead of ministers being in opposition to civil servants, a recalcitrant policy environment becomes the adversary" (p. 426). Implicit in Rose's (1987) position is a more responsible, reciprocal, and respectful relationship between elected officials and bureaucrats. The missing ingredient is an explicit moral perspective that includes citizens.

Peters (1995), in speculating about the purpose of the politics–administration dichotomy, suggests that it allows administrators to participate in organizational, as opposed to partisan, politics, without being held accountable for the outcomes of their actions. He believes that, in the guise of legal or technical rationality, administrators can engage in policy making, avoid political interference in their decisions, and make unacceptable decisions more palatable to the public. But politicians, too, benefit from the dichotomy, particularly in influencing difficult decisions made by bureaucrats who are not electorally accountable. Rather than remove political influence, the separation of political and administrative functions simply makes it harder for citizens to identify or control.

We can conclude, therefore, that both bureaucrats and politicians are parties to deception of citizens and that both are selective in their application of democratic theory. In this sense, political–administrative relations might be characterized as an artful arrangement designed to promote the comfort and convenience of political and administrative actors at the highest levels rather than the development and participation of citizenship. Peters (1995), however, only hints at the meaning of this artifice for the quality of governance, and he provides no remedies in his discussion.

Like theory, ethics is perceived by many as of little or no value in the real world of governance. However, like theory, ethics is embedded in both political and administrative practice and is, therefore, inseparable from governance. Practitioners do not function without theory or moral purpose, and scholars must maintain a morally informed connection with practice. Thus, practitioners and scholars, ideally, promote a collaborative relationship involving moral as well as theoretical critique, understanding, and cooperative building and blending of theory and practice.

Integrity, intelligence, and imagination in governance can be enhanced if practitioners and scholars alike are active, morally alert critics of conventional wisdom. A key element of enhanced integrity, intelligence, and imagination in governance is the moral point of view. The moral point of view in political and administrative thought, choice, and action includes justification, the provision of good reasons as opposed to only efficiency and expediency, and the application of judgment to technical and political expertise. For the political or administrative practitioner, it means functioning as a critical thinker rather than an ideologue or passive instrument of the status quo.

The purpose of applying the moral point of view is to discover the underlying moral content and moral categories of political and administrative thought and practice, not to superimpose arbitrary rules. Moreover, ethical theory must be practical. It must help practitioners make sense of their situations, it must be explicable in ordinary language, and it must be testable through experience. Accordingly, the theorist's essential responsibility is not to his or her career or profession or theoretical elegance but, rather, to the moral nexus shared with the practitioner and thus to the power and probity of public service.

Both legislators and administrators are moral agents and, therefore, moral exemplars for private citizens, although in different ways, as noted earlier in this book. In principal-agent theory, an agent is a person who acts in behalf of another, the principal. In the public arena, agents have multiple principals. The legislator, for example, is the agent of the district from which he or she is elected, the voters who supported him or her, campaign contributors, interest groups, his or her party, and by extension, his or her country. Public administrators, too, have multiple principals or constituencies, including legislators, interest groups, and private citizens. In both cases, multiple principals mean conflicting priorities and the exercise of discretion and judgment.

Multiple principals, therefore, signify complexity. But a deeper issue arises when an agent acts in behalf of an abstract principal such as morality itself. If, as we noted in Chapter 1, a person believes that he or she is morally obligated, apart from or in addition to obligations to individuals or institutions, then morality becomes his or her principal. Morality as a principal, however, enjoys a different status from other principals. When conflicting principals impose conflicting priorities on an agent, morality is not simply one among many to be balanced against the others. Morality becomes the paramount principal.

The moral agent expresses concern for moral values as ultimate ends, meaning that moral values leaven self-interest in the pursuit of moral objectives, such as the promotion of equality. But moral agency extends beyond individuals to organizations as well. Moral organizations have a moral mission and strive to achieve morally justified goal; an example is public agencies that exist to serve values that society considers significant enough to support through political and economic means. In the end, however, legislators and public administrators are not ideal or morally perfect public officials, but flesh-and-blood individuals who, by virtue of their respective roles and responsibilities, are required to make moral choices for and with the rest of us.

We turn now to James Svara's (1999) complementarity model, which seeks to advance our understanding of American political–administrative relations but could apply to any political culture. Like Rose's (1987) concept of political interpenetration of the civil service, complementarity acknowledges the value of mutual respect, reciprocity, and responsibility between politicians and bureaucrats. The problem is no longer adversarial political–administrative relations but, in Rose's (1987) words, "a recalcitrant policy environment" (p. 426).

The fundamental question, however, still remains unanswered: What difference do more cooperative political–administrative relations make in the lives of citizens? Like other scholars, Svara (1999) contributes to our understanding of political–administrative relations but fails to address directly the significant challenge concerning their connection to the quality of governance. Even if politicians and administrators communicate, cooperate, and coordinate in textbook fashion, citizen-centered or higher-quality governance will not necessarily result. Therefore, something more is needed than the recognition of political–administrative interdependence if we wish to broaden the debate to include the voices of citizens as well as the interactions of insiders, specialists, and policy entrepreneurs.

What is needed is a commitment to moral agency and moral citizenship. These elements add a critical feature to political–administrative relations and policy discourse, namely, active, explicit attention to the moral dimensions inherent in the decisions and actions that affect citizens in particular and governance in general. Inquiry into the principles and values at stake in deliberations about possible policy responses to particular problems becomes as routine in political–administrative relations as identifying the salient interests involved.

From this perspective, complementarity can be justified on both moral and practical grounds. It is more in keeping with respect for human dignity and responsible autonomy than the timeworn politics–administration dichotomy, however conceived, and the truncated, impoverished administrative role is replaced by reciprocity, respect, and legitimacy. On the practical level, it can facilitate more effective design and delivery of public policy to citizens, as elected officials and administrators simultaneously serve as agents of the public interest and of particular constituencies. The dialectic between the ideal and the real persists until the two are virtually indistinguishable.

But shifting political–administrative relations in theory and practice from an insiders' game to a morally conscious, citizen-centered process requires more than general prescriptions and proscriptions. What is needed, in addition to moral agency and moral citizenship, is a genuine level of trust in and of government. Without trust in the integrity of public officials and institutions, morally informed renewal of governance is unlikely — thus, the importance of moral exemplars. However, trust is difficult to create and easy to damage or even destroy. Indeed, institutions across the spectrum, including universities, corporations, medicine, and the media as well as government, have experienced a decline in trust.

According to Kenneth Ruscio (1996), "The decline in trust is due to the growing perception that elected officials, administrators, and citizens seek to maximize their self-interest, and the system provides every opportunity for them to do so" (p. 464). Political–administrative relations, as currently conceived and conducted, are characterized more by collusion and connivance than genuine trust. Thus, if elected officials and administrators do not trust one another, in the office and in the media, it is unreasonable to believe that trust in government will be engendered in the citizenry. Trust, like charity, begins at home.

But, again, the creation of trust, like reform in general, is daunting. Although it is easy to defend trust in principle, establishing and sustaining it in practice is a different matter. In the case of political–administrative relations, elected officials and bureaucrats engage each other in a series of compromises and concessions — their *modus vivendi* — which serves their respective interests and manages the governance process with varying degrees of skill, effectiveness, and responsibility. Whether or to what degree trust is part of the equation in particular circumstances is an empirical question worthy of investigation.

The complexity of political–administrative relations has provided a rich research agenda for many scholars over many decades. As a result, we have available detailed descriptions, images, and analyses of political–administrative relations in many polities across the globe. The glaring omission is the two-level question: the moral relationship between political and administrative officials themselves, and the moral relationship between political and administrative officials, citizens, and the quality of governance. On both levels, moral agency, citizenship, and trust apply.

That bureaucrats do, indeed, participate in policy making has long been common knowledge. The issue is the meaning and importance of such participation for policy outcomes. Therefore, it is time for scholars themselves to exercise moral agency in their research, to go beyond conventional treatments, and to ask the moral question. As adherents to democratic theory, it is incumbent on them to consider not only the propriety of administrative policy making but also the nexus between prudence and principle. As long as both legislators and administrators claim to act in the name of and on the authority of citizens, scholars are responsible for assessing this claim on moral as well as political grounds.

Rose (1987), Peters (1995), and Svara (1999) offer incipient insights into the moral dimensions of political–administrative relations. Each implicitly recognizes that mere description of legislative–bureaucratic interaction takes us only so far in our understanding of what is, in fact, the implementation of democratic theory. Therefore, these scholars are to be commended for opening the door to higher-order research, for viewing political–administrative relations through a different lens, and for beginning to ask fresh questions. Although their discomfort with the moral aridity of the status quo may be only inchoate, it is the precondition for change. If public officials do not consider such issues as inequality from a moral perspective, for example, then the likelihood of change is dim indeed.

On both the practitioner and scholarly levels, then, what is required, first of all, is a kind of transformational leadership in which the status quo is unfrozen and a new set of assumptions, incentives, and objectives is established (Burns, 1978). For practitioners with a serious interest in resolving such problems as inequality, the benefits of moral agency and citizenship, enveloped in trust, are obvious. Clear moral positions, coupled with political and administrative skills and strategies, are formidable opponents of the merely expedient, familiar, and comfortable in the policy arena. In the academic arena, clear moral positions, coupled with sophisticated research and communications skills and strategies, are equally essential requirements. Together, they can contribute both to the creation of a new set of profiles and competencies for public officials and to the advancement of democratic discourse and decision making in the governance process.

INVESTMENT IN CHANGE

In principle, the benefits of investing in change to engender moral agency and moral citizenship would seem to be self-evident. We know, however, that value-based reform can be contentious and controversial. In this context, we argue that ethics codes, ethics training, and accountability are the beginning, rather than the end, of the ethics conversation. On the surface, it may appear that we understand the meaning of these topics and can easily incorporate them into organizational policies and procedures. In fact, however, their meaning, as well as their implications, requires discernment and much more consideration than they typically receive in public organizations. For example, what are ethics codes designed to do? What is ethics training intended to accomplish? Do ethics codes and ethics training produce more accountable public administrators? The answers to these questions are hardly obvious or simple.

Consider the two major images that we have of public administrators in the United States (Moore, 1995). First is the faithful agent or servant of elected officials whose only moral duty is to do what he or she is told and to provide expertise to legislators and organizational superiors. This image reflects the classic politics–administration dichotomy in which the administrator is a technician whose only interest is in the implementation of policy designed by the legislative branch. The second image is the public administrator as an independent actor whose own moral views are inseparable from his or her administrative responsibilities, including policy design and organizational dissent. This image reflects the practical abandonment of the politics–administration dichotomy and the acknowledgment of the administrator's role in policy, which by definition involves the interpretation of values.

Which of these two images is more appealing — the faithful agent or the independent moral actor? As citizens, we tend to be ambivalent. On the one hand, we fear and even recoil from public officials who blindly follow orders and who are not accountable — sometimes referred to as the Eichmann syndrome, in which the obedient Nazi or, more recently, the obedient soldier at Abu Ghraib does only what he or she is told. On the other hand, we fear and mistrust public administrators who express their own moral views because we worry that, being unelected, they may pursue ideas contrary to those of society in general or legislators in particular. In either case, as citizens, we are uncertain about our expectations of public service, and as public administrators, we are unclear about what ethics in government actually means.

Imagine a public administrator assigned the responsibility to design both a code of ethics and an ethics training program for his or her agency. Where should he or she start? How might he or she begin to think about fulfilling this assignment in a way that reflects well on him or her and adds value to his or her organization? Where could he or she look for guidance? One place to look might be the Code of Ethics of the American Society for Public Administration (1994). Divided into five major sections, the American Society for Public Administration code encourages members to serve the public interest, respect the constitution and the law, demonstrate personal integrity, promote ethical organizations, and strive for professional excellence. As a general statement of the essence of public administration, the code is exemplary. The challenge lies in the interpretation and implementation of the code, with its exhortations to "exercise discretionary authority to promote the public interest," "to be prepared to make decisions that may not be popular," "to work to improve and change laws and policies that are counterproductive and obsolete," "to provide organization members with an administrative means for dissent," "to promote accountability through appropriate controls and procedures," and "to encourage organizations to adopt, distribute, and periodically review a code of ethics as a living document." These half-dozen admonitions, along with the 26 others in the code, impose a heavy personal and professional burden on public administrators because they go well beyond the legal and financial concerns often found in codes of ethics. Interpreting, implementing, and applying them, both in the design of training programs and on the job, therefore is a difficult problem. Thus, it is hard to disagree with the content of the American Society for Public Administration Code of Ethics, but it is equally hard to know how to make it real.

Ethics training is common in private as well as public organizations. It tends to be rule- or compliance-oriented, legalistic, and infrequent. If it is evaluated, it is often by the number of complaints the organization receives from citizens or customers or by the litigation avoided. In this sense, ethics training is a kind of risk-management device designed to prevent problems, produce stakeholder confidence in the organization, and increase public trust. As an element of organizational change, its effectiveness is difficult to discern or measure.

The purposes of ethics training often include what is referred to as a high road and a low road. The high road is aspirational, reflected in the American Society for Public Administration code, with an emphasis on the development of employees' ability to identify ethical issues or dilemmas in their everyday decision making, to think through them ethically, and to resolve them more or less satisfactorily. The low road or defensive mode refers to an emphasis on laws and regulations. However framed, training should be seen as part of an organization's entire system of ethics activities, including top management commitment, ethics as a criterion in hiring and promotion, and on-the-job application and reinforcement. If nothing else, trainers need to distinguish between "knowing" and "knowing how" because ethical knowledge involves both knowing that certain behavior is wrong or that a dilemma demands resolution and knowing how to meet one's responsibility in these respects (West and Berman, 2004).

Moving to accountability, we often hear demands that people in government be held accountable (Behn, 2001). We have an elaborate accountability structure in government: auditors, inspectors general, and independent counsels, and the United States General Accounting Office were recently renamed the Government Accountability Office. But what does accountability actually mean? More often than not, it seems to mean blame and punishment, which can take various forms, including job loss, a prison term, a lawsuit, a subpoena, or humiliation by a legislative committee. Sometimes, accountability means accountable or answerable for fairness finances, and performance. A key problem, however, is that holding people accountable for performance while also holding them accountable for finances and fairness, tends to create a dilemma. The rules for finances and fairness can obstruct performance, as innovation is penalized, flexibility is limited, and excellence is not encouraged, let alone rewarded. Therefore, we confront the accountability dilemma, the tradeoff between accountability for finances and fairness and accountability for performance: Should public administrators be held accountable for complying with procedures for finances and fairness or for producing results through performance? It is much easier to do the first, as we are often unclear or do not agree on the results that we want public agencies to produce in the first place.

Before turning to our proposal for value-based change, we summarize the discussion thus far with the following four points. First, change, including the introduction of meaningful ethics codes and ethics training, as well as a revised understanding of accountability, is a major challenge. Today, despite the globalization of ethics, it is difficult to find credible, empirical evidence of more ethical individuals and institutions across the world. This is not surprising, given the daunting nature of change, the multiple perspectives on administrative ethics, and the need for consistent and committed leadership. Prospective change may have academic appeal, but a practitioner tends to see it through a different lens and will be concerned about the likelihood of resistance and disruption in the organization, the willingness of managers and employees to embrace the reform, and the specific benefits to be derived. Although organizations change all the time in their operations, procedures, and technologies, introducing ethical change into an organization's culture is a different matter.

Second, public organizations today are probably as ethical as they know how to be in the context of the conventional understanding of ethics that tends to prevail in most agencies. Survey data show that most public organizations have no consistent approach to ethics and that employees often flounder when confronted with ethical challenges. Ethical decision making is not well understood, so in this morally confused and confusing environment, public agencies grasp at whatever ethical straws they can find. Often, the important thing is to have a code of ethics on the wall and in the handbook. Thus, the question is: What does it take to translate the noble sentiments of ethics codes into concrete skills and behaviors among public administrators? This takes us to point three: ethics training.

Like codes of ethics, ethics training is widespread in public agencies, often described as a key supplement to an effective ethics code. Ethics training is required at the federal level as well as in many states and cities and is a conventional method for promoting compliance with statutory, regulatory, or administrative standards. Discretion, judgment, and independent moral choice are usually not considered. Thus, as currently constituted, ethics training generally does not translate the noble sentiments in ethics codes into practical skills and behaviors. This, in turn, reflects our ambivalence about the kind of public administrator that we prefer — the faithful servant or the independent moral actor — and the tilt toward the compliance or low-road approach. We suggest, therefore, that we must decide this question before ethics training can produce the desired skills and behaviors in the public service.

Fourth and finally, we may be able to reframe our understanding of accountability if we first acknowledge that public administrators do, indeed, exercise discretion which, by definition, entails independence, choice, and judgment. In fact, without discretion, there is no accountability (Behn, 2001). If an elected official or political appointee refuses to delegate to public administrators the discretion that they need to manage their organizations and to implement their programs, either by imposing detailed rules or requiring approval for every decision, then they clearly cannot hold those public administrators accountable. But delegating discretion demands trust. Therefore, accountability means both discretion and trust, as opposed to micromanagement or wink-and-nod management, as the only way to achieve accountability as well as results in public administration.

CONCLUSION

Value-based, citizen-centered governance may seem chimerical, a utopian fantasy concocted by academics who have the leisure to spin visionary tales rather than face the challenges of the real world. We submit, however, that nothing is more practical than a vision, than imagination placed in service of the public interest. Although differences of views and emphases abound, the essential point is consistently to ask ourselves the timeless question: How are we to live? In our judgment, asking this question and answering it with intelligence and integrity, whether on the personal, professional, or policy level, is to apply practical wisdom to both the travails and triumphs that life brings.

In this spirit, then, we issue the following call for translating the Blacksburg Manifesto–Unified Ethic, revised political–administrative relations, and investment in change into a revitalized understanding and enactment of governance. Part of our intent is to implant Kant's kingdom of ends at all levels; not as some sectarian or moralistic revival, but as a more comprehensive focus on the recalcitrant policy environment, rather than timeworn adversarial politics. This does not signify an end to ideology or partisanship but, instead, it marks a commitment to morally grounded, morally explicit political and policy discourse. It signifies serious struggle with the question of how we shall live, in which the moral dimensions of our decisions are as routine or embedded in our considerations as cost-benefit analysis, risk management, and performance review.

Our proposal resembles Terry L. Cooper's (1991) call for "The Restoration of Citizenship in the Practice of Public Administration," in which university education in public administration, professional associations, and the workplace are implicated in the need for change. We, too, call on public administration/public affairs education programs, professional associations, and institutions of governance to participate in the development of the kind of moral agency and moral citizenship discussed in this book. At the educational level, we encourage both undergraduate and graduate programs to incorporate into their curricula courses in ethics and citizenship, while acknowledging the limited impact of such a step thus far, given the fact that most practitioners do not have formal academic training in public administration and that academic exposure to these topics is necessary but not nearly sufficient in the long run. In this respect, similar steps taken with undergraduate and graduate programs in colleges of business, law schools, medical schools, and others may prove equally relevant.

With regard to professional associations, we, like Cooper, also recommend programs, awards, and conferences. But besides the American Society for Public Administration, the National Association of Schools of Public Affairs and Administration, and the International City/County Management Association, we call on such organizations as the National Academy of Public Administration, the International Association of Schools and Institutes of Administration, and the Organization for Economic Cooperation and Development to sponsor working conferences focused on the design and delivery of training programs to fulfill the three requirements for change outlined in this chapter. Again, we also recommend the participation of trade associations, corporations, think tanks, and professional associations in business, law, medicine, and other fields.

Finally, on the political–governmental level, we recommend the involvement of supportive national, state, and local legislators, as well as administrators, who are committed to the transparency of process in the context of our three requirements for reform. Bureaucratic discretion, judgment, and independence, for example, would be openly and fully addressed rather than hidden behind the counterproductive adversarial relations referred to earlier. In the spirit of focusing our efforts and resources on the recalcitrant policy environment instead of engaging in the satisfaction of short-term interests, such high-level political and administrative involvement would cast refreshing sunlight on governance and, in the process, contribute to the development of citizen knowledge and action.

Moral reform of public service, like reform, in general, is a political act, not simply a technical exercise. It seeks to reconfigure the role of the public servant, first, by acknowledging the governance responsibilities inherent in public service and, second, by holding the public servant up as a moral agent and exemplar for both professionals and citizens to emulate. But the nobility of public service notwithstanding, American society is not now ready to embrace the dignity, honor, and legitimacy of the men and women whose lives are devoted to the enactment of our collective values. Most parents do not encourage their children to become bureaucrats, and academic civic education programs fail to address public service in any meaningful or positive way. Candidates for public office continue to scapegoat bureaucracy and bureaucrats, government is business's junior partner when it comes to efficiency and effectiveness, and the achievements of public servants tend to be unknown to the citizenry at large. Public servants as moral agents and moral exemplars is an alien concept. Therefore, the establishment of common ground and a common future across professions, sectors, and citizens is fundamentally a matter of cultural change, requiring the understanding, commitment, and energy of individuals and institutions at all levels and in all regions of the country. We believe that our citizens and our public servants deserve no less.

REFERENCES

Aberbach, J. A., R. D. Putnam, and B. A. Rockman. 1981. *Bureaucrats and Politicians in Western Democracies.* Cambridge, MA: Harvard University Press.

American Society for Public Adminstration. 1994. *Code of Ethics.*

Behn, R. D. 2001. *Rethinking Democratic Accountability.* Washington, D.C.: Brookings Institution Press.

Burns, J. M. 1978. *Leadership.* New York: Harper & Row.

Campbell, C. 1988. The Political Roles of Senior Government Officials in Advanced Democracies. *British Journal of Political Science.* 18(2):243–272.

Cooper, T. L. 1991. *An Ethic of Citizenship for Public Administration.* Englewood Cliffs, NJ: Prentice Hall.

Cooper, T. L., and N. D. Wright, eds. 1992. *Exemplary Public Administrators.* San Francisco: Jossey-Bass.

Dunn, D. 1997. *Politics and Administration at the Top: Lessons from Down Under.* Pittsburgh: University of Pittsburgh Press.

Frederickson, H. G. 1980 New Public Administration. Tuscaloosa: University of Alabama Press.

Garofalo, C. and D. Geuras. 1999. *Ethics in the Public Service: The Moral Mind at Work.* Washington, D.C.: Georgetown University Press.

Hart, D. K. 1992. The Moral Exemplar in an Organizational Society. In *Exemplary Public Administrators*, eds. T. L. Cooper and N. D. Wright, pp. 9–29. San Francisco: Jossey-Bass.

Israel, R. 2002. Roger's Rules for Public Administrators Working with Policy Makers. *PA Times.* 25(9):5–6.

Kettl, D. F. 2003. *The Global Public Management Revolution.* Washington, D.C.: Brookings Institution Press.

———. 2002. *The Transformation of Governance.* Baltimore, MD: The Johns Hopkins University Press.

Lee, M. 2002. Politicians and Administrators: A Partnership Doomed to a Superior– Subordinate Relationship. *PA Times.* 25(9):6.

Moore, M. H. 1995. *Creating Public Value.* Cambridge, MA: Harvard University Press.

Mouritizen, P. E., and J. H. Svara. 2002. *Leadership at the Apex: Politicians and Administrators in Western Local Governments.* Pittsburgh, PA: University of Pittsburgh Press.

Peters, B. G. 1995. *The Politics of Bureaucracy*, 4th ed. White Plains, New York: Longman.

Rose, R. 1987. Steering the Ship of State: One Tiller but Two Hands. *British Journal of Political Science*. 17(4):409–433.

Ruscio, K. P. 1996. Trust, Democracy, and Public Management: A Theoretical Argument. *Journal of Public Administration Research and Theory*. 6:461–477.

Smith, B. L. R., ed. 1984. *The Higher Civil Service in Europe and Canada: Lessons for the United States*. Washington, D.C.: The Brookings Institution.

Smith, L. W., and S. Millick. 2002. Partnering for the People: Alliances between Career Administrators and Political Appointees in Federal Agencies. *PA Times*. 25(9):4.

Svara, J. H. 1999. Complementarity of Politics and Administration as a Legitimate Alternative to the Dichotomy Model. *Administration and Society*. 30(6):676–705.

Wamsley, G. et al. 1990. *Refounding Public Administration*. Newbury Park, CA: Sage.

West, J. P., and E. M. Berman. 2004. Ethics Training in U. S. Cities: Content, Pedagogy, and Impact. *Public Integrity*. 6(3):189–206.

Wilson, G. K., and A. Barker. 2003. Bureaucrats and Politicians in Britain. *Governance*. 16(3):349–373.

Index